DATE DUE

Uncertain Refuge

Uncertain Refuge

ITALY AND THE JEWS DURING THE HOLOCAUST

Nicola Caracciolo

TRANSLATED AND EDITED BY

Florette Rechnitz Koffler and Richard Koffler

Foreword by Renzo De Felice

Prologue by Mario Toscano

University of Illinois Press   Urbana and Chicago

Gli ebrei e l'Italia durante la guerra, 1940–45 © 1986 by Bonacci Editore S.R.L.
English-language translation published in 1995 by the University of Illinois Press
under agreement with Bonacci Editore S.R.L.
Manufactured in the United States of America
1   2   3   4   5   C   P   5   4   3   2   1

This book is printed on acid-free paper.

Library of Congress Cataloging-in-Publication Data

Caracciolo, Nicola.
    [Ebrei e l'Italia durante la guerra, 1940–45. English]
    Uncertain refuge : Italy and the Jews during the Holocaust /
Nicola Caracciolo ; translated and edited by Florette Rechnitz
Koffler and Richard Koffler ; foreword by Renzo De Felice ; prologue
by Mario Toscano.
        p.   cm.
    Includes bibliographical references.
    ISBN 0-252-01923-7 (cloth). — ISBN 0-252-06424-0 (paper)
    1. Jews—Italy—History—20th century. 2. Holocaust, Jewish
(1939–1945)—Italy—Personal narratives. 3. World War, 1939–1945—
Jews—Rescue—Italy. 4. Italy—Ethnic relations. I. Rechnitz
Koffler, Florette. II. Koffler, Richard. III. Title.
DS135.I8C3713   1995
945'.004924—dc20   94-16156
                                                                        CIP

To
Liza Silberman Rechnitz
John Rechnitz
and
Charles Rechnitz
In Memoriam

Contents

APPENDIXES

Acknowledgments

Apart from the fact that all translations are of necessity collaborations, even if the first collaborator is often silent and need not be among the living, this book is a collaboration on several levels at once. It contains an English version of interviews conducted, for the most part, in Italian, some of it ill- and faintly remembered Italian, with a smattering of dialects thrown in, at various places in Italy, Israel, and France. The translators are indebted to Radiotelevisione Italiana, for whose documentary program the interviews were conducted, and to Nicola Caracciolo, the journalist who shaped the documentary and did the interviewing. He is the author of the book that served as a source for us. We are also indebted to those who granted him interviews, some of them famous in their own right, others people with unknown names, whose collective presence haunts these pages and lends them immediacy. Some of those interviewed were alive in the mid-1980s but now are gone, as the inescapable time limit for oral histories of survivors and rescuers in the European Holocaust approaches.

We owe another sort of debt to colleagues, some of them our friends. Sandro Gerbi, financial columnist for *La Repubblica*, warned us several years ago during a visit to our home to be careful; we hope we have heeded his advice. Susan Zuccotti of Columbia University, who went first and furthest among American historians of the Holocaust in Italy, gave selflessly of her time and expertise, going over an early draft of our translation line by line, spotting flaws and questionable judgments with her acute eye and long memory, and steering our work in the right direction. Rabbi Arthur Hertzberg, magisterial historian of Jewish thought and experience over centuries and continents, served as an example of the necessary absorption of coexisting irreconcilables and made himself available to us from time to time. Sister Perpetua Deane, O.P., our colleague in Romance languages at St.

Thomas Aquinas College, offered a different sort of example, embodying for two displaced scholars of the Jewish faith the central thread of a decency, catholic and humane, that connects her with Father Benedetto and with lesser known sisters and brothers in orders some fifty years ago whose good works of rescue mark these pages. Stanford Lyman of Florida Atlantic University, a sociologist and polymath, made us aware of the striking evidence that Matsuoka, the Japanese foreign minister who signed the Pact of Steel with Ribbentrop and Ciano in 1939, was prepared (as his Italian counterpart was) to resist the coming war against the Jews, and that the other Axis partner did some rescuing of its own in the Fugu Plan. Stjepan Meštrović of Texas A&M, Durkheim restorer and chronicler of received opinions on the Third Balkan War, offered helpful comments on the Ustasha, the Chetniks, and the Jews in the lands of Yugoslavia.

Other kinds of support for our endeavor mattered enormously to us. John Barth of the reference staff at the St. Thomas Aquinas Library electronically extended the resources of a small liberal arts college to accommodate our inordinate bibliographic demands. In its own way, the Teaneck Public Library also catered to our needs and surprised us constantly with its holdings. To Richard Martin, executive editor at the University of Illinois Press, we want to express our gratitude for his patience and wise counsel; to his colleague at the press, Jane Mohraz, manuscript editor, our appreciation for the care she devoted to our intent in copyediting an unconventional scholarly project with an unusual range of language. We are grateful to the Italian Cultural Center in New York for some useful leads and, once again, to Radiotelevisione Italiana for allowing us to adapt images by its cinematographer, Bruno Mazza, from Caracciolo's two-part RAI-TV documentary *Il coraggio e la pietà*. All of the frame enlargements in the book, with the exception of a photograph of Count Pietromarchi from the 1940s and of the archival document with the comment in Mussolini's handwriting, were copyrighted by Radiotelevisione Italiana in 1986 and are used with permission. We are also grateful to Informed Solutions in Teaneck, New Jersey, for exploiting the high technology needed to capture images from the RAI footage and release them as halftones in these pages. This is a better and certainly a livelier book for all of their efforts and assistance. For errors inevitable or otherwise, the translators credit only themselves. *Traduttore traditore.*

Finally, but for bereavements of those in our family who had survived another of Hitler's wartime alliances and later the grim times and gray regime that followed the war, we would have dedicated the English version of this book to our son, Daniel Koffler. He deserved more of our time in his middle childhood than this book allowed. Instead, it commemorates the Rechnitz side of our family, all of whom took an interest in the project as it unfolded. In common with the survivors who speak in these pages, they too were rescued in Italy.

FRK and RK

Foreword

Renzo De Felice

To understand and assess accurately the Italian position during World War II on the "Jewish question" and the Holocaust and, consequently, the far from negligible amount of help—in proportion to the number of Jews in Italy and the zones of Italian military occupation—the Italians offered to the Jews, one must have some essential reference data. The following observations are useful for anyone not already steeped in knowledge of the history and character of Italian Judaism and Italian Fascism, which was quite different from Nazism:

a. In Italy racism was unknown, and anti-Semitism did not have a real tradition of its own or a mass presence. Catholic anti-Semitism was kept within circumscribed limits and, in any case, was counterbalanced in the 1930s by a rejection of "pagan" Nazi racism.

b. The Jews were integrated into Italian society, and a good part of them had put themselves on the path to assimilation. To this one should then add their sparse number (fewer than fifty thousand) and their geographic distribution, in effect limited to central and northern Italy and numerically significant only in a few places. The process of the Risorgimento, the struggle for national unification in the nineteenth century, had brought with it the emancipation of the Jews, who had participated largely and had been fully recognized in the unified state, with stances of genuine patriotism and even, in the early twentieth century, of nationalism. Italian participation in World War I had also found large support among the Italian Jews, whether for national and patriotic reasons or with a view toward the liberation of the Jewish subjects of Austria-Hungary.

c. Except for almost singular and completely marginal cases (such as that of Giovanni Preziosi), Italian Fascism was not anti-Semitic. So much was this the case that Italian Jews reacted to it in the same way other Italians did: they accepted it or rejected it on the basis of motivations that quite rarely depended on their being Jewish.

There were some Jews in the Fascist regime from its origins. Until 1938, Jews held important administrative, economic, and political offices under Fascism. Guido Jung was Minister of Finance from 1932 to 1935; some of Mussolini's most sought-out economic advisers were Jewish.

In exercising its own foreign policy, the Fascist government had no scruples about maintaining relations with the Zionist movement (and not only with revisionists). Italy between the two wars was one of the European countries that most helped and sheltered the Jewish refugees from Central and Eastern Europe. And, in the time prior to the Rome-Berlin axis, Mussolini tried to curb Hitler's anti-Semitism, to the point of coming into open clash with the Nazis right after the failed putsch of Vienna in 1934.

d. The anti-Semitic and racist turn of Mussolini in 1938 was essentially dictated, on one level (the more properly anti-Semitic one), by considerations of practical politics (to eliminate an element so loud in its dissonance that it made the Axis scarcely credible abroad) and, on another, by preoccupations connected with colonial policy (relations between Italians and indigenous populations) and with the idea of a Fascist "New Man."

e. The racial legislation of 1938–39, however, had and was intended to have a different character, more moderate and "civilized," than the Nazi racial legislation had. Mussolini's conception of a "parallel war" is in a certain sense anticipated by it, especially as far as the role of Italian sympathizers was concerned. Despite its racial policy, the regime, politically open-minded, continued—while utilizing the Arab card to undermine the British—to defer in its plans to Mediterranean Jewry, in order above all to undercut the Germans.

f. The racial laws were received unfavorably by the vast majority of Italians, whether because such laws offended their sense of humanity or because they were considered a symptom of the generally unpopular alliance with Germany. Even a fair number of Fascists received them unfavorably, and there are plenty of cases of Fascism's exponents of the highest rank who tried at least to mitigate them. The most celebrated case is that of Italo Balbo,[1] but there were others. Many cases of anti-Semitism on the part of Fascist exponents, rather than being real anti-Semitism, were dictated by opportunism or the desire to make the Fascist regime more intransigent and bring it closer to the Nazis.

g. Until the establishment of the Italian Social Republic (the RSI) in 1943,[2] the executive branch of the Italian state, the Foreign Ministry, and the armed forces in general applied the racial laws in a restricted spirit, avoiding excesses and at times using bland procedures that ended up favoring the Jews, particularly in the occupied zones. So clearly did they do so that in February 1943 anti-Fascists could maintain that the Italian request to the French authorities to suspend the provision for the removal of Jews from the zone of Italian occupation (to hand them over to the Germans) had been made in order to have it on record to their credit, in expectation of a separate peace or the collapse of Germany.

Until July 25, 1943,[3] Mussolini, who had been informed of the fate that the Jews deported by the Germans would meet, responded in formally positive terms to German requests (all the more pressing since the end of 1942) to hand over the Jews in the Italian-occupied zones, particularly in Yugoslavia. All the while, however, he authorized the military commands to make up any excuse they wished "so as not to hand over even a single Jew."

Nor, finally, can one underestimate the fact that on at least two occasions, Mussolini authorized resorting to Jewish officers with naval expertise, who had been removed from the service on racial grounds.[4] The fact that in both cases the interested parties accepted, together with the fact that, immediately after July 25, various Jewish officers asked to be recalled to service to "defend the fatherland," is in turn indicative of the degree of integration and naturalization of a portion of Italian Jewry.

h. The really dramatic shift in the anti-Semitic policy of Fascism took place only with the advent of the Italian Social Republic, largely under the domination of the Germans.

Once these general reference points have been put into clear view, it is possible to begin to examine the help Italians offered the Jews during World War II. There are two particularly important features of such help.

The first has essentially to do with the Jews of the Italian-occupied zones in France, Yugoslavia, and Greece. This is the one to which scholars have, in a certain sense, devoted more attention. We recall above all the works of Leon Poliakov and Jacques Sabille for France and Tunisia and of Daniel Carpi for Yugoslavia and Greece, not to mention the more general work of Salvatore Loi.[5] The picture that emerges from their work is sufficiently well known that we need not expand on it. It will suffice to say that later research in the archives of the Foreign Ministry and in the archive of the Historical Office of the Italian State not only has confirmed such a picture but also has enriched it with new elements that are worth knowing and, we hope, soon will be known.

The second aspect has to do directly with the Jews who were in Italy from September 1943 to April 1945. No studies exist on this specific period,[6] but several elements can be inferred from studies on the Fascist anti-Semitic policy, in particular from those of the present writer and those of Giuseppe Mayda and Meir Michaelis.[7]

To these two most important features one could add some others that have only an indirect connection with the problem of help for the Jews but are far from devoid of significance; or that have to do with cases in countries not under Italian occupation, cases in which individual Jews were helped. Among the former, to give only two examples, are the possibility of leaving Italy, which, until the U.S. entry into the war, the Jews who were in the country retained; and Mussolini's persistence, even beyond the date known up to now, in his plans to resettle Italian Jews and Jewish refugees in Italy into Ethiopia. And since we have touched on Ethiopia, it should also be said that meaningful elements for evaluating the Italian position on the Jews can be inferred from the vicissitudes of the Jewish community in Libya, in particular during the two-year period of 1939–40, when Balbo was governor of the colony—the aforementioned Italo Balbo, who managed to obtain from Mussolini the nonapplicability of the racial laws to the Libyan Jews.

As for help offered individual Jews or small groups of Jews in territories directly controlled by the Germans, it ought to be recorded that on various occasions Italian diplomatic representatives enabled some Jews to pass for Italian who were nothing of the kind, thus succeeding in getting them to safety. Various cases of rescue took place even in Poland, thanks to the Italian military authorities present there, members of the Italian Red Cross (the CRI), and individual Italian citizens. In April 1943, for example, a Jewish couple (on the recommendation, it seems, of the Duke of Bergamo) was transported clandestinely from Lvov into Italy on a hospital train of the CRI. While the available documentation does not provide the names of the two Jews, we know those of the two persons who organized their escape: Paola Menada, inspector of the voluntary nurses of the CRI; and Second Lieutenant Fulchero, a doctor.

To evaluate the help offered the Jews by the Italian population in the period of the RSI and the German occupation of Italy, it is appropriate to start with a statistical consideration. According to the most reliable estimates made by the Center for Contemporary Jewish Documentation (CDEC) in Milan,[8] in this period about 1,000 Jews fought in the Resistance; from 5,000 to 6,000 crossed into Switzerland; almost 4,000 were already present in or were able to reach the southern regions liberated by the Allies; and about 7,000, finally, were deported or killed in Italy. The Jews rescued in the zones controlled by the RSI and the Germans would therefore have been about 27,000.[9] That number is not very high in itself but is significant, especially in comparison with the proportions rescued in other countries; it can be explained in large part only thanks to the solidarity displayed toward the Jews, Italian and foreign, by the population of Italy.

A particularly meaningful contribution to this rescue effort was certainly provided by the peasant populations of central and northern Italy. Although their ambit did not lack for elements that were pro-Fascist or fearful of the grave sanctions facing anyone accused of harboring or abetting Jews, the solidarity practiced by the rural populations, especially in the zones of the Alps and Apennines, was fundamental for the Jews who took refuge in those zones to be able to evade the persecution and the discomforts of their surroundings.

Despite the availability of written and oral testimony and also a body of memoirs by Jewish participants, until now no investigation has been completed that would characterize this attitude, study the reasons for it, and evaluate it, beyond the declaration of a vague humanitarianism and a Christian solidarity. These are constant values typical of peasant culture, whose variations depend on traditions and "memories" that are particular and/or local. We have drawn heavily on the testimony of two Italian Jews, Augusto Segre and Giancarlo Sacerdoti,[10] who are diverse enough in their attitude toward Judaism, in their age, in their origin, and in the surroundings in which they were sheltered—one in the Langhe hills of Piedmont, in a reality characterized by a notable mutual penetration of peasants and partisan bands; the other in the Apennine mountains near Bologna, where this rapport was less intense and continual. From that testimony, we arrive at an early schematization of motives at the root of this attitude, which allows us to characterize such behavior on the part of the rural populations as the product of a "cultural" patrimony, pushing them toward the recognition of the common values of humanity that were crushed by the persecutors. At times this recognition may be distinguished from tones of authentic piety and may be animated by a basic sense of justice.

A persecuted Jew seemed immune from faults and, as such, deserving of help. The sole limit, sometimes difficult to overcome, on the practical accomplishment of this feeling of solidarity was represented by the need to protect one's possessions—the house, the cattle, the fields, the genuine and only reason for one's life, which urged one toward prudence, toward the least possible compromise: to provide immediate help without going so far as more permanent shelter. The latter was more easily granted wherever the presence of groups of partisans constituted, at one and the same time, a safeguard and a warning.

A second component of peasant solidarity can be recognized in the growing weight of the war, which involved a sense of greater and greater distance from the conflict, of hostility when confronted with those who had unleashed the war, of nostalgia and preoccupation with children and relatives scattered about after the disbanding of the Italian army, all of which impelled one to help the Jews, who had been reduced to the condition of fugitives. Nor should we overlook, particularly with the population of the Alps, the persistence of a traditional hostility vis-à-vis the Germans, connected with the experiences of World War I and the recent dramatic experiences of the ARMIR, the Italian army in Russia.

The extent to which the diffusion of a positive image of the Jew could matter is a theme still open to research. A single but meaningful example is offered by *Memorie di vita ebraica* (Memoirs of Jewish Life) by Augusto Segre, regarding the countryside of Monferrato, where the recollection of the honesty of a Jew represented for the local peasants an example of correct behavior that ought to repaid by practicing the same rules of human solidarity.

Available evidence suggests that the number of Jews hidden in urban centers was notably lower than the number of Jews who found refuge in the countryside. Nor can that be surprising, if we think for a moment of the much greater risks to be run in such centers, both by the Jews and by those who might shelter them. That also helps explain the fact that anyone in the cities who provided shelter for some Jews had as a rule already been in contact with them earlier, knew them either directly or through friends and safe relatives, or else was connected with the Resistance movement. And the fact that the opposite situation existed in the countryside, where Jews in the vast majority of cases were unknown to anyone who offered them shelter or aid. In cities the help offered by the church was a lot more consistent, above all with shelter in religious places. In Rome, during the German occupation, the Jews given shelter in religious buildings (about 180 of the innumerable congregations) were over 3,700. DELASEM,[11] the main Jewish relief organization, was in effect run by the Capuchin Father Marie-Benoît,[12] who had already gone to such pains earlier for the Jews of Marseille, Cannes, and Nice and had tried to make possible their transfer into Italy and from there into North Africa.

Nor, finally, did the Italian aid for the Jews stop with the end of the conflict. Among all the European countries, Italy was, between 1945 and 1948—that is, between the end of World War II and the birth of the state of Israel—the one that endeavored the most to help and promote the clandestine emigration to Palestine of the Jews saved from the Holocaust. It did so notwithstanding the difficulties this could cause, and in some cases did cause, its government with England. Ada Sereni's book *I clandestini del mare* already offers useful evidence about this important page in the history of both European and Italian Jewry,[13] but soon it will be possible to know a lot more about it: Tel Aviv University, in fact, has in progress a complete research project on this subject, which has been announced with notable fanfare.

In regard to what has been said up to this point, the testimony gathered by Nicola Caracciolo, from which this volume offers an ample selection, constitutes a direct source. This testimony is certainly secondary historical documentation, in the more exact sense, but at the same time it is of primary importance in capturing the drama and the problems that lay behind the events to which the witnesses refer. Much of it may appear to be almost confined to "human interest" and therefore too "simple," not to say simplistic; too personal, elementary—void, in short, of meaning, of "historical" importance. In reality, if you know how to read it, it constitutes, as we have said, a direct source of primary importance. And not only for the ends of a "true" history, that is, a living one, not merely lifted from books, a history of people rather than categories, rather than ideas more or less artificially deduced from schemas constructed a posteriori. It also constitutes source materials for a history (with a capital *h*) that, as such, can utilize any sort of documentary "material" and draw everything possible from it.

Among the numerous starting points it offers toward this end, we wish to indicate only one, which seems to us, moreover, among the most salient. It is not hard to note a certain difference, occasionally striking, between the testimony of the Italian Jews and that of the foreign Jews, especially if the succession of events to which the latter refer took place in the Italian-occupied zones rather than in territory occupied by other armies. The testimony of the foreign Jews is more spontaneous—less reticent in some cases. Above all, it is more likely to set itself apart by a widespread, often enthusiastic sense of recognition and admiration for how much the Italians did for the witnesses themselves and did to help Jews in general. The testimony of the Italian Jews is more critical, sometimes even bitter, and in some cases less spontaneous. To explain this difference, it is helpful to some extent to have a better understanding of the complex reality of European Jewry between the two world wars and, within its ambit, of the particular reality of Italian Jewry.

Far and away the majority of foreign Jews who came into contact with Italians during World War II had spent time in or hailed from countries where the Jews had lived and were living before the Nazi occupation in a more or less assumed condition of moral and sometimes civil inferiority. They had come from countries in which anti-Semitism was alive, or at least right on the surface; from countries, finally, into which, except for unusual cases, the Jews were not integrated and were far less assimilated. Certainly among the Jews of Eastern Europe and the Balkans, among Greek Jews and French Jews, there were differences within this general pattern. But all told, the differences were not really decisive, as the vicissitudes of 1940–42 had shown. It is therefore easy to understand that the Italian attitude toward them appeared and remained in their memory in a most favorable light. Perhaps this was so because in very many instances it was the reason for their survival; perhaps because it proved quite unexpected for them, and they were indebted to it not only for their lives but for something often just as important: faith in "other people," evidence that even among enemies there were human beings who looked upon the Jews the same way they did upon others.

The state of mind, the psychological attitude of the Italian Jews, was different at that time and, in a certain sense, remains so or can remain so up to the present time. For they had been used to an entirely different historical context, had been strongly integrated into Italian society, and had quite often put themselves on the path to assimilation. To them, the introduction of racial discrimination in 1938 was and has remained traumatic, notwithstanding the demonstrations of solidarity and the help offered them by so many Italians. We understand how, in certain cases, such a trauma may remain so deep, so morally disturbing, as to arouse in them a state of mind opposite to the one aroused among their ordinary coreligionists from other countries by the aid and solidarity of the Italians. While the foreign Jews found Italians to be capable of positive feelings, for the Italian Jews moral wounds were added to the material ones—chief among these, disappointment for the betrayal perpetrated in their presence by a collectivity in which they used to feel deeply that they were participants.

That the aftereffects of this trauma may sometimes not yet have been placated in those who have lived it in their own person is a fact that, on the one hand, must cause us all the more to understand the extent to which the wretched anti-Semitic policy of Fascism, even in its relative "moderation," has been fraught with consequences we do not often even think about. On the other, it must make us all the more diligent to unmask and rebuff any form of explicit anti-Semitism, above all the camouflaged sort. The wounds of anti-Semitism are among the deepest and most difficult to heal, for if they leave their mark on the bodies, they leave it no less on the souls of everyone: victims, executioners, more or less innocent or passive onlookers. Every fact, every document that one records for us is a step for civilized humanity on the road to victory over prejudice, deception, and barbarism.

Introduction

Florette Rechnitz Koffler and
Richard Koffler

In the mid-1980s the Italian journalist Nicola Caracciolo interviewed for a television documentary a wide array of survivors of the *other* World War II, the one Lucy Dawidowicz aptly called "the war against the Jews."[1] Many of those he interviewed were Italian Jews, though a significant number were not. Some of the latter were, instead, foreign Jews who had found their way into Italy as refugees from discrimination and persecution in their native countries; others were Jews living in the parts of southern France, Yugoslavia, Greece, and even Russia occupied by the Italian army during the war. Still others, a small and distinct group unto themselves, were non-Jews who had rescued or had overseen efforts to rescue Jews from the areas occupied by the German army, including most signally, after September 8, 1943—that terrible date to which these interviews recur time and again, like the antiphon to a dirge—in Italy itself. Among the Gentiles interviewed were priests, diplomats, and simple peasants in the countryside, north and south.

Caracciolo's interviews were interspliced with newsreel footage and photographs taken from archives, with voice-over narration, portraying the domestic policies and foreign relations of the later part of the Fascist era as these bore upon the situation of the Jews. The live interviews with the witnesses and participants chosen by Caracciolo were conducted in Italian in Italy and in Israel; the fact that the one-time refugees could remember a language they had not used for forty years is more impressive to us, perhaps, than it was to Caracciolo and his team. The film, entitled *Il coraggio e la pietà* (Courage and Compassion)—a glance at the title of Marcel Ophuls's documentary *Le cha-*

grin et la pitié (released in English as *The Sorrow and the Pity*), which explores French collaboration under the Vichy regime—took two years to assemble and edit into two segments, each an hour long, which were shown over the second network of RAI-TV in 1986.

"The task was not intended," Caracciolo tells us, "as a dispassionate and 'neutral' examination of the facts." He began, instead, with a premise, conveyed in his introduction to the Italian edition of this book: "that the Italians in the war years remained immune to that terrifying psychological epidemic . . . which was anti-Semitism, at least in its homicidal, Nazi form."[2] Or as he put it to his historical consultant in Israel, Daniel Carpi, in the first interview in this volume, "Do you mean, then, Professor, that the Italians behaved better than everyone else in Europe at that tragic moment?" Carpi's answer, from his fastness in Tel Aviv, was a nuanced yes. The film, despite Caracciolo's intentions—and far from being a weakness, this speaks for its honesty and the complexity of the experience it renders—is not always so sure, particularly in the course of interviews with some of the Italian Jews, when the testimony becomes, as Renzo De Felice puts it in the foreword to this book, "more critical, sometimes even bitter, and in some cases less spontaneous."

What Caracciolo has done with these interviews in their published form is to have restored to their full length, and in somewhat different order from that of his film, transcripts that had been cut, moved around in interspersed segments, and sometimes eliminated altogether. A documentary journalist under well-understood constraints, he had previously edited many hours of material down to two hours, of which only half to two-thirds was the actual testimony. He has added a foreword by De Felice, who advised him in the making of the film and in whose series the volume found a subsequent home, conveying the underlying social history in broad strokes; a separate historical essay by another consultant to the program, the diplomatic historian Mario Toscano, rigorously conveying the chronology of anti-Semitism in Italy in its increasing severity, even before the armistice of July 1943 and the direct German intervention that followed in September; and a brief bibliography by Toscano. We have further annotated these texts, added the appendixes, and amplified that bibliography with suggestions for further reading.

Caracciolo's premise contains an engaging paradox: "The Fascist government, which had also with its racial laws gravely reduced the civil rights of the Jews, took on, with respect to the genocide, something of the role of their protector."[3] In Italy, where the memories of the two-year civil war fought between the partisans of the Resistance and the combined armies of Germans and Fascist loyalists of Mussolini's "Social Republic" do not easily yield to historical distancing, the revisionist thesis embedded here remains suspect. Nor do those who were thrown out of jobs and schools and dispossessed, the relatives of the slain and the deported, find much solace in it or gratitude to the government that made the pact of "bitter friendship" (to use F. W. Deakin's telling phrase).[4] The evidence for official protection of both Italian and foreign Jews in these pages is striking though. We would point to the interviews with the late Ambassador Roberto Ducci, Ambassador Egidio Ortona, and Professor Daniel Carpi for direct testimony and scholarly corroboration. Whatever Mussolini's own equivocations, however limited the Italians might have been in their putative administrative autonomy by their stronger ally, until September 1943 the government not only disregarded German pressures to hand Jews over to the Germans but also rebuffed orders to do so by almost overt defiance and ensnared them in bureaucratic subterfuge.[5]

Here we arrive at a vital distinction between the role of bureaucracy in the National Socialist regime and its role in the Fascist regime. The "final solution" may have been thought up by Hitler's ideologues, but it remained for the bureaucracy to plan it and arrive, technologically and politically, at its implementation. As the sociologist Zygmunt Bauman puts it, following Raul Hilberg and Hannah Arendt:

> the Holocaust is so crucial to our understanding of the modern bureaucratic mode of rationalization not only, and not primarily, because it reminds us . . . just how formal and ethically blind is the bureaucratic pursuit of efficiency. Its significance is not fully expressed either once we realize to what extent mass murder on an unprecedented scale depended on the availability of well-developed and firmly entrenched skills and habits of meticulous and precise division of labour, of maintaining a smooth flow of command and information, or of impersonal, well-synchronized co-ordination of autonomous yet complementary actions: on those skills and habits, in short, which best grow and thrive in the atmosphere of the office. The light shed by the Holocaust on our knowledge of bureaucratic rationality is at its most dazzling once we realize the extent to which the very idea of the *Endlösung* was an outcome of the bureaucratic culture.[6]

An outcome of the bureaucratic culture *in Germany,* one should qualify Bauman's otherwise perceptive remark; undoubtedly an outcome of the bureaucratic culture in Vichy France as well. In Italy, however, the bureaucratic stance was rather different, as Ambassador Ducci indicated in his interview: "However much I can try to speak of myself and my office, we found a bunch of reasons that let us keep the thing on the back burner without ever complying with the German request, and at the same time to have plausible enough pretexts or reasons to justify the lack of action before the German authorities." In a similar vein, we can cite Carpi's comments on the military and diplomatic correspondence: "here there's an organized action on which practically *everyone* was in agreement. It's hard to find anyone who opposed it. That is, the correspondence at the Foreign Ministry between Roatta and Count Pietromarchi, between Pietromarchi and Vittorio Castellani, the liaison officer with the Second Army in Croatia, was an open correspondence, notwithstanding the Duce's order . . . to hand over the Croatian Jews to the Germans. . . ."

In short, the bureaucratic hierarchies of the Italian state were acting in the ethically sighted pursuit of a willed inefficiency in the face of an inhumane order that, Fascists or not and notwithstanding the Duce's order (itself fraught with purposeful if cynical ambiguity), they would *not* carry out. The refusal to yield to the mandate of the "final solution" was accompanied at the administrative level by countless acts of decency on the part of officers, noncommissioned soldiers, *carabinieri*, local police, and even officials of the Italian concentration camps in the country and in the zones of Italian occupation, all the way to the doomed Russian front. Witness the statement by Marco Hermann, a Jewish orphan Italian soldiers found in Lvov, sheltered at the barracks there, and brought back with them all the way to Udine when the defeated army withdrew from Russia in the bitter late winter of 1943: "I wasn't the only one. Perhaps it was a humanitarian tradition displayed by the Italian soldiers, to take with them orphans from parts of the world where they found themselves, because in Udine I also met many little orphaned Russian boys who were brought by the Italian soldiers when they returned to Italy from Russia."

Some other themes emerge from a careful reading, or should we say instead, a careful listening to the narrative accounts and overtones contained in these interviews. One is the role of the Roman Catholic church. Until 1939 and the outbreak of the war it was headed by Pope Pius XI Ratti, who signed the Concordat with Mussolini but was willing to confront Hitler and National Socialist racial theories in his unpublished 1937 encyclical *Mit brennenden Sorge* (With Burning Anxiety), intentionally drafted in German.[7] He was succeeded, a scant half-year before Hitler invaded Poland, by Pope Pius XII Pacelli, whose silence on the deportations and unwillingness to jeopardize the Vatican's officially neutral position with the Third Reich encamped in Rome could not have served to inspire Italian clerics to risk offering help and sanctuary to imperiled Jews.

Yet the simple fact, attested to many times in the interviews in these pages, is that men and women in religious orders risked their lives over and over again to save the lives of Jews and to offer them shelter and escape. Father Pierre Marie-Benoît, a French Capuchin priest called Father Benedetto by the Italians, speaks of a plan to rescue tens of thousands of Jews by removing them to North Africa. After Father Benedetto describes how he managed to obtain an audience with the pope through a sympathetic Vatican official in order to present this rescue plan, Caracciolo asks him about the pope's attitude. The priest's reply is instructive: "Good. I spoke of the French police, who were acting pretty much against the Jews and working with the Germans . . . arresting the Jews. The Italian police were protecting them instead. The pope made this observation: 'No one would have believed that in France there would have been such an attitude.' In addition, he told me, 'I will study this and have it studied, your requests'—and that sort of thing." That sort of thing, we should point out, is neither the indifference of Hochhuth's *Deputy* nor the moral courage—we are tempted to call it saintliness—of Benedetto himself.[8]

Within the church hierarchy there were exemplary figures, whose names crop up in passing throughout these pages. Izak Itai (Josef Ithai), a Croatian Jew who rescued a group of German and Austrian refugee children in Zagreb and brought them safely into Italy, recounts how immediately after the German occupation of September 8, 1943, the aged Monsignor Pelati saved a large group of Jewish children from the SS at Nonontola by placing them in the abbey. Bernard Grosser, working at the time with the Jewish rescue organization DELASEM in Genoa, speaks of the trust shown him and the material assistance his organization received from Cardinal Francesco Borgoncini Duca in Rome and Father Francesco Repetto, secretary to the archbishop of Genoa. Olga Di Veroli, whose family had a small store in the Roman ghetto where they lived, recalls how Monsignor Quadraroli, a Vatican secretary, knowing they were Jewish, provided false identity papers for her two brothers and sent her mother and one of her two sisters along with Olga to refuge in a convent.[9] Massimo Ottolenghi, a lawyer in Turin, recalls how a Monsignor Ulla, a Salesian priest, sheltered Jews in the Lanzo valleys of Piedmont.

Comparable attitudes manifest themselves in these pages on a local level as well—the level of the parish, the neighborhood, the postage stamp of native soil (to use Faulkner) that has suffered invasion and violation. Many of those interviewed speak of taking shelter and refuge in convents and monasteries, a dangerous act for the orders that did the sheltering. Among Caracciolo's paired interviews are two parish priests, Father Libero Raganella in Rome and Father Aldo Brunacci in Assisi. What emerges from the first interview is that Father Raganella, disarmingly modest and ironic, would break the chains on cloister gates to get Roman Jews to safe havens; among those he rescued, temporarily, was the partisan Lello Perugia, also interviewed here. Just before a Yom Kippur raid by the Germans on October 9, 1943, Rabbi Elio Toaff's entire congregation at Ancona was evacuated—one of the few Jewish communities so spared during that dreadful autumn—because a local priest, Father Bernardino, might have tipped the rabbi off that the raid was coming. (We should note, however, that Toaff does not mention Father Bernardino in his interview with Caracciolo, and the story is hard to authenticate.)[10]

"That simple people went to some trouble to protect the Jews was well known," writes Caracciolo.[11] Some, we should add, went to greater trouble than others. In his foreword to this volume Renzo De Felice, author of perhaps the major biography of Mussolini as well as the major history of the Jews in this dark era in Italy, singles out "the peasant populations of central and northern Italy" for their "particularly meaningful contribution to this rescue effort." There is no need for us to review the motives De Felice posits for the actions of the rural populations in the mountains. Instead, we would refer to the testimony on this subject gathered by Caracciolo, particularly the testimonies by the Israelis in the early section of the book and the members of the Di Girolamo family in the Apennines and the Giordana sisters in the Alps at the end of the book.

Two aspects are striking here. One is that the peasants had little contact with Italian Jews; the Jewish refugees from southern France and Yugoslavia (to say nothing of more distant lands and sites of earlier persecution) who made their way into Italy must have seemed foreign indeed, remote, incomprehensible in their speech, *other*. The imperatives of the racial laws of November 1938 could be ignored in the countryside; not so the imperatives of the German invasion of September 8, 1943, which the peasants could not have avoided seeing and hearing. Yet they hid and sheltered even the foreign Jews (like Ariel Leo Koffler and the children of Villa Emma).

The second harks back to Carpi's remarks to Caracciolo about the singularity of this response—of how differently the rural populations behaved elsewhere. One thinks inevitably here about the rural universe of the extermination camps themselves, whose surrounding populations in Poland are so memorably evoked by Claude Lanzmann in *Shoah*— the world of Jerzy Kosinski's *Painted Bird*.[12] One thinks of Le Chambon-sur-Lignon, the rural village in the Loire Valley described by Philip

Hallie in *Lest Innocent Blood Be Shed*,[13] so isolated and rare a counter-instance in a France marked by capitulation, suspicion, and Vichyite persecution of Jews. (Le Chambon, we should perhaps remind the reader, is a largely Protestant community, whereas the rural communities where Jews were sheltered in Italy, with the exception of certain Waldensian communities in the Piedmont, were Catholic.)

The realities of Italian urban life and of Jewish-Gentile relations in those centers where the Jewish communities congregated (and where, years later, Caracciolo would conduct most of his interviews) were far more complex even prior to September 1943. We need to consider the fact of divisions between Fascists, those without real politics, and anti-Fascists within the Jewish communities themselves; among the anti-Fascist Jews; and between the Left (itself schismatically divided) and the Zionists. We should not allow ourselves to be *overly* amused at the ineptness and absurdity of the Racial Office in Turin described by Massimo Ottolenghi or at the comeuppance of the physically repugnant anti-Semite on the tram in Rome at the hands of Giacoma Limentani's beautiful mother. The investigations of the OVRA—Mussolini's secret police, mentioned in several of the interviews by function but never by that feared acronym—affected the lives of all Jews with a known anti-Fascist in the family. The acts of persecution described in these interviews, the humiliations and loss of employment and status, the imprisonment and confinement of opponents whose Jewishness made them easier to identify, and the tergiversations of the Duce's policy are just as poignant and memorable as the contrapuntal notes on which Caracciolo dwells. Both are true, instances of the kind of complex truth embodied in the testimonies of oral history and reduced at peril to a single, beneficent strand.

After September 1943, most of the Italian peninsula becomes yet another zone of occupation by German forces, including the SS. Significant numbers of Italian Jews (and they are well represented among Caracciolo's interviewees) take an active part in the Resistance. For many others, including a large portion of the foreign Jewish refugees still in Italy and still arriving, the relatively safe haven yields to the roundups, mass shootings, Gestapo interrogations, incarcerations, disappearances, and eventual deportations to extermination camps that are the signature of these occupations. The Holocaust, as Susan Zuccotti puts it, comes to Italy. While the statistics adduced by CDEC—drawn from the archives on which all such historical investigations must rest and summarized here by Mario Toscano—support in their general outlines the success of the efforts by many Italians in high places and low to resist, defy, and thwart the Holocaust, we would do well to regard that success as relative, provisional, statistical. These interviews also contain their tragic dimension, a note of kaddish rather than celebration.

That note is struck first of all, and most resonantly, by the five interviewees who are survivors of Auschwitz: Nedo Fiano, Emilio Foà, Primo Levi, Lello Perugia, and Giuliana Tedeschi. The only one well known outside of Italy is Levi, the author of Auschwitz memoirs and of fiction and essays that are also Auschwitz memoirs of a sort, who died in 1987, a scant year after this interview, probably a suicide. Fiano tells Caracciolo that he "never completely left the camp." Foà is the sole survivor of a group of forty-four people, mostly aged, including his father and uncle, deported together from Mantua. Three of Perugia's four brothers deported with him to Auschwitz perished there; he remembers (as part of the "collective madness" of that time and place) that German schoolboys aged six or seven stoned his train on the tracks leading toward Poland. Tedeschi's two young daughters were rescued from deportation by nuns and a devoted housekeeper. Her husband was murdered at Auschwitz, and on her own return, her younger daughter would not recognize her or sleep in the same room with her for a full month.

These are the direct survivors, but there are others who are vicarious survivors, indirect casualties of the Holocaust, touched forever by the same murderous hand. Elisa Della Pergola tells how her father was picked up by the SS in Genoa and was never seen again; she would later learn that he had been among the last shot by the Germans when the Russian army was about to arrive at Auschwitz. Marco Hermann, the orphan whom we have already mentioned, lost his father, mother, brother, and two sisters, along with the entire Jewish community of Lvov.

The most affecting of all as narratives, perhaps, are those of Carla Ovazza and Olga Di Veroli.[14] Ovazza, a child of the haute bourgeoisie, recounts grimly, almost stoicly, how her uncle Ettore Ovazza—a supporter of Fascism from the early days to almost the end—and his family were betrayed to the SS and slaughtered by them. Unwilling to change his political views or to emigrate as his brothers' branches of the family did, Ettore Ovazza was destined to be consumed by the social order he had helped construct. The story takes on a tragic dimension, like the Greek fable of the sculptor Perillos, who lent his craft to the construction of the hollow brazen bull for the tyrant Phalaris, only to be roasted alive inside his creation with the tyrant's other victims.

Ovazza's tale furnishes a counterpoint to the one Levi recounted about the mason from Piedmont, who had been sent to Germany for paid construction work at Auschwitz and would later became a sub-conscious "victim" of the machine into whose service he had been impressed. Both, in their different ways, are exemplary tales of horrific role reversals, told in the sober, reflective language of the safe, normal, present quotidian existence. Conveyed with searing, self-directed ironies, they are akin to some of Franz Kafka's narratives. In Ovazza's case, the dominant tones of her account find their gentle complement in the narrator's "discovery" of her Jewishness, when she is rejected by a schoolmistress and classmates to whom she had been unthinkingly attached. Her own family was fortunate enough, or perhaps prescient enough, to have spent the war years in the United States.[15] The bitterness lingered on her return, and lingers still, so that the fate of her uncle's family is presented as a tragedy without catharsis or consolation.

Di Veroli's is the saddest interview of all those Caracciolo conducted for his documentary. She came, as we have noted earlier, from a family of shopkeepers in the Roman ghetto, far more humble in position than Ovazza's. Speaking in a language modulating between Italian and Roman dialect, not even knowing for large stretches who her journalist interlocutor is, she tells how all of her family had been wiped out by the occupiers in one manner or another by the war's end. Two cousins with her surname, a father and his fourteen-year-old son, were massacred in a German reprisal at the Ardeatine Caves. Some seventy other members of her family, including her father and her married sister's family, perished at Auschwitz. Since the war and her mother's subsequent death, she has made more than one visit to Auschwitz, a pilgrimage of sorts, out of an unfulfillable and inexorable longing for the peace of those tormented souls and for her own soul's peace:

> I hope that God, blessed be His name, will give me the strength to return there. Because look, over there a really strange thing happened. Because the first time I went there (I'm speaking about more than twenty years ago) it was raining so hard, and my mother always used to tell me, "I'm convinced that you are the only person who will go to those camps one day, because you have more courage than anyone." "Remember this," she says. "Bring me a fistful of that soil and kiss the ground for me." And when I went, there are witnesses who saw it: It was raining, and I threw myself down, face forward, spattered with mud, right in the middle where the entrance to the camp was. Then they told me, "Come on, lady, you've fallen." I say, "No, stop." I pulled myself back on my feet. I don't know, look, I was clean the way you are now, look. When I went, unfortunately, my mother was no more, so I brought a fistful of earth from a crematory oven, not that it was from those dead,

but it was a fistful of that soil, the soil of Auschwitz. I put it in a little bag and took it to my mother's grave before I returned home. I say, "Mama, I carried out your wish the best way I could."

Throughout these interviews the verb *salvare* recurs, which we have rendered as *rescue* and, when *rescue* would not fit, as *save*. The Italian verb is inextricably bound up with theological connotations that we tried, to the extent possible, to avoid. Here we are of one mind with Lawrence L. Langer, who finds spiritual uplift inappropriate to the experience recounted in the Holocaust testimonies he has studied at great length in the Fortunoff Video Archives at Yale. His book is subtitled *The Ruins of Memory,* and it follows the Auschwitz memoirs of Charlotte Delbo in setting apart the "deep memory" of the camps from the "common memory" of life before and after that dehumanizing experience. Langer welcomes Delbo's "departure from the familiar approach that tries to entice the Auschwitz experience, and others like it, into the uncongenial sanctuaries of a redeeming *salvation* [emphasis added]."[16]

Clearly the memories recounted in the testimonies in this book have more fortunate outcomes, at least for those interviewed, than the camps had. To the extent that the common memories of those rescued allow them to express gratitude—unqualified in the instances of the foreign Jews, sometimes rueful and disenchanted in the lengthier instances of the Italian Jews—these interviews speak for themselves and make Caracciolo's case. The gratitude, as Carpi indicates, is deserved and earned. The historical statistics advanced by Toscano bear out this judgment. But we also hear in this book the discordant and irreconcilable voices of deep memory, for which gratitude is beside the point—voices beyond rescue, even now, fifty years after the events. For these, we must be grateful to Caracciolo and his camera and tape. He has captured these accounts of the remembered truth in their bittersweet complexity: a web of joy and grieving still.

Prologue

The Jews in Italy and the Anti-Semitic Policy of Fascism

Mario Toscano

After they had achieved equal rights during the Risorgimento, Italian Jews quickly began to fit into the fabric of the country, taking an active role in its social, economic, cultural, and political life. As time went by, Judaism assumed by degrees a more exclusively religious connotation, of a private and domestic character; for Italian adherents, it did not entail a reason for separation from the surrounding society. Furthermore, between the end of the nineteenth century and the beginning of the twentieth, not even the residual forms of anti-Jewish prejudice or the new anti-Zionist demonstrations of nationalistic and Catholic milieus—already limited as they were by the scant importance of Italian Zionism and by its mostly cultural and philanthropic character—represented significant obstacles to achieving an ever stronger integration within Italian society.

But together with the particular characteristics of the process of emancipation of Italian Jewry and the specific nature of its history, compared with other European countries, there was a fundamental reason why it was hard for anti-Jewish feeling to spread in Italy: the small number of Jews there. According to the 1911 census, the Italians who declared themselves as practicing the Jewish faith amounted to 32,825 (in an overall population of 34,671,400); according to the 1931 census, which included the important community of Trieste that had become a part of the kingdom of Italy after World War I, their numbers rose to 39,112 among 41,176,700 citizens. The census of

1938, taken on the basis of racial rather than religious criteria, furnished the number of 47,252 Italian Jews, to which 10,173 foreign Jews were added, the latter to a large extent residents of Italy for many years and integrated in the life of the Italian Jewish communities.[1] The Jewish presence in Italy was therefore, by percentage and as a whole, rather modest and appeared significant in only a few cities of the central and northern regions: Trieste, Leghorn, Venice, Rome, Milan.

The rise of Fascism to power in October 1922, notwithstanding the presence of some Jews among its ranks, from the outset caused uncertainty and mistrust in the Jewish community, which were destined to last for some years, until the new regime was stabilized. Toward the end of the 1920s, despite the problems (common to all Italians) due to the establishment of an authoritarian regime, the relations between Fascism in power and the Jews appeared to have improved notably, and the Jewish communities enjoyed a climate of substantial religious freedom in a peaceful coexistence among fellow citizens. At the start of the 1930s, the situation seemed positive; in 1932 Mussolini declared to Emil Ludwig that in Italy anti-Semitism did not exist.[2] In a few years' time, however, Fascist policy was destined to change radically through the convergence of internal and international factors.

Hitler's rise to power in Germany involved a gradual change in Mussolini's policy, and that of Fascism, with regard to the Jews: this policy in fact favored a renewal of the pro-German and anti-Semitic Fascist currents and primed a rapid change in the international political situation. The change evidenced itself in particular during the second half of the 1930s, in a sharpening of the contrast between Fascism and the Western democracies and in its growing closeness to Nazi Germany. This change in the international context was accompanied by an important internal change: its basic characterization of itself as a totalitarian regime, looking toward maximum internal unity; toward the full mobilization of all its material and "moral" energies; toward the creation of citizens adequate to its goals, in accord with the myth of the "New Italian," bearer of a Roman and imperial civilization, freed of the debris of democracy, of "bourgeois" pacifism, of the "disintegrating" Jewish mentality.

Therefore while in 1933–34 Mussolini could still give himself airs as protector of the Jews, without allowing a fissure on this account in the potential development of relations with Nazi Germany, in March 1934, after minor skirmishes, the first violently anti-Jewish campaign erupted in the press in Italy. The situation, internal and international, was not yet such as to turn anti-Semitism into a practical political factor in Italy, but the first die had been cast.

In the second half of the 1930s, the crucial shift in the policy of Fascism toward Jews was determined by the international consequences of the war in Ethiopia and the Spanish Civil War; during this period, as far as the Jews are concerned, Mussolini's mistrust of Zionism was growing. Zionism was held to be an instrument of English imperialism and Judaism and was considered hostile to Italy and Fascism. The concurrent internal shift in the regime fused its internal and international interests in an anti-Jewish function. The gradual consolidation, between 1936 and 1938, of the ties between Fascism and Nazism made it necessary to eliminate any reason for potential friction between the two regimes. Without any explicit Nazi request to move in such a direction, during the second half of the 1930s Fascist Italy was moving toward marginalizing its Jewish citizens, with the purpose of achieving its totalitarian internal objectives and its expansionist external ones.

Starting in 1936–38, the rhythm of anti-Jewish events and measures was becoming emphatic: in September 1936 the anti-Semitic polemics in the press were resumed; in October the Rome-Berlin axis was created; in December began the removal of the Jewish contributors to *Popolo d'Italia;*[3] in April 1937, after a brief pause, the anti-Jewish press campaign recommenced, stimulated by the publication of the book by Paolo Orano, *Gli ebrei in Italia* (The Jews in Italy);[4] in September Mussolini went to Germany; in November, on the occasion of Ribbentrop's visit to Rome, Italy joined the anti-Comintern pact. In this circumstance, Mussolini and Ciano[5] informed the minister of the Reich on the developments of the anti-Jewish campaign in Italy; on December 11 Italy announced it would be leaving the League of Nations. In the first days of 1938 the Italian press was fully committed to the anti-Semitic campaign; on February 16 *Informazione Diplomatica* No. 14 was published, the first official display of Italian anti-Semitism, edited by Mussolini personally. In it, after having denied the intention of initiating an anti-Jewish policy, he specified that the regime reserved the right "to keep a watch upon the activities of Jews recently arrived in our country and to see to it that the share of the Jews in the national life as a whole should not be disproportionate to the intrinsic merits of individuals and to the numerical importance of their community."[6] It was a matter of "a masterpiece of anti-Semitic propaganda," in accord with Mussolini's own definition of the term.

In April Ciano refused to meet with Goldmann, an important exponent of Zionism;[7] from May 3 to 9 Hitler's visit to Italy took place. On July 14 the *Manifesto della razza* (Manifesto of the Race) was published,[8] which declared among other things that "the population of Italy today is of Aryan origin and its civilization is Aryan" (point

4) and that "the Jews do not belong to the Italian race" (point 9). On July 19 came a notice that the Central Office of Demography at the Ministry of Internal Affairs had been transformed into the Central Directorship for Demography and Race, the central bureaucratic and administrative nucleus of the anti-Semitic policy that the regime was setting out to put into effect.[9] On August 5, 1938, *Informazione Diplomatica* No. 18 informed its readers that "to discriminate doesn't mean to persecute" and that the participation of the Italian Jews in the life of the country had to correspond to the ratio of one to a thousand for the Italian population. At the same time, the first anti-Semitic provision appeared, prohibiting foreign Jewish students from enrolling in the schools of the kingdom for the year 1938–39. From August on, despite the lack of approval for every legal measure with respect to the Italian Jews, arrangements were already being put into effect to remove Jews from public office.

Other measures were undertaken on September 2 and 3: foreign Jews were barred from taking up residence in the kingdom, in Libya, and in the islands of the Aegean Sea; those already in residence had to leave within six months; further, Italian citizenship was revoked for whoever had obtained it after January 1, 1919. Some did leave; others were able to remain on the peninsula. Italian Jews, for their part, were excluded from teaching on any level whatsoever; all students of the "Hebrew race" were forbidden to attend public schools. Only students already enrolled in the universities could finish their studies.

In view of the adoption of new provisions, the Office of Demography and Race completed a census of foreign and Italian Jews, elaborating specialized statistics by categories, laying the bases for a census of Jewish possessions, with continually updated data.

In the night of October 6 the Grand Council, with the opposition of only Balbo, De Bono, and Federzoni,[10] approved a "Declaration on Race" in which, among other things, a prohibition against marriages between Italians and those belonging to races other than the Aryan race was established; expulsion of foreign Jews from the kingdom was decided on; the criteria for belonging to the Hebrew "race" were specified; discrimination in favor of Jews who had high patriotic or Fascist merit was settled upon; and the general lines of exclusion of Jews from employment of certain kinds and from the professions, and the limits to their property rights, were also settled. Racism would become the subject matter of university courses.

Specific legislative measures followed shortly after this generalized declaration: with DL (legal decree) No. 1728 of November 17, 1938, detailed "Measures for the Defense of the Italian Race" were taken, which confirmed the declarations of the Grand Council and translated them into detailed legal standards.

In the application of these anti-Semitic measures, the rules established to concede extenuations and "Aryanizations" fostered sensational instances of corruption; at the same time, however, Demography and Race was preparing new restrictive measures. In June of 1940, in connection with Italy's entry into the war, a decision was made for the internment of about two hundred Italian Jews regarded as "dangerous"; others were added in the following years, up to something over a thousand. On the basis of the legal decree of September 4, 1940, relative to the aforesaid "enemies," the government began to put into effect the progressive internment and concentration of foreign Jews in camps that, while differing profoundly from those organized by the Germans, still represented an instrument of coercion and degradation.[11] Despite the blows they had suffered, the Italian Jews tried to bring moral and material aid of their own to their foreign coreligionists, often refugees separated from their own countries in order to escape persecution or else stateless people with Italian papers, through the establishment of DELASEM (Delegation for Assistance to Jewish Emigrants, December 1939),[12] a creation of the Union of Italian Jewish Communities. The camps were situated principally in the central and southern regions; there were numerous places of confinement in the Veneto as well.

On May 6, 1942, the Ministry of Internal Affairs, in accord with the Ministry of Corporations, established a civil summons for purposes of work, which was to be served on those belonging to the "Hebrew race" between the ages of eighteen and forty-five; bureaucratic and administrative problems, however, limited the effectiveness of the measure.

Inside the country, even though in a manner perceptibly different from what happened in territories controlled by the Nazis, Jews were subjected to restrictive measures and confined in a condition of marginality. Outside, the position of the Ministry of Foreign Affairs differed from that of the Internal Ministry with respect to Jews who were in zones where anti-Semitic arrangements were in force and who were considered to be Italian citizens. The Foreign Ministry and the armed forces took the same position in the conquered territories in France, Greece, and Yugoslavia, into which Jews were rushing to enjoy the protection offered by the Italian troops as distinguished from the treatment by the Germans and their collaborationists—a behavior motivated by humanitarian and political considerations and destined to last until September 8, 1943.

The fall of the Fascist government (July 25, 1943) and the establishment of the Badoglio government did not lead to a radical change in the situation: the racial legislation, apart from some secondary modifications, survived, and with it the bureaucratic apparatus put in place to enforce it. In the same period, some of the projects dreamed up by certain leaders of Italian Jewry to transfer Jews in danger—to the southern regions of the country (or somewhere else, from the Côte d'Azur to North Africa)—remained a dead letter.[13] September 8 caught the vast majority of Jews, Italian and foreign, in a position of great risk and discomfort. The crucial phase of the tragedy of persecution was beginning, one that involved above all the Jews who were in the central and southern regions of Italy and in the occupied territories. The Jews interned in Yugoslavia, liberated on September 8, made individual attempts to reach safety;[14] for those in the French zone, once the attempts to organize their transfer failed, only a few were able safely to elude the dragnets carried out immediately by the Germans;[15] the lot of the Greek Jews was frightful.[16]

In the new situation, characterized by the dominant presence of the Germans, the ambiguous earlier policy of "discriminating without persecuting" was no longer feasible. The very measures adopted by the RSI (the Italian Social Republic), as grave as they were—even when (following Nazi logic) they had not aimed at the deportation and extermination of the Jews but at putting them in concentration camps, postponing the solution to the "problem" for an uncertain future— expressed positions that were not tenable with respect to the reality of events.

On the other hand, the condition of the Jews, already quite precarious, was made still more difficult, if possible, by the new measures: in November 1943 the Verona white paper declared in point 7 that "those belonging to the Hebrew race are foreigners. During this war they belong to an enemy nationality."[17] On November 30, 1943, a circular from the Ministry of Internal Affairs established concentration camps for the Jews in apposite places.[18] A legal decree of January 4, 1944, established new prohibitions on Jewish property rights, making their situation frightful. A new exacerbation of the legislation was delineated by a legal decree of April 16, 1945, ten days before the liberation.

But for some time now the Jew hunt had been begun and developed. It was conducted directly by the Germans and, in some circumstances (Venice), by Italians. In these circumstances there was no lack of instances of denunciation and informing; but there also emerged some signal and important episodes of solidarity.

The violent persecutions began the day after September 8 with the massacres of Lago Maggiore and the Val d'Aosta;[19] on October 16, 1943, the raid on the Jews of Rome was carried out;[20] on December 31, 1943, and August 17, 1944, it was the turn of the Jews of Venice.[21] Seventy-five Jews were slaughtered in the Ardeatine Caves on March 24, 1944.[22] Between October 18, 1943, and December 14, 1944, fifteen convoys of Jews left Italy for the extermination camps. The arrests, deportations, and killings went on to the very end.

According to the research of the CDEC,[23] the number of deportees from Italy and from Italian territories outside of the metropolitan centers was 8,369, of whom 6,244 were Italian citizens; there were 980 survivors (of whom 515 were Italian citizens). In addition, 292 perished in prisons and concentration camps in Italy.

While the tragedy was playing itself out, however, demonstrations of solidarity and resistance were not lacking. Though reduced to a clandestine existence, DELASEM, with the fundamental assistance of Catholics in religious orders, was able to bring help to large numbers of the persecuted.[24] About two thousand Jews, a very high percentage of the total population of the Jewish community, entered the ranks of the Resistance in that same period, to regain through the partisan struggle their own freedom and the freedom of their country.[25]

The Interviews

PROFESSOR DANIEL CARPI

NICOLA CARACCIOLO: Well, Professor, have you devoted a lot of time to this problem of relations between Italians and Jews during the war?

DANIEL CARPI: Yes. It was something that began a bit by chance. Fifteen years ago I decided to give a seminar, a course here at Tel Aviv University, on the Jews of Western Europe, and I got my hands on documents having to do with the Jews in southern France and a whole complicated story. Almost, I'd say, a detective story.

N.C.: And that is?

D.C.: . . . On the position of the Italians vis-à-vis the Jews. That is, an Italian police chief, Lospinoso, who was sent into southern France by the Italian government to look into Jewish questions. Having been advised by a Capuchin friar, Pierre Marie-Benoît, and by a French Jew, Italo Angelo Donati,[1] he decided not to collaborate with the Germans and not to hand over to the Germans the Jews of the South of France, but on the contrary to vanish, not to let himself be seen.

Professor Daniel Carpi, Tel Aviv University

N.C.: And the same thing also happened in Croatia, no? And in Greece?

D.C.: Well now, from that time on I began to study, to see what the position of the Italians was, and what emerged was a really interesting picture, a unique one, I'd say, for the history of the Holocaust.

N.C.: Why unique?

D.C.: Why unique? Because in a period in which, in all of occupied Europe, the Germans were able to draw on help from at least a part of the local populations, including the Vichy government, certainly from the Croatian Ustasha, to give some examples . . .

N.C.: And in Italy?

D.C.: On the contrary, the Italians, who were allied with the Germans, refused to collaborate and helped the Jews: in the first place, Jews who had Italian citizenship, and in the second place, also Croatian Jews or Greek ones in Salonica, or French ones, or Polish refugees in France. And this is, in the history of the Holocaust, a unique example.

N.C.: Why unique?

D.C.: Because, in a period in which a large part of the peoples of Europe were collaborating with the Germans, at least on this issue, the Italians, who were the Germans' allies, on this very issue, this matter, were unwilling to collaborate, and so they saved thousands and thousands of Jews.

N.C.: Well, Professor, we know a good deal about how the common people, let's say this, peasants, ordinary soldiers, workers, merchants, helped the Jews . . .

D.C.: You see, here there are, one can say, two levels: there's the level of simple people (I am speaking of the occupied countries), that is, Italian soldiers who were in Croatia or in France, soldiers who tried spontaneously to help these people without knowing exactly why, only because they were persecuted, because they were innocent people and persecuted not as Jews or non-Jews; the other level, which is perhaps more important, or at least has another importance, is the level of help that was given in an organized way, more or less planned, by both Italian diplomats and a large part of the military commands.

N.C.: If you permit, in fact I've got a personal recollection about this.

D.C.: Tell me.

N.C.: In brief, as a young journalist during the Algerian War, at the moment when there was a revolt by the French extremists against De Gaulle in 1962—the OAS—we Italian journalists in Algiers got on well with one of De Gaulle's police chiefs, a man named Goldenberg. Someone who would help us quite a lot, by giving us news and developments just for being Italian journalists. At a certain point I asked him the reason for this, and he told me that when he was fourteen, he was of a Jewish family, and he was standing in the station at Grenoble to be brought into Germany, to Auschwitz, an Italian officer, whom he didn't know, saw this boy there, took pity on him, let him leave, and rescued him.

D.C.: Oh, yes, but here in Israel you find these episodes by the thousands: someone who was hidden under an Italian officer's bed, someone who was brought from Cracow to Italy, young children, orphans found that way on the street, on the streets of some village in Galicia or in Poland, and rescued, then brought to Italy, who took part later on in the partisan struggle, or . . . The interesting thing is that we find a very broad curve of these cases: it runs from Grenoble, as you say . . . to Tunisia, to Croatia, which is the principal country, Croatia and Dalmatia, Albania and . . . Salonica, that is, it's really an important curve and a unique chapter in the history of the Holocaust.

N.C.: Well, then, I repeat the question, *why* is it unique?

D.C.: Because apart from the level of the common people that we also find in some, not many, but in some of the European countries such as Holland and Denmark, here there's an organized action on which practically *everyone* was in agreement. It's hard to find anyone who opposed it. That is, the correspondence at the Foreign Ministry between Roatta and Count Pietromarchi, between Pietromarchi and Vittorio Castellani, the liaison officer with the Second Army in Croatia, was an open correspondence, notwithstanding the Duce's order (which I'll let you see afterward) to hand over the Croatian Jews to the Germans; or the Italian diplomats, precisely . . . First I would remember Count Luca Pietromarchi, Ambassador Ducci, Vittorio Castellani, and Blasco D'Ajeta.

N.C.: Pellegrino Ghigi.

D.C.: Pellegrino Ghigi. I've certainly forgotten many names, I'm sorry to say, which would deserve to be recalled. But it's significant that the correspondence between them was completely open, which means they weren't afraid that this might provoke a reaction from the police. That is, it was an action they took for clearly humanitarian reasons—

Count Luca Pietromarchi, chief of the Department of Occupied Territories, Italian Foreign Ministry. This archival photograph dates from the period of the Italian occupation of parts of France and Yugoslavia. (Courtesy of RAI-TV)

namely, they were unwilling to partake in genocide. They might have had . . . have been of one opinion or another, but there was a limit beyond which they were unwilling to go: from racial persecution to genocide.

N.C.: Do you mean, then, Professor, that the Italians behaved better than everyone else in Europe at that tragic moment?

D.C.: I'd say yes, the Italians showed in any case that even in a period of darkness, a period in which, I'd almost say, the sun of civilization grew dark over the greater part of the countries of Europe, at that moment the position of the majority of Italians, and not only in Italy—this is the interesting point—was positive.

N.C.: Were there black sheep?

D.C.: Look, there would have been someone here or there, certainly not at a high level, it's hard to find him, but he didn't leave a trace. There would have been somebody. The great majority, not the average, the great majority behaved well.

N.C.: And Mussolini?

D.C.: Mussolini, the position of Mussolini isn't clear. I'd say it's ambiguous.

N.C.: Why ambiguous?

D.C.: It's clear, yes, yet ambiguous. That is, Mussolini washed his hands of it somewhat, he had neither the will nor the courage to take a clear position. When the Germans came and put pressure on Mussolini so he would give the order to hand over the Croatian Jews to the Germans, Mussolini gave this order, he wrote "*nulla osta*"* on it.[2]

N.C.: Is there a document?

D.C.: A document that proves it clearly. Other times Mussolini said to the generals or to the diplomats, "You do it, find an excuse, say that you don't have the boats to carry them to Trieste." Mussolini, to be sure, didn't share the Nazis' opinion on the genocide, but Mussolini had neither the character nor the courage nor the good faith of his aides to decide not to cross this Rubicon.

N.C.: And Ciano? How do you view him?

D.C.: Ciano? The position of Ciano is very clear. Ciano looked out for Italian interests. Ciano was against consignment to the Germans of the Jews of Salonica, of Tunisia, of all places. He saw, as I was saying, the role of political interest: to hand over the Croatian Jews or the Greek Jews to the Germans meant a great blow to Italian prestige in the Balkans, a great blow to Italian economic interests. Ciano was looking out for both aspects, whether out of political interest or (as I believe) because he, too, was clearly in moral agreement with those who tried to oppose the German orders.

N.C.: Listen, that's one of the things generally said so much now in Italy when we talk, so much is said about the faults of the Italians. Is this, instead, a story in which the Italians cut a better figure than many others?

D.C.: Than almost all the others, yes. I don't know why Italians today keep this chapter almost hidden away. I think that Italians are almost afraid that to emphasize what Italian diplomats or military men did during the World War II could be interpreted as apologetics for Fascism, which it isn't, it surely isn't. Well, from this viewpoint it's a lot

---

* *Nulla osta* = *nihil obstat*—in the jargon of Italian diplomacy, no official objection to a recommended action.

more comfortable for me than for a scholar in Italy. I am here in Tel Aviv, at Tel Aviv University; we aren't suspected of Fascism.

Here we speak from an Israeli perspective, that is, it's of interest to us to comprehend that in that darkness, of which I was speaking, which descended upon Europe, there were also some rays of light, there was also a moment of . . . of . . .

N.C.: Of humanity.

D.C.: Of humanity and of—I'd almost put it this way—the light of reason not being lost, when there was someone who said, "Gentlemen, you cannot proceed in this manner; it's not conceivable."

I think that it's important to emphasize that the action of the Italians, at least in Croatia, was not applied uniquely vis-à-vis the Jews, but at the beginning, on the contrary, in Croatia, the Italians thought it their duty to impede the massacre of the Serbs and I think of the Gypsies as well.

BLANKA STERN AND OTHERS[3]

NICOLA CARACCIOLO: How did the people in Italy behave toward you?

BLANKA STERN: It was a very different atmosphere than the one we escaped from. There was humanity, we became people again, or to put it the way one of the Italians did, he said, "They're not Catholic, but we're all Christian," that is to say, we're all human. We were received very well everywhere.

N.C.: Is there anyone in particular you want to remember?

B.S.: There is. I expressly wanted to remember a woman, because . . . Mrs. Irma Andriol, from Sozzano—she was, they said then, the wife of the town secretary—she was a brave woman. When September 8 arrived we knew that we had to escape again—I was eight-months pregnant—escape, but how? And this lady, Irma Andriol, who died a month ago, came at night, brought us blank identity cards, and told us to attach our photographs to them. Then we returned the identity cards to her, she put the official stamp of the municipality on them, we in turn wrote some falsified names on them, we were Stareni rather than Stern—and that's how we were saved. So I'd like to say that the Italians weren't just good people, human, but also that they had courage, because this woman was in danger. I want to add something. It's well known that the Germans used psychological systems to make us, the others, the Jews, a very inferior race. We were no longer hu-

The restaurant in Jerusalem. *Left to right:* Ita Lador, Nada Volhaim, and Blanka Stern, speaking to Nicola Caracciolo, who has his back to the camera.

man, we had no rights; when we arrived in Italy the people restored our sense of being human, they restored our sense of humanity, in fact, our feeling of being part of the entire human race.

NADA VOLHAIM

NADA VOLHAIM: There is, in fact . . . yes, I remember a certain person who saved my life—a Dr. Elio Del Giudice.

NICOLA CARACCIOLO: From where?

N.V.: From Rome. He hid me for almost nine months in his apartment . . . and this was a danger for him and a grave danger for his family, because you couldn't hide a Jewess, it was forbidden under penalty of death, naturally.

ERNA NACHMIAS

NICOLA CARACCIOLO: And you, Mrs. Nachmias, is there any Italian you remember?

The restaurant in Jerusalem. Erna Nachmias, speaking, is in the center. The woman to her left and the man to her right are not identified.

ERNA NACHMIAS: Yes, I can tell you that all of us lived in great fear in Split for two and a half years, but when we saw an Italian *carabiniere* or any Italian, my heart was light, because they were so kind to us. And they loved the children so much. One evening—I've got to tell you this. I had three little children. The youngest was two years old, he was playing outside and fell. I saw so much blood, I didn't know what to do. It was past curfew. I took my son and started to go. My husband says, "Where are you going, it's curfew, aren't you afraid?" "Not afraid, I've got to go to the hospital." On the street I ran into a *carabiniere*: "Lady, where are you going now?" "I'm going to the hospital." "But how, you know, you *do* know, there's a curfew now?" "I know." "Do you know where the hospital is?" "No." "Ah, lady, I'll take you there." The *carabiniere* took me to the hospital. I told him, "Many thanks," in fact—we came, there were so many people and so many soldiers. Then the doctor came, he put a bandage on, everything for the little one, and he said, "Lady, you can go home, everything's all right." I look at the clock: twelve. The cops! I don't know what to do now, I was afraid to go. I can't go home, I don't know where I am—What do I do? I'll stay until tomorrow morning, fine. I see the *carabiniere*. "But officer. . . ." "Lady, I am waiting for you." "Officer, how is it that you're waiting for me?" "I'll accompany you home." I told the *carabiniere* that they'd killed our entire family, because nobody is left, out of the entire large family there are only my husband, myself, and three children and a nephew—that's all that's left of our family. I told the *carabiniere* everything, and he had a heart like all Italians who were so kind to us, he accompanied me all the way home. I said, "Officer, come, come in, a glass [*sic*] of coffee, my husband must also thank you for what you've done for us." "Lady, I did my duty." "Sir, I am telling you this, it's something one cannot forget, I . . ."

N.C.: Do you remember this *carabiniere*'s name?

E.N.: I don't remember, I don't remember—I'm sorry, I was so confused that I don't remember. I said, "Come in, Officer." "No, lady, I did my duty, I've got a home and children, too. I did this with a lot of pleasure." [*Laughter.*]

MARCELLO HOFFMAN

NICOLA CARACCIOLO: [*reading*] "To my friend, Marcello, fondly— Alessandro Bersani" of Nonantola—do you want to show us this pho-

Marcello Hoffman

tograph? [*Holds up photograph for close up.*] Thank you. What is there within this story?

MARCELLO HOFFMAN: This was a friend who helped me when we . . . escaped from Nonantola[4] to Switzerland.

N.C.: What did he do?

M.H.: When the Germans entered the town we all ran out of our large house, Villa Emma, where we were lodging.

N.C.: Yes?

M.H.: Everyone escaped to a different place—I and three friends of mine to the home of a peasant. Every evening this boy came to us, bringing cheese, bread, things to eat. And when we escaped to Switzerland I received a letter from him via the Red Cross. . . .

N.C.: What did it say?

M.H.: And he said that when we escaped from Nonantola . . . there was a woman who had denounced him for having helped us. And he wrote, "I don't regret that I helped you." And these words are with me forever.

SLATA GLICK

SLATA GLICK: Ah . . . I have some memories—my whole family escaped, that is my parents and my sister, we escaped from Slovenia, which was occupied by the Italians, and then they sent us to internment in Italy, to a small village called Montiglio. . . .

NICOLA CARACCIOLO: Where is it?

S.G.: In the Province of Asti. . . .

N.C.: What memories do you have?

S.G.: Oh, some beautiful memories. It was a tiny village, with kind and very warm people, and they helped us a whole lot. We had friends. I remember a lady named Renata, who was a dressmaker, and she really helped us a lot. My sister learned to sew from her, and my sister went back to the village a year or two ago and visited her, and there was certainly great joy. And I could say that they were all very kind. I could tell you that the village "*podestà*"* helped us escape,

*An appointed municipal official, differing from an elected mayor (who would be a *sindaco*).

then brought us falsified papers and people to take us over the Alps to get into Switzerland.

ERVIN GOMBOSH

ERVIN GOMBOSH: There was someone in Bologna who helped me a lot, who obtained all the fake papers for me, because I lived in Bologna until 1942, and his name was Mario Finzi . . . who afterwards in 1943 or 1944 was shot by the Germans.

ALIZA ALMOSLINO

NICOLA CARACCIOLO: Whose photograph is this?

ALIZA ALMOSLINO: It's of a priest, Don Dante Sala* of Carpi, Province of Modena, who saved our lives during the world war.

N.C.: What did he do?

A.A.: He hid us in his apartment and then organized our escape to Switzerland. He found out where we should go, and we escaped to Switzerland.

ABRAHAM COHEN

ABRAHAM COHEN: My name is Cohen Abraham—my wife, unfortunately, is no longer alive. We were in Italy for a long time, from 1941 till 1943.

NICOLA CARACCIOLO: And where did you stay?

A.C.: I don't want to go into details, but I can only tell you that the Italians (first of all the Olivetti family) saved my life, and Gertrude's, who is no longer living, and all the Olivettis gave us moral and financial help. After all, the Catholic Church also helped me a lot, and the last time they found a place for me to stay, a priest went with me from Ivrea to Azeglio on a bicycle during the month of December. It was bad weather.

N.C.: Do you remember this priest's name?

---

*The title "Don," by which Mrs. Almoslino refers to Father Sala, is an honorific, often given to priests, even simple parish priests, in Italy.

A.C.: Oh, I don't know anymore, I don't know anymore. We went for kilometers with this priest, from Ivrea to Azeglio. There we found another priest and he found a place for me to stay, and two days later my wife came, and when we went to our lodgings, we found everything arranged for us. This is only one instance of how the Italians saved our lives.

WOMAN (UNIDENTIFIED)

WOMAN (unidentified): We were in Asolo, Province of Treviso, we were together with Italians. They were very, very good to us, and a lady I remember very well, her name is Ida Zorzetto—the entire Zorzetto family helped us a lot, a lot.

NICOLA CARACCIOLO: What did they do?

WOMAN: They gave us food and almost every day—because what they gave us wasn't enough, and she had a good heart and always thought that we were hungry—she always gave us something, a morsel of polenta, a morsel of something else, it was always this way.

A MAN'S VOICE

A MAN'S VOICE: Thanks so much to the Italian people. . . .

ITA LADOR

ITA LADOR: I have a little story about the concentration camp at Ferramonti;[5] there were so many children there, they started a school.

One day a Jewish man from Milan comes with toys for the children, and there was a party and every child gets a toy. There was an Italian captain there, whose job was the sanitation for the camp, the water in the barracks, the latrines. He lived in the camp with his wife and three children. Every day his children left for school and in the afternoon they played with the Jewish children in the camp. And when the man from Milan came and every child received a toy, the captain comes over and says, "But why don't you invite my children too, they're at home and crying, please invite my children too." That's my story.

AN UNIDENTIFIED VOICE

AN UNIDENTIFIED VOICE:* I like Italy so much because I like the Italians who are so good and had such good hearts with us. We were poor, we were, we had nothing to eat, they came to us: "Lady, you need this," they saw the little ones, they always wanted to help us. I like Italy, and I want, whenever I can, when there's a possibility, I'll go to Italy with so much pleasure.

MR. DORON AND BERNARD GROSSER

NICOLA CARACCIOLO: Mr. Doron, you are the secretary of the association [called] Gratitude to the Population of Italy.

DORON: We have begun to send letters to all those who we know had been in Italy. I believe we have sent about a thousand letters, we've received three hundred replies containing over a thousand names. Unfortunately many people died in those days and we don't know where a great number of others are to be found, because in those days, I believe, in Italy or in areas under Italian protection there were seven or eight thousand Yugoslavs. There were two or three thousand on the island of Arbe,[6] because afterwards I went back with the partisans and found that many had died, but in Italy itself there were six thousand Yugoslavian Jews, and of these six thousand I believe that almost all were saved.

N.C.: And how did this happen? To whom do we owe it?

D.: I'll tell you what happened in our place in September 1943, after the armistice. We were seventy persons interned in the Province of Treviso, in a village called Asolo—and on that day the secretary of the local government called us. He told us it was better to run away, because the Germans are coming, you don't know what will happen, and he gave all of us, as they say, false identity cards. Not really false, he just changed the names, and on the cards it was written that everyone had been born in southern Italy: Palermo, in those places where the Allies were—and this way we started to run away, not all at one time. Every one of the seventy people in my place was saved.

---

*This is the last interview conducted at the Jerusalem restaurant, evidently in some haste, and hence the uncertainties about the source.

N.C.: And how was this book made, would you show it to me?

D.: [*showing him a page*] This is one of the three hundred pages of the album. We printed the sheets, and at the top of each one there is the inscription "gratitude to the Italian people." To the population, and afterwards we printed the names of all those people who told us where they were born and where they were in Italy during the war.

N.C.: How did you come up with this idea?

D.: We were thinking about this for many years, that is, what the Italian people did for us. It was most difficult to understand why they behaved this way during wartime. It wasn't just the ordinary people, but also the authorities, the police force, the *carabinieri*, everyone helped when he could. Perhaps there were a very few who didn't act this way, but they were extremely few, we didn't hear them. We were given false I.D. cards and were always helped with food of various sorts. They gave us more than they gave to the Italian Jews. So we didn't go hungry during wartime.

N.C.: And you, Mr. Grosser, are the president of the Gratitude to the Population of Italy Association. How did it happen?

BERNARD GROSSER: During the war I was living in Italy, in Genoa, and I was working in collaboration with Lelio Valobra, president of DELASEM.[7]

N.C.: What was that?

B.G.: The Delegation for Assistance to Emigrants, a Jewish relief organization for the victims of the persecutions, which was in existence in Italy, with the authorities' permission, until September 8, 1943.

N.C.: Your group was helping the Jewish refugees. How many arrived from Central Europe during that period?

B.G.: We don't know the exact number. There were thousands, maybe even tens of thousands of refugees, from every part of Europe.

N.C.: In short, then, people who had escaped from death.

B.G.: Of course . . .

N.C.: I would like to ask you this question. In that very period, that is, in 1939, before Italy entered the war, for a Jew who escaped, let's say from Poland or Germany, was it easier to enter Italy, France, or England?

B.G.: Italy . . .

N.C.: That is, the Italian government was the most open with respect to the refugees among all European governments—can that be said?

B.G.: Without a doubt, without a doubt, without a doubt . . .

N.C.: What sort of relations did you have with the Italian authorities in those days?

B.G.: I had relations with police headquarters in Genoa and with two commissioners, Dr. Veneziani and Dr. Mollo. I was in touch with them daily to get transit visas and various permits for . . .

N.C.: And how did they act?

B.G.: Well—extremely well. They helped in a really unbelievable manner, for . . . one couldn't believe that the police would behave this way.

N.C.: And who was their boss? Was it Carmine Senise in those days?

B.G.: No, no, no, Senise is [*sic*] in Rome. At the Genoa police headquarters their boss was the chief commissioner, a really magnificent person.

N.C.: What was his name?

B.G.: I don't remember any longer. I'm very sorry. These commissioners were always asking the deputy chief of police for some permits, and he agreed—I can't remember his name, he too was a really exceptional person who helped us a whole lot.

N.C.: In those days did Valobra have contacts in the upper echelons?

B.G.: Attorney Valobra knew the chief of police, Senise, personally.

N.C.: Yes—and how did Senise act in this matter?

B.G.: Very well, really very well, because we've seen the results. In that period of time no Jewish refugee from abroad and no one from Italy was expelled. And we got all that we asked for.

N.C.: How high up did the protection go? In your opinion, was there someone on top of Senise? From what you know . . .

B.G.: I cannot give you a firm answer. Clearly there were other personalities who helped us, but I cannot say. If you are interested, I can tell you about Cardinal Borgoncini Duca's involvement.

N.C.: But of course . . .

B.G.: We needed someone to intercede with the Interior Ministry on behalf of a person, and then I was advised to turn to Cardinal Borgon-cini Duca, and I went to Rome, and . . . when I entered the waiting room I announced myself, Bernardo Grosser, secretary of the Genoa chapter of DELASEM, and when Borgoncini Duca heard my name while step-ping outside his office, he called me instantly and didn't make me wait. There were about twenty people waiting in the antechamber, he took me in quickly. I entered his office and he turned to talk to me in He-brew. At that point I asked him to talk to me in Italian because it was easier for me, and he asked me what it was that I needed. Then I ex-plained the entire case to him, and so on, and when I was finished the cardinal took a piece of blank paper with his letterhead, signed it, and said, "Mr. Grosser, by all means write what it is you need and take it with you." This is an act that impressed me greatly. I was very pleased indeed to have been shown such trust by the cardinal.

N.C.: And did you get the impression that the church involved itself in this matter? Did it show solidarity with you, that is, did it help you or not?

B.G.: I don't know what the church's decisions were. I can only tell you that all the contacts I had with priests of various kinds were excellent—they all helped, we weren't rejected by any of them. I must recall here Don Repetto, who in those days was secretary to the archbishop of Genoa and who helped us print the passes, the false ID cards.[8]

N.C.: Listen, where did the money you had come from? In other words, how did the organization function?

B.G.: Before the United States entered the war we received money from the American Joint Distribution Committee. They were very big, they sent us really large amounts. When the United States entered the war . . . Then we no longer had direct contact with the United States, we couldn't receive money from that source, and there was an inter-mediary at . . . in St. Gall, Mr. Sally Mayer, who received the money from the "Joint" and sent us this money from Switzerland.[9]

N.C.: Did you have difficulty in getting the money? I mean, did the revenue officials let it go through?

B.G.: There was a money exchange in Rome, and they were without a doubt agreeable. There was no difficulty.

N.C.: Mr. Grosser, you functioned at DELASEM until September 8, 1943, right? There, then, wasn't it strange that a Jewish organization such as yours was operating in an Axis country? Did you ever ask your-self how this was possible?

B.G.: Well, we never asked ourselves how this was possible because we were in Italy, and we were dealing with Italians, and all that was necessary to assist those poor unfortunates, the refugees, the persecuted, in general, Italy was doing. Italians understood the situation of these people very well, so we had no difficulties. During a time of persecution almost all over the world, I had so much help, so much assistance from the Italians, and also goodwill, friendship, caring, and all these things.

N.C.: Then tell me, Mr. Grosser, about how many people could DELASEM have rescued?

B.G.: I've got to tell you, as for being rescued, they were rescued by Italians, DELASEM was an organization for help, for assistance; it was available to the refugees in every sense, with counsel, money, with anything it could do. But help, real help, I've got to say that it was Italy that gave it.

N.C.: And were many Jews helped in this way?

B.G.: Very many, especially all the Jews who passed through Genoa, because they were going in transit through the port of Genoa, they emigrated from there, we had in the port of Genoa a group of our employees who were helping the refugees set out on vessels, and so on.

N.C.: Any concrete instance of Italian help?

B.G.: When I was still with the committee for refugees in Milan—it was called COMASSEBIT at that time, at the time it was closed—because the committee was closed down in a really unusual manner, that is to say, we still had work, it was closed suddenly, within an hour . . .

N.C.: What year was that?

B.G.: That was in the summer of 1939, because Hitler had called Mussolini and reprimanded him for accepting refugees and offering help, et cetera. Therefore these committees were closed down, and we had to leave our office without documents, without the archive, without anything. We were no longer able to be of any help to the refugees in Milan, and it turned out that all of the refugees who were living in furnished rooms . . . and apartments were not thrown out by the Italians who gave them lodging.

N.C.: So you're saying all of the refugees who were renting furnished rooms in homes or boardinghouses could continue to stay there without paying.

B.G.: Nobody threw a refugee out. On the contrary, I know of cases where the families gave them free food.

N.C.: How many of these refugees were there?

B.G.: Thousands, I don't know exactly how many, because after forty years, it's hard to remember the exact numbers.

N.C. And the police? You had become friendly with the Genoa police?

B.G.: Naturally, because when you have daily contact with someone you become his friend. And once as it happened I went to police headquarters to see Dr. Veneziani and ask him for another of many favors. Then he looks me in the face and says, "Look here, Grosser, you're awfully pale, I have a feeling you're not eating enough." He opens a drawer and pulls out a loaf of bread, this long, and tells me, "Here, take the bread." I said, "No, Dr. Veneziani, I cannot accept it because everything is rationed. You, too, must have your rations and I cannot accept this gift." "Grosser, take this bread!" in this tone—and then I said, "No, I'm sorry, I won't take it." Then he opens a drawer and pulls out a revolver and says, "Grosser, take this bread." Then I took it. This was something that really made a great impression on me.

Then, this other thing happened, when I was running around downtown Genoa, and someone comes near me and says, "Look, I'm a police agent, and I have an order to pick you up. Grosser, do me a favor, don't go around the city like this, go home and stay there." When I'm some ten or twelve steps away from that agent, another plainclothes agent comes and says, "Listen, Grosser, I'm with the police, don't run around town so much, because I've got orders to bring you in. Go home, hide there, and this way we forget about it." And this was a most lovely action on the part of the police.

COMMANDER YEHOSHA HALEVY

NICOLA CARACCIOLO: So, what do you think of the Italians, commander?

YEHOSHA HALEVY: What do I think of the Italians?

N.C.: With respect to this whole question.

Y.H.: They're a magnificent people—do you say "magnificent"?—magnificent. The best people in Europe. And possibly in the world.

N.C.: Are you convinced that they helped you?

Y.H.: The Italians saved our lives, two or three times. We came from Bratislava, in a steamship with Jews escaping from the Germans, but I don't speak enough Italian.

MARCO HERMANN

NICOLA CARACCIOLO: Well, Mr. Hermann, how did you arrive in Italy?

MARCO HERMANN: The story's a little complicated: in a few words, I came with the Italian troops who were retreating from Russia in June 1943.

N.C.: Where from?

M.H.: I was born in Lvov and lived there till 1943.

N.C.: And your parents?

M.H.: And my parents were also deported in the summer of 1942, and . . .

N.C.: And you?

M.H.: I stayed, alone with my brother, outside the ghetto, and we were helped by the Italian soldiers who were traveling toward the Russian front.

N.C.: What became of you?

M.H.: We were homeless boys, and we got our food, in large part, from the Italian soldiers next to an Italian barracks, which was a command post. We spent the winter of 1942–43 in the cellar of an unfinished house, next to the Italians. But in the spring of 1943 we were arrested, and *I* managed to escape, I was all by myself then . . .

N.C.: What happened to your brother?

M.H.: He ended up in that horrible concentration camp, that extermination camp that was in Lvov.[10]

N.C.: And he died?

M.H.: Yes, he died. My father, too, I know he was shot there when he came down with typhus.

N.C.: And your mother?

M.H.: My mother was taken away with two younger sisters, and I don't know where she was taken to finish like the entire Jewish population of Lvov.

N.C.: Then you alone were left . . . and the Italian soldiers took care of you in some way . . .

M.H.: Yes, in June I was able to reach their barracks, they invited me to come inside. There I became their mascot. After a few days, when they started on their homeward journey, they took me with them. And so I arrived in Udine in June of 1943.

N.C.: And what did they say at the moment they took you away with them?

M.H.: We didn't speak about anything specific, in any particular way, because I wasn't the only one. Perhaps it was a humanitarian tradition displayed by the Italian soldiers, to take with them orphans from parts of the world where they found themselves, because in Udine I also met many little orphaned Russian children who were brought by the Italian soldiers when they returned to Italy from Russia.

N.C.: And what happened later on?

M.H.: On September 8 they divided the children among the various Italian soldiers who wanted to take them home.

N.C.: In other words, on September 8 that unit, like the rest of the Italian army, was disbanded. But before that happened, twenty soldiers were found to take care of the twenty young refugees.

M.H.: That's right. But unfortunately we didn't get far. When we arrived in Mestre, we were taken prisoners by the Germans and were put on a train going to Germany.

N.C.: But you were able to escape . . .

M.H.: Yes, in a little village north of Verona, I jumped off the train with another Russian boy—his name is Vassily Popov, who still lives in Italy, in Ghiemme in Novara Province—and from there we arrived at the houses of those soldiers who wanted to adopt us, but we only had the soldiers' letters.

N.C.: And there you lived, you lived with the family of the soldier who wanted to take care of you?

M.H.: Yes. . . .

N.C.: And what happened to the soldier?

M.H.: He was captured.

N.C.: What was his name?

M.H.: Giovanni Ferro, from Canischio Canavese, which was then in the province of Aosta. I did not see him again until 1961, when I took my first trip to Italy after the war, because in 1945, when I left Italy to return to Lvov in search of my family, thinking that perhaps someone was still alive, he had not yet returned from prison in Germany.

N.C.: Did you find anyone alive?

M.H.: I didn't find anyone but an uncle who returned from Russia, my mother's brother, who had been inside Russia and returned.

N.C.: Later on in Canischio you joined the partisans, am I right?

M.H.: Yes, in the same village. In the meantime I also studied until May 1944, because four well-to-do families allowed me to study in a boarding school, in a town six kilometers away from Canischio, a town called Cuorgné. Then in June 1944, by chance, I witnessed a meeting between Italian partisans and some Czech soldiers who had escaped from the Germans to that village, and there I joined the forty-ninth attack brigade called Garibaldi, which wasn't yet a brigade then, more of a band of Resistance fighters, but soon afterward became a brigade.

IZAK ITAI (JOSEF ITHAI)

IZAK ITAI (Josef Ithai):[11] In 1941 at the time of the German invasion I was in Zagreb. I was responsible for some forty German and Austrian Jewish children whom I got out of Austria. Their parents had been arrested by the Nazis. They were practically orphans. I was able to save all of them, together with about the same number of Yugoslavian Jewish children who were later added to the group thanks to the Italians. So, we had been under the Germans in Zagreb. The Germans had prohibited Jews from traveling by train. We were lucky and did not run into them. Forty children and a few adults, whom I got to help us. We arrived in the Italian zone. And the officers of the Italian Army asked, "But what is this? Children on the train in wartime? The entire train is full of children." I then told them that these are Jewish orphans running away from the Germans and then I heard "Children, children," and a general gave the order that we could enter.

NICOLA CARACCIOLO: And were you afraid of being deported?

I.I.: Naturally, it wasn't that we were afraid, we knew that for certain, and this "boy" you see here, Ariel Leo Koffler, told me, "You don't know, you don't know what the Germans are like, but we in Vienna had met up with them already." Then I was able to enter the Italian-occupied zone in the province of Ljubljana.

N.C.: How did you do it?

I.I.: I told you I was a little crazy, I took the children and we got on a train. In every station the Italian soldiers gave the children sugar and candy. They were wonderful. That was the first time the children met friendly soldiers.

Then from Yugoslavia they sent us to Italy, to Nonantola, near Modena. We were stopped for hours in Verona because the Germans had asked that we be handed over to them.

N.C.: And this would have meant death.

I.I.: Naturally. The general of the *carabinieri* in Croatia, Giuseppe Pièche,[12] decided that we should go to Nonantola and not to Auschwitz. And the train left for Modena. Not for Germany.

N.C.: Then you owe your lives to this General Pièche?

I.I. Yes, yes—not only do we, but so do many, many other Jews. He is one of the best of the Italians who did so many things on behalf of the Jews.

N.C.: What were your relations with the people there in Nonantola?[13]

I.I.: Good relations, certainly, with all of them: Fascists, non-Fascists, anti-Fascists, with all. The entire population of Nonantola became our friends. Of course some were friendlier than others, but the entire population was very, very much in favor of the children at Villa Emma.

N.C.: And what happened when September 8 came?

I.I.: On September 8, that was a sad time again. Koffler told me, "You'll see, the Germans always arrive wherever we are." We saw the SS command near Villa Emma, and since we didn't want to have anything to do with the SS, well, that same night I took the young children to the Nonantola Abbey. The old monsignor, Pelati, said, "In the name of the Lord, come in"—then we went in, twenty boys and the youngest girls, the girls too.

N.C.: And where were the other boys hidden?

I.I.: The others were hidden in the village, in the homes of the inhabitants, and the entire population knew it.

N.C.: No one said anything to the Germans.

I.I.: Yes, no one spoke to the Germans. And then we found a way to get to Switzerland. It's true that we did have to pay the smugglers. And this, too, is a complicated story.

N.C.: Listen, Mr. Itai, what do you think of what the Italians did with respect to the Jews during the war?

I.I.: We haven't yet spoken enough about what the Italian people—not the regime, but the Italian people—did for the Jews. It is one of the most beautiful things in the time of the Holocaust, one of the moments that consoled the Jewish people. Because the Italian people, and Italian officers, no matter what the regime, helped the Jews: Jews from Yugoslavia, Jews from Greece, Jews from France—and saved thousands and thousands of Jews.

ARIEL LEO KOFFLER

NICOLA CARACCIOLO: Mr. Koffler, what was your experience in Nonantola? How did things go?

ARIEL LEO KOFFLER: Well, life at Villa Emma was already a period far along into those times, it was almost the next to last place before my liberation. And I think that among all of those bad periods, the life I led at Villa Emma was the most joyful and the happiest.

N.C.: Why do you say this?

A.L.K.: For different reasons. First of all, we were no longer in a war zone like before, when we had been in Slovenia, and then we tried to live as normal a life as possible in those times. We studied, we worked on the land, we had good relations with the townsfolk of Nonantola, who wouldn't (I think) before we arrived have known what it means to be a Jew. And all of this went quite well until July 25.

N.C.: And on September 8 . . .

A.L.K.: And then on September 8 when the armistice was declared, because in those times right after September 8 the German army—which even before that was in Italy, but afterwards felt like the master—had occupied Italy.

N.C.: And at that time you didn't go to Switzerland with the other Jewish boys of Nonantola.

A.L.K.: No.

N.C.: Instead you went to the South. Can you tell us about this journey?

A.L.K.: On September 16, a week after we left the villa, I decided to head toward the South, because my aim was to go through the lines, for by now I already knew from the radio that the English and American troops had landed in southern Italy. So that morning I went to the station—that is, Nonantola is on the Modena-Ferrara line. In those times the train was still operating. I got aboard the train, and just as the train had entered the station at Ferrara, I was outside the compartment always on the lookout from the window. I saw many German trucks that were really near the railroad tracks, and I understood that I must not enter the station on this train. So I got off the train when it was still in motion, but two or three hundred meters before it entered the station, so it wasn't moving very fast. In brief, I got off, then hid in the countryside, and after several hours headed south. And so I went, and made it all the way on foot from Ferrara to a small town in the province of Chieti, a town called Fara Filiorum Petri. It's a small town in the Abruzzi. The distance, I think, is something like 300 or 350 kilometers, and that's what I did on foot.

By day I rested under the trees or in the countryside, and toward five or six, when it was already dark, I went on. In fact I went on the whole night. I always avoided the main highways and always kept to the countryside, but near the highway, so that I always looked to the left to see the sea, and so I would know in what direction I was going: it was the Adriatic Sea. On September 23 or 24, I think, I arrived in that town there, and then there was an Italian there called Vincenzo Di Girolamo.

N.C.: Where was this man?

A.L.K.: In Fara Filiorum Petri. I entered his house and told him that I was an Italian soldier who wanted to go home, and my home was in Chieti. In fact, I told him a tale, because I held fake ID cards. Ones I'd gotten in Nonantola. I had to hold two cards, one saying that I was German and the other that I was Italian. To the Italians I always showed the German card and to the Germans the one that I was Italian, and that way . . . I was able to reach Fara Filiorum Petri. After two or three days at the Di Girolamos' my conscience kind of told me that it wasn't right that I should pretend to be someone I wasn't, precisely when he was so kind, treating me as a guest, giving me shelter, and I told him, "Vincenzo, I've got to tell you something, I'm not Italian, I'm Jewish, I'm fleeing the Germans." And he knew by now what "Jewish" meant because in that town there was a Jewish family that was interned somewhere. And then one day he went somewhere else, and I waited for him in the countryside, a patrol of *carabinieri* from the village went by, they stopped close to me, and in fact on that day I didn't have my ID cards with me. They began to talk, I said that I was from here. In brief, they brought me in a car to town and to their police station and did not interrogate me at all. I was in a closed room. Towards eleven o'clock at night I heard someone outside saying that the door was opening, and I knew Vincenzo's voice: "Leo, leave right away." I left, he took me, and we climbed up on the hills, because his house wasn't on the hills, nor in the center of the town. And then he went with me into the countryside, close to a cave, put me inside, built a little haystack to hide the entrance to the cave, told me "not to worry about anything," and left me some food. And he also tells me, "Tomorrow my sons or I will come bring you something to eat and drink. Don't leave the cave." So I stayed for seven or eight days. Then he came, brought me back to his house, and said, "The danger is over."

N.C.: Many thanks. One question: have you seen any more of it, or gone anymore to this Fara Filiorum Petri? Did you see the town again?

A.L.K.: Oh, sir, I am like a member of the Di Girolamo family.[14]

ELENA AND LOT MINERVI

NICOLA CARACCIOLO: After September 8 how did people act toward you?

ELENA MINERVI: Wonderfully. We always ran away, one time after another, and when there was danger the *carabinieri* would send friends to warn us.

N.C.: And the people?

E.M.: Ah, really extraordinary.

N.C.: What did they do?

E.M.: During that whole period I was wearing a brooch with a Jewish symbol, the six-pointed star. I did it partly to prove something, and I never heard anything but friendly words. Then, after 1943, naturally you couldn't do that, but every time we needed help we always found somebody who would help us, somebody who would warn us to escape at the right moment, and somebody who would wait for us and would give us shelter.

N.C.: Where was this?

E.M.: We spent September 8 at Senigallia, then we went on to Ancona, to the Pinocchio at my grandmother's villa. From there we fled again to the home of my father's tenant farmers, who kept us until once again the *carabinieri* sent someone to warn us to escape, and these farmers themselves found another peasant family who sheltered us.

N.C.: What was their name?

E.M.: Well, my father's tenants the Pigliapocos, and the others I think I might have forgotten, the Rafagnas. Anyhow, they were truly extraordinary, and my father's tenants in particular.

A few years ago we went to look for these Pigliapocos.

N.C.: [*turning toward Mr. Minervi*] And what was *your* experience?

LOT MINERVI: We were in Florence on September 8, and it seemed as if the Americans were going to land in the area near Leghorn—anyway, this is what people were saying. So we stayed close to the city. And then, seeing that things weren't getting better, we went to the Aretino, at La Verna.

N.C.: Did anyone hide you? Or help you?

L.M.: In La Verna, a little village downhill from the monastery, just about everyone knew the Jewish families there, because the summer before they had been on vacation there. But both the monks in the cloister and the people in the village very likely knew everything, yet they never said a word, not even when the SS Division Hermann Göring was in those parts for a mopping up operation, and we were hidden under a roof for a week—not one word was said.

N.C.: The whole village kept the secret?

L.M.: The whole village, completely. Even the man who had once been the village Fascist, who seemed to be the most dangerous, didn't open his mouth.

E.M.: As for us in the Marches, as I was telling you before, the sentence that the villagers uttered upon liberation was this: "We all knew that you were Jewish, but we didn't disclose it to anyone." There was a feeling that you could trust everyone.

FERI AND ZLATA NOIMAN

FERI NOIMAN: I was in Ferramonti in March of 1942, we arrived from Rhodes.

NICOLA CARACCIOLO: How did the Italians treat you?

ZLATA NOIMAN: Very well. I can tell so many stories, all of them beautiful, as to how the Italians were with us.

N.C.: And you?

F.N.: Yes, I can only tell the nicest things in the world, because the Italians saved our 509 people when our ship was sinking next to an island made of stones, nothing . . . nothing, not one green thing, nothing.

N.C.: And you, Mrs. Noiman, what experiences did you have?

Z.N.: Before coming to Italy, nothing. I knew that the Italian people had joined the fight on the German side; I thought them no better than the Germans. But when I arrived in Italy and stayed there a year and a half, then I saw that the Italian people were different, that they are very good people, with a heart. And now if I can I'll tell you an episode about what an Italian Fascist is, since we were so frightened of them. In this little village where I was interned there was a pharmacist.

N.C.: What little village was that?

Z.N.: It was Castelnuovo Don Bosco, in the Asti province of Piedmont. He was a pharmacist, and everyone said of him that he was a big Fascist, and we were a little afraid. I was very young. It was a year and a half since we, the Jewish refugees, had been there. He never said hello to anyone, he didn't speak with the interned Jews. A few days before our departure for Ferramonti I was walking near his pharmacy, and he says to me, "Hello, Miss," and I was really frightened. What does he want with me? After a year and a half during which he never said hello? And he tells me, "Come in, come in. Come for a while inside my pharmacy, I have something to give you, a present."—"What is it?"—"I heard they are sending you to Ferramonti, it's in Calabria, and I know there is a lot of malaria there. I prepared some quinine for you, and some other medicine as well, if it's needed." I couldn't comprehend how this man, who all this time never spoke with anyone about us, now wants to offer me medicine as a gift. And at the end he told me that when I got to the concentration camp, if I needed anything, he was leaving me his address, all I have to do is write him a card, he would send me whatever I needed. I only wanted to tell you this to show you what an Italian heart is like, because even though he was a Fascist, he was a grand one.

N.C.: And how is it that they brought you to Ferramonti? And how was the camp?

F.N.: The Italians took responsibility for our people, they took all five hundred of us to Ferramonti, which is in Calabria in southern Italy. We came to Italy where for us it was already wonderful, because Rhodes was no paradise.

N.C.: And how did it happen that you decided to get married at Ferramonti?

F.N.: And then, when we were already in Ferramonti, my wife came to the camp from northern Italy. On May 15, 1943, we met and became friends, and on August 31 we got married, eight days before the arrival of the British.

N.C.: Weren't you afraid to get married under those circumstances?

F.N.: No, because the Italians let us, we weren't the only couple. . . . There were many newly wedded couples, Mr. Citron also got married at Ferramonti. There were many couples like ourselves, and this is what we wanted to say again: how good the Italians were with us.

N.C.: Weren't you afraid that something might happen? That the Nazis might arrive?

F.N.: No, not at all.

Z.N.: We weren't afraid.

N.C.: How did the officers of the camp behave? The ordinary soldiers?

F.N.: Very well. At our wedding, we received something from the marshal commandant of the camp. We received a gift. And the marshal even came to our wedding. Every couple that married at Ferramonti got a room.

N.C.: And the people, there in Calabria, how were they?

Z.N.: In the beginning we didn't have much to do with the people because this was a closed camp. We met them during the very last days, when we fled the camp because we were afraid. When the Germans retreated north from Sicily, the commandant told us, "You can leave the camp and go into the mountains, because I don't know what will happen tomorrow, because the Germans might do something." Then we left for a few days and went into the mountains in Calabria, until the British arrived. At that time we had our first contacts with the people. It was very beautiful. They were . . .

F.N.: Very primitive, but they're . . .

Z.N.: But they've got a warm heart, really a warm heart. They gave us their hospitality and they hid us.

N.C.: Let's go back to your wedding, though. How old were you then, Mrs. Noiman?

Z.N.: Me? I was twenty-one years old.

N.C.: [*turning to Mr. Noiman*] And you?

F.N.: Twenty-three years old.

N.C.: And why did you decide to get married at Ferramonti?

Z.N.: Ah, we were in love, too, but I was alone and didn't want to stay alone in this world.

N.C.: And what happened to the rest of your family?

Z.N.: In Yugoslavia, all dead.

N.C.: Where did they die?

Z.N.: In the concentration camps there were the Germans but also the Ustasha, and they put an end to my entire family. I was left alone, and I told myself, "I want to get married and have a family." I was alone.

N.C.: Have you been happy through these years?

Z.N.: I've been happy.

N.C.: How long have you been married?

F.N.: Forty-one years.

N.C.: And have you been happy, too, Mr. Noiman?

F.N.: Yes, and we're still happy. And we hope to have many more years together.

N.C.: Excuse my question, but could one say, could *you* say, that you owe this happiness . . . your life, to the Italians?

Z.N.: Yes, it's true.

EMMY RAPHAEL NACHMIAS

EMMY RAPHAEL NACHMIAS: The Italian troops rescued me, and I have to tell you the story of how they did it.

NICOLA CARACCIOLO: What happened?

E.R.N.: What happened was this. In that time of the Germans, which was so difficult for all of the Jews, I was in Salonica, and every day we did everything in our power to escape from the Germans, from the deportations. When the deportations began to get more severe, then I took advantage of knowing a little Italian. I seized a little courage to stay alive and went alone, just like that, to the office of a captain, Riccardo Curti, whom I didn't yet know.

N.C.: Where was this, in Salonica?

E.R.N.: In Salonica, and he was commandant of the Greek railways at that time. So I presented myself there and they opened the door for me, he greeted me, he said, "Sit down," but I couldn't tell him anything, I said that I came to get a safe-conduct. And he told me to go to the Greek police, and "Why did you come here?" And I said, "But can't I be here?" Then he said to me, "Will you tell me the reason?" I told him that I was afraid to speak in the office. Then he said to me, "You come to my house at seven in the evening."

I left the same way, and thought for many hours about whether or not I should go, and told my brother everything. And my brother told me, "You won't do well to go, because you don't know what can happen." I replied that I have nothing to lose there, haven't *any*thing, I always used this word. Then I went to his place, waited for him at his home, and told him, "I'm Jewish." He was listening to me in calm, but suddenly he got up and says to me, "What?!" . . . So he was afraid. Then he says, "Listen, tell me again." "Nothing, I want to go to Athens, I want a pass, and the Greek police won't give me one because I'm Jewish." Then he said to me, "Poor, pretty little Jewish girl, but I admire your courage, I admire it so that I've got to do something for you."

He took the telephone and spoke with the Athens command: "Yes, yes, I can have her travel as a civilian on the troop train." They told him yes, and he prepared a safe-conduct for me with my name, Emmy Raphael (that was my name then). Then . . . he told me, "But it's dangerous for you to come alone another time here to the office of the command, opposite there's a concentration camp. I'll send a *carabiniere,* he'll take you from your home and you come with him to take the train."

I didn't believe these words, but in the morning an Italian came, an Italian *carabiniere,* and he was looking for the name Emmy Raphael. Everybody was afraid, everyone said, "Poor girl, they came to take you, who knows what you did?" No one knew why this *carabiniere* came— in the family, when he entered, my mother wept, she said to me, "You're going away, you're young, God knows what will become of us." And so I left with the *carabiniere* till we got to the station. They gave me a false safe-conduct. The *carabiniere* told me, "From today on you will be Bianca Fontolan." That's how I put myself on the train.

N.C.: And did you see this captain anymore?

E.R.N.: No. I wanted to ascertain, how do you say it, whether Captain Curti is still alive.

ASAF KANSI

NICOLA CARACCIOLO: And your story?

ASAF KANSI: My story is the following. I escaped from the concentration camp of Skoplje in Yugoslavia, from which four thousand Jews went to the ovens of Auschwitz. A day earlier I escaped and went directly to the place of my friend, the Italian consul, La Rosa.

N.C.: La Rosa?

A.K.: La Rosa. If Mr. La Rosa hears my voice he'll be very, very, very happy to learn that his friend, his good friend, his cordial friend Giuseppe Kansi is still alive, after so much, in my eighty-fourth year.

JOSSEPE PAPO, M.D.

NICOLA CARACCIOLO: What end did your brother meet with?

JOSSEPE PAPO: He was slaughtered in February 1942.

N.C.: And what about the rest of you?

J.P.: Well, they threw us out of the plant, and we rented a room from a Jewish family right in Karlovac. The plant was a bit outside of town, and here, in substance, is where the story of how the Italians really saved us begins. The apartment had two entries—one entry led to our room. Next door an Italian officer had rented a room, because the Italian officers were lodged with various families. That was mine and my mother's great luck, as far as the raids were concerned. They were

Jossepe Papo, M.D., in Israel

meant to capture the Jews. And they were carried out by the members of the Ustasha.

Now we hadn't known that the Italians were opposed to this situation, troubled by it, and one night they carried out a definitive raid against the Jews. In the city there were about ten thousand Jews: a few dozen of them were left, and even these were deported later on. Now that night the Ustasha soldiers arrived and knocked on the main door of this family's apartment, and they deported all of them, husband, wife, two young girls. A son managed to escape by jumping out of the window on the balcony. At that moment, when the Italian cavalry major who lived there saw what was happening, he let out one of those shrieks and didn't allow them to enter our room, mine and my mother's.

N.C.: What was this officer's name?

J.P.: I believe, I don't remember exactly, I believe his name was Pichetti. A small man, thin, he smoked a lot and was drinking coffee whenever I saw him. The major took me, put me under his bed, protected me in this fashion, not letting these people, the Ustasha, not letting them rummage about looking for me and my mother.

N.C.: And your mother?

J.P.: My mother stayed locked in her room. Whatever fate would have to be, would have to be.

N.C.: And your mother was saved, too?

J.P.: Yes, my mother was saved. Anyhow these people didn't find us. And the next day the major stationed a picket in front of our room.

N.C.: How old were you?

J.P.: I was thirteen and a few months. And, in fact, he ordered us not to open the door to anyone for any reason. Nevertheless, the next morning the Ustasha came back. They saw us but didn't take us away. And we kept ourselves locked in the house for . . . I believe two or three weeks.

N.C.: Under the protection of this major?

J.P.: Under the protection of this major who, as I say, placed a military guard in front of the door and didn't allow anyone to come in. One fine evening he told us, "Get your suitcases, we're taking you away." And at four in the morning, it was September 4, 1942, a military truck arrived, and we went downstairs in the dark and got on the truck in complete darkness. We heard some voices. We knew nothing at all. And the truck left, made another round of the city, stopped, picked up two or three other people, and from that point took its place in a military column. This truck was camouflaged in a sense, placed between tanks and a small cavalry unit so as to resemble a military convoy. But it was formed in order to get eight Jews in hiding out of Karlovac and take them to the Italian-occupied zone. After some ups and downs we ended up at Metlika, where we were interned. There I befriended many Italians in the military. One was a military doctor, and I was there when he took care of the wounded, and during that time *I* decided to study medicine, too. And so it was that I made it the purpose of my life.

ALBERT SAMUEL, M.D.

NICOLA CARACCIOLO: Doctor Samuel, what's your story?

ALBERT SAMUEL: My story? Before the war I was working in Skoplje in Macedonia. When the Italians came to Priština I decided to relocate myself and my family, my father, mother, and all the others, in order to be under the Italians and not under the Germans.

N.C.: What difference was there?

A.S.: There was a great difference—first, the humaneness of the Italian authorities cannot be compared with the savagery of the German or Bulgarian authorities.

N.C.: And then what did you do, Doctor?

A.S.: I came to Priština from Skoplje and I was the community physician, not for the Jewish community but for the Albanian community of Priština. I worked for five or six months. After six months the Germans wanted to take us to concentration camps. But the Italians said, "No, we'll take them all, not only the women and the children, but the men also." And this way they rescued us, then took us to Berat.

DAN DANKO STERNBERG

NICOLA CARACCIOLO: Here we are, Mr. Dan Sternberg. What experiences did you have during the war?

DAN DANKO STERNBERG: My father was among those presiding over the Jewish community, and that was the reason we were among the last ones to be arrested. I had an uncle, married to a Christian woman. When those raids started I went over to his house to sleep every evening. I went to my uncle's place because it was safer there, he had a Christian wife. One morning I returned to my house and saw my parents with an Ustasha policeman. A Croat, a Croatian Fascist, an Ustasha, just like all those in Pavelić's regime. My father saw me, I remember it this way: he saw me and stopped himself, said something to the Ustasha, he probably gave him some bribe, because he called me. I went to him, and he told me, "They're deporting us now, your mother and me. Try to reach your brother." My brother, seven years older than I, was in Dalmatia, in the Italian-controlled territory.

N.C.: And then?

D.D.S.: And then he said to me, "Goodbye. I don't know when we'll see each other again."

N.C.: Did you ever see your parents again?

D.D.S.: No, no.

N.C.: They're dead?

D.D.S.: I know they died in Auschwitz, but I don't know how, they'd been deported.

N.C.: And you did reach Dalmatia, after many vicissitudes. How were relations with the Italians? . . .

D.D.S.: The city of Mostar was on the border. It was a very important Yugoslavian city, eighty kilometers from the sea. I believe that was the beginning of the Italian-occupied zone, and it was there that I saw Italian officers for the first time. And I remember they had more smiling, more human faces than the others, so it seemed to me. There was a bald captain who loved girls.

FATHER PIERRE MARIE-BENOÎT (FATHER MARIA BENEDETTO)

NICOLA CARACCIOLO: Father, would you tell us what your relations were with the Italian authorities on the problem of the Jews during the war?

PIERRE MARIE-BENOÎT: But I didn't have direct contact with Italian authorities. All that I did I began upon the advice of Angelo Donati.[15]

Father Pierre Marie-Benoît, called Father Benedetto by the Italians

N.C.: And what did you do?

P.M.-B.: Angelo Donati asked me two things. The first time he asked me . . . he says, "Since you speak Italian, you should go to the commissioner of police, Lospinoso, to discuss a bit with him the problem of the Jews." And I went, accompanied by a Jewish man, and we did indeed speak of this problem. I explained that the thought is a humane thought, and that for the church there is no reason to persecute the Jews, but that one must treat them humanely. We got on well, as far as I understand, and so remained friendly with Lospinoso. And then after a short time Donati told me that he had prepared a plan of his for a transfer, but quite an important one: it had to do with bringing 30,000 . . . 40,000 Jewish refugees in the Italian-controlled zone of France into Italy in the first stage and later on, in a second stage, from Italy into Africa.[16] Lospinoso had already told me, "You should see the Italian generals. . . ." But he had no time to act on this . . . because the time went by very quickly. . . . And instead Donati said something else to me: "You see, when you get back to Italy you should go to the pope and recommend our plan to him, and ask the pope to support it with the Italian government."

N.C.: And did you go to the pope?

P.M.-B.: When I got back to Italy I prepared for my audience with a certain difficulty. I'm calling on my superior and he says to me, "It's not possible because the pope is no longer receiving private audiences." But then he tells me, "You prepare something in writing to present to the pope." And I put something in writing and show it to my superior, and I know that he went then to Monsignor Micara. And after a few days he calls me, and he tells me, "Now I've obtained the audience, let's go together to the pope." And so I was presented to the pope by my general superior.

N.C.: And what had you written in this report?

P.M.-B.: I was quite embarrassed because Donati hadn't given me anything. I knew everything, but as I told you, approximately, I had no particulars this way, and being afraid of saying too much, I talked about 10,000, 15,000 Jews. Instead, Donati was talking about 30 or 40 or 50,000.

N.C.: Yes. . . .

P.M.-B.: And then I spoke on how to facilitate the departure for Spain,[17] and then I asked the pope directly to act upon the Italian government to prepare this great plan of Donati's.

There, on the whole that's the way I spoke to the main points of my request.

N.C.: What was the pope's attitude?

P.M.-B.: Good. I spoke of the French police, who were acting pretty much against the Jews and working with the Germans . . . arresting the Jews. The Italian police were protecting them instead. The pope made this observation: "No one would have believed that in France there would have been such an attitude." In addition, he told me, "I will study this and have it studied, your requests"—and that sort of thing.

N.C.: And then came the twenty-fifth of July, and nothing more was done with it.[18]

ENZO CAVAGLION

NICOLA CARACCIOLO: Then, after the eighth of September, the Jewish refugees from France came here to Cuneo.

ENZO CAVAGLION: Here in Borgo San Dalmazzo, a village at the bot-

Enzo Cavaglion

tom of the valley, was the arrival spot for the Jewish refugees from Saint-Martin-Vésubie.

N.C.: How many were there?

E.C.: We are speaking of over eleven hundred refugees, originally from the "forced residence" of Saint-Martin-Vésubie.

N.C.: How did the people treat them?

E.C.: Well, they received them in a praiseworthy manner. It's useless to emphasize how tremendously the population made itself available to the refugees, and I am speaking about the poor people, the peasants in the mountains who are among the poorest classes we had and still have in the area. Their homes were also open in order to offer help. Indeed, if we can say that many were saved, it's precisely because of this tremendously available local population. So it's a positive thing, and if the population hadn't been so open to the Jewish refugees from Saint-Martin-Vésubie, certainly seven hundred people wouldn't have been saved.

N.C.: Over seven hundred out of the twelve hundred who arrived from France were saved.

E.C.: Oh, yes, if you figure that we have the number of eleven hundred refugees from Saint-Martin-Vésubie; of these, from the documents that we've had in hand, it turns out that the Germans caught 350. The difference is made up of people who were rescued, a notable number thanks to the help of the population. I went to meet them, I used to leave from Cuneo, which had just been taken by the Germans, and would have to go to Valdieri, where the first partisan band, GL, was being formed, led and guided by Duccio Galimberti and Livio Bianco.

N.C.: There are the seven hundred. And you met these Jews who came from France?

E.C.: Yes, I had some news of these Jews and so on and so forth, but I didn't have a true perception of what might happen, and when I found myself in Valle Gesso I was amazed. I saw coming toward me people in tatters, desperate, discouraged, deceived, because they thought they would find freedom, they believed they would find the Allies, not the Germans.

N.C.: They thought that the war was over.

E.C.: Well, at least in this period, in September 1943, the forecasts were like that for everyone, even for ourselves. That's why when I saw them, I wanted to tell them that I was a Jew, too, but they wouldn't believe it. They were so consumed that they didn't believe me. I had to say some prayers, some prayers in Hebrew, so that they would understand that I was Jewish as well, that I was with them to help them.

N.C.: They didn't have any trust?

E.C.: They didn't have any trust, and this was acceptable, it was logical, it was natural, it was clear. For several years now they had been moving about Europe. They were people coming from Poland, from Germany itself, from Austria. I have very dear friends whom I helped rescue and who still live in Brussels. They had come from Austria. Think about the "vicious circle" they had traveled.

N.C.: And in France they had been captured under the protection of the Italian army.

E.C.: There you have it, a very interesting question. Here's the distinction we can make between the German and the Italian occupation authorities. You know, France was more or less divided into two parts: in the north were the Germans, and in the southern part there was the Fourth Army, the Italian one. Naturally the sensitivity, the love that the Italian people would show their neighbor is well known, even on this occasion, in the attitude of an army of occupation toward the Jews.

N.C.: And what happened at that time?

E.C.: What happened was this, a very interesting thing, yes. The question is: what was Saint-Martin-Vésubie? It was a *résidence forcée,* an involuntary home—if you will—where the Italian authorities, seeing the arrival from northern France of this tide of persecuted refugees, had to make some arrangements, had to place them somewhere. And they found this most beautiful place for them to stay, Saint-Martin-Vésubie, a tourist spot in the Maritime Alps. It was the famous police commissioner Lospinoso who arranged everything.[19] The Italian authorities and the Italian army asked for the best hotels and there they settled the Jews. There was a synagogue, weddings took place, children were born, and some people died.[20]

These were the Jews who arrived in Borgo San Dalmazzo, amid the dismantled Fourth Army, behind another dismantled army, in ruin. I can't conceal from you that here, too, there emerges the soldier, the man of the people, who helps transport these people, brings them, with bundles on them or without, with children, old folk, women, some ill. And brings them all the way to Entracque, to Valdieri—but you should have seen the state in which these Jews arrived. They had been at an altitude of three thousand meters. The hills we call "the Windows," the "Cherry Tree Hill," come close to three thousand meters. We were in September, and the season is relatively cold. It was a crossing that is difficult even for a good mountain climber. Imagine eleven hundred people of all ages; there were three-month-old babies who were born there during those months. And they arrived here, they arrived in Borgo, they arrive in Entracque Valdieri. And they find themselves like this, people without a country who imagined they would find here a quiet, free place. "At least"—they thought—"there are no more Germans," and instead things happened quite differently. Exactly three days later, let's say, the ring was closing. The German jeeps arrived in Saint-Martin-Vésubie, the German jeeps would arrive from Cuneo, too. So the ring was closed and they fell into the trap.

N.C.: And then there was this proclamation . . .

E.C.: And there was this proclamation, a very strong one signed by Commander Müller, not well known, but who was also Peiper's right arm. I mean General Peiper who painted the town red both here and at Boves, afterwards also in the Ardennes if you know the story of this notorious character well. The proclamation threatened anyone caught without papers, documents, et cetera, including the families that sheltered these poor people, with being shot instantly.

N.C.: Therefore the people who were hiding Jews knew they were risking their lives.

E.C.: Yes, they knew it, and that is the praiseworthy point about the people, that although they knew—because the proclamation wasn't just for Borgo, it was for Valdieri, for all the important centers—they hid the Jews nevertheless.

LIA CORINALDI

NICOLA CARACCIOLO: Then tell me your experience at the Jewish school in those years?

LIA CORINALDI: The Jewish school was very lovely, the Jewish high school was founded in 1938 and lasted till 1943, because it wasn't possible to continue after that. In order to offer schooling to the Jewish children who were excluded from the public schools, this type of high school was formed in those centers of the Jewish community where there was already a Jewish elementary school, and it was established with the high school teachers who had been thrown out of the public schools, with some excellent teachers. The high school was a very lovely experience, because, think about it: to be able to teach in a non-Fascist way during the Fascist period, with a freedom that wouldn't have been possible in the public school, this really represented a very beautiful experience.

N.C.: And how did the children manage?

L.C.: We had to do the same programs as in the public school and the same tests, that is to say the authorized tests, and so all the tests were made according to the Fascist directives, but we had a freedom of expression and pedagogy, a freedom to teach, that we would not have had in the public school. In the meantime we were not obliged to swallow that Fascist brew, and the kids were very good, there were small classes and they attained the best results. When the children took the state examinations . . .

N.C.: They *could* take the state exams?

L.C.: They could take the state exams, and they placed among the first, they were very good.

N.C.: In other words, they were not discriminated against by the examination commission?

L.C.: At that time, no; later, it was no longer possible.

N.C.: But, quite to the contrary, someone told me that often the examination commissions displayed a certain friendliness when a Jewish child was questioned.

L.C.: Yes, indeed, in intellectual circles there was this kind of friendliness. But they were really good, well prepared. They were extremely good.[21]

FATHER LIBERO RAGANELLA AND MR. DELL'ARICCIA

NICOLA CARACCIOLO: Are you from San Lorenzo,* Don Libero**?

---

*A quarter in Rome, centered on the church of San Lorenzo.

**As we have seen in the instances of Father Sala and Father Repetto, the honorific title "Don," by which the interviewer addresses Father Raganella, is often given to humble priests in Italy.

Father Libero Raganella and Mr. Dell'Ariccia, his lifelong friend

LIBERO RAGANELLA: Yes, I was born in San Lorenzo, and in fact after leaving to pursue my studies for the priesthood, I returned in 1938, and here I still am in 1985. . . .

N.C.: And so you know the area very well. . . .

L.R.: Of course, even too well. . . .

N.C.: During the war, how did the people act regarding the Jewish problem?

L.R.: Ah, here in San Lorenzo there never was a Jewish problem because the Jews in San Lorenzo were exactly like everybody else—respect for one another, mutual friendship, and when the need came, mutual assistance—therefore there never was in San Lorenzo the problem of the Jews. Even when the racial laws came from outside, here in San Lorenzo there were no racial laws because friendship and acquaintance mattered more than those very racial laws, so therefore there never was this problem. On the contrary, I could add for you this specific occurrence. There was a family with three sons and a daughter. The three boys came to our school, here at the seminary, and the girl went to school with the nuns, and when these three boys . . . We would say, during the hour of religion, "You can go out because you're not at all obliged to follow our religious instruction, since you're of another religion." And instead they didn't want to go out and said, "But no, we don't mind it, we are like the rest," so that even from the very point of religion there was no difference: they were Jewish, the others were Christian. Everyone followed his own religion, but from morning till evening always together, always the one like the other.

N.C.: [*turning to Mr. Dell'Ariccia*] And you, Mr. Dell'Ariccia?

MR. DELL'ARICCIA: It's the same. . . .

N.C.: You're Jewish?

D'A.: Yes. . . .

N.C.: And you've always been here in San Lorenzo . . .

D'A.: Always, our family has been here in these parts practically from 1887, we've always been welcome, all our families. Father Libero himself is a witness—there has never been, let's say during the time of the so-called racial law . . .

N.C.: And how did the people act toward you?

D'A.: In the best way. Look, it's touching how everyone acted identically, how we were always helped, when let's say on the day when the reprisals occurred and people were arrested. We were helped by people who sheltered us in their homes. Look, there are no words, let's say, to praise the entire population enough, all the people . . .

N.C.: And Don Libero?

D'A.: Don Libero, well, one can't even begin to tell how he treated us all, look. I don't believe that a man like Don Libero will ever be born again.

N.C.: Then you owe him a debt of gratitude . . .

D'A.: A debt of everything, of everything, gratitude . . .

L.R.: That's why he pays for my morning coffee.

N.C.: Would you tell us this story, Don Libero?

L.R.: When the rounding up of the Jews after September 8 had just begun . . .

D'A.: Ah, yes, the first roundup happened on October 16 . . .

L.R.: October 16. Then I took this family whose children came to our school, in order to bring them to a safe place, to hide them so that they wouldn't possibly fall into the hands of the Germans. But while walking, because other means of transport didn't exist, with several kinds of luggage in our hands, we arrived at Largo Santa Susanna hard by Piazza San Bernardo. Since the curfew hour had begun, I was afraid that we'd be on the street during curfew, which would have really been the end of them and of me. Then I remembered that next to the church of Santa Susanna there was a cloister, and then I thought: I'll go inside here and put them in a safe place in the cloister. I spoke with the Mother Superior, but she didn't want to hear about it, "Because," she says, "Here in the cloister I cannot receive anyone and especially since these are men, boys," she says, "It's impossible, in fact . . . It can't be done, it can't be done." I insisted, so that in the end we came to an agreement, and I told the Mother Superior, "You take off the chain of the cloister gate in such a way that I then push the gate open—that's to say, *I* broke the chain, not you—and take these people to safety, because otherwise we're at risk of causing their deaths. It's better with a cloister broken into here than to cause the death of people in the middle of the street." And this way I got them inside. The next day, I went to the Vicarate to tell what happened, that is, that I'd broken into the cloister, and the answer was "You did well."

N.C.: And what was the attitude of the Vicarate toward this entire situation?

L.R.: The attitude of the Vicarate was this: there were appeals, not orders, but appeals, first of all to help all the Jews for whom the Germans were searching after the roundup that occurred; and also to help all those who needed it. To such an extent that here in this seminary we were hosts to six high officers of the Italian army, dressed as priests in order not to show that they were officers, and I provided each one of them with a postal pass, because I had a relative on Via Mercede who was working for the post office. Since she trusted me, I introduced all of these men to her and I made postcards with their own pictures on them, but the names belonged to priests who were in southern Italy. That's how all of them got their own regular ID cards. You understand, that's how one tried to help. Now, getting back to the Jews, I hid some, among whom were Lello Perugia,[22] Angelino, and the others. I hid them here with the Sisters of the Garden, who are here by the Walls, and they stayed there for some time, until they decided to move away from Rome, where (even though they were in the convent) they were afraid that there might be an attack by the Germans at any moment. They preferred to go to Tufo, in the Abruzzi. There they met with a misfortune, because they were captured by the Germans and afterward taken to Germany, to the concentration camps, and when the war was over only two came back to look for me. Out of five who had been taken away, three had been killed, I don't know how, in the concentration camps, and two returned and are still living in Rome.

N.C.: Tell me one thing. Do you believe that the people of San Lorenzo behaved well toward the Jews?

L.R.: Yes, all of them. No one here in San Lorenzo ever had anything against the Jews.

N.C.: And did they really help them?

L.R.: They helped them as their means allowed, because certainly in those days the means for help were not exceptional, on account of all the restrictions you had to live with during the "German" times. It wasn't as if you could help greatly, but those who could even took them into their homes and kept them in hiding.

N.C.: And you, Mr. Dell'Ariccia, how did you save yourself?

D'A.: And we, since here in the quarter we had the bombardment and then later, let's put it this way, the first glimmerings, we also escaped to a village in the Abruzzi, a village called Sante Marie—then we had to run away from there, because they sent a German command and . . .

N.C.: And did the people over there help you too?

D'A.: There Father Libero has always been commendable. . . .

N.C.: And in the village in the Abruzzi?

D'A.: And in the village in the Abruzzi where we were, in Sante Marie, we had a Catholic family. I have no words to tell you what this family did for us.

N.C.: And did they know that you were Jews?

D'A.: Yes, yes, they knew it, in fact when we arrived there in the village, in Sante Marie, we found the entire house ready, even with provisions of food, and up to now we still have, let's call it, a brotherly friendship, how shall I put it, like this . . . Then, from that place, from Sante Marie, we had to go away, because they sent a German command, and we reached our relatives at Tufo di Carsoli, and then we were surrounded by the Germans, and whoever could manage to escape and get into a house or run to the forest did so. These cousins of mine weren't able to hide and were captured. We managed to escape and let's say we were saved this way, and we came to Rome without knowing where more or less to go. And we found two friends from the quarter, and someone else who suggested something, and some others who wanted us in their home. In fact, a family did hide us.

N.C.: And they, too, knew that you were Jewish.

D'A.: Everyone knew us, because we've been here in this quarter for a lifetime. Everyone wanted to put whichever of us here in their own homes, and in fact my brother and me in one house, mother and father in another, my sisters the same way, always sheltered by other people, let's say from the quarter, who knew us. And this way they sheltered all of us.

L.R.: Then there is the story of Di Nola, another Jew, who had instead married a Catholic woman. And he, too, came to ask me for help, and I found another place with some other sisters, but outside San Lorenzo in order to be able to hide him. And even though the wife was Catholic, and therefore could have stayed in peace because nothing would have been done to her by the Germans, she wanted to follow her husband and stay with him so that if something happened to him, "It would have to happen to me, too." In short, in this way if nothing else she showed that she loved her husband.

D'A.: There are so many cases like this. . . .

L.R.: Yes, because there were quite a few, quite a few Jews who were married to Catholics. . . .

D'A.: Yes . . . there are so many mixed marriages. . . .

L.R.: Just as, on the other hand, there are Jewish women who married Catholic men. And in these cases it has been seen that in danger they did not separate, they did not attempt to save themselves without thinking of the husband or wife.

D'A.: They were more united . . .

L.R.: They were united, and despite the difference that discrimination could seem to suggest at these moments, race and religion had no effect, neither did the racial laws or the religious laws. They remained united and both people were facing the danger together, no matter what that might be.

D'A.: No, look, in San Lorenzo proper there was no racism. . . .

N.C.: And in Rome?

L.R.: But in Rome, look, more or less, I think that . . . the same way people behaved here in San Lorenzo they also behaved in the other quarters.

D'A.: Here in Rome it isn't that the racial laws had much of an effect—yes, there might have been . . . some hothead who might have tried to apply them, but the people didn't feel the effects of this. Look, I'll tell you this about the family that sheltered us in Sante Marie in the Abruzzi. I'll say even more, that the head of the family, who now, poor soul, is no more, was called (or anyway we called him) Zio Sante,* because his name was Santino Di Vitto. He was, let's say, quite a convinced Fascist, quite. He knew about us, but with all that he didn't behave badly, because even if they were Fascists, they still treated us very well. This man's behavior was commendable, this . . . In fact, after the liberation, someone had him captured because he was a Fascist, and yet he always was a great human being. He was taken to prison, down to Regina Coeli. . . . And we, the families who had all been sheltered, let's say, by him, even assisted with food, got together and found a lawyer and in a few days we had him freed from Regina Coeli. But it's true that in Sante Marie we were . . . Look, without exaggerating, beyond the seven or eight families of Roman Jews that he protected because he was practically the local bigwig because he was in charge of the tax collector's office for the town, in other words he ran the show, did you understand?

N.C.: I understood . . . I understood . . .

D'A.: Look, he was a praiseworthy man, he was unsurpassed from any point of view.

N.C.: I understood . . .

D'A.: And there are so many such cases . . . So, so, so, so, many . . .

OLGA DI VEROLI

NICOLA CARACCIOLO: Tell us then, Mrs. Di Veroli,[23] how were you rescued?

*Zio Sante = "Uncle Sante."

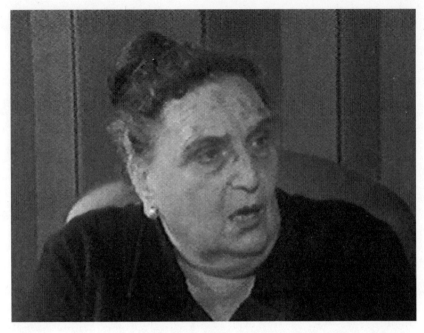

The late Olga Di Veroli

OLGA DI VEROLI: Well, on the morning of October 16 we were in the Rome ghetto, or rather during the night we heard shots, and we were a little worried because this was not a normal thing, beyond the existing bombardments. At six in the morning we heard a loud, repeated ring. It was a girl of about twelve or thirteen who lived on the floor above, and she told me, she says, "Quickly tell your papa and two brothers to run away, because the Germans are here, they're on a raid and they're taking everyone in." Then I went to my father and mother's room and told my papa what was going on. We leaned out over the street and saw these Germans with machine guns going back and forth like real madmen. Then my father said, he says, "Well, get dressed and let's go away immediately." We—the girls, that is, my sister and I (I was barely twenty then), my sister says, "No, Papa, we women will stay at home, that way we'll say that the men went to work." And my brother says, "No, no, no, no, let's all go away." Since we had a wholesale business one block away from where we lived, he said, "Let's do one thing, let's go to the store, since at this hour they won't come there." He says, "Look, I'll whistle. At the first whistle the store is open, at the second one the path is clear." Except that we heard the first whistle and then sent mother ahead, then the two boys, then my sister, and I was the last one left in the entryway. While I'm walking like this—I was still in my nightgown, with an overcoat on top because it was raining a good deal that morning—a soldier saw me, but I didn't know whether he was German, or what his nationality was, because I didn't know uniforms. He looked straight at me and almost crossed the street, and he told me, he says, "Run away." He made a movement to indicate "Run away." I say, "No, I'm sorry," I say, "but I'm not running away," I say, because let's say I was afraid of doing my family harm. At a certain point this man made a gesture toward me, he gave a mute signal as if to say, "You look at me," and with his hand he gestured, "Run, run, run away!" I still remained motionless because, I'm telling you the truth, somewhat from fear, somewhat from terror, I'm saying, but what's wrong with me?—then he motioned toward me with his hands, "Run, run away!" He took the machine gun that he had with the barrel pointing upward, turned it around as if to let me see that he wouldn't shoot me, and then gestured behind himself like this: "Run!" I went away, I kept on walking, and after I saw him at a distance of about thirty-forty meters I went to the store. Papa asked, "How come you were so late?" and I say, "Papa, there was a soldier dressed in such and such a way in green, you could tell he wasn't German, he was an Austrian."[24] We stayed there for a few hours. Then my father said, "We can't stay here, we have no provisions, no water, we don't have anything." You know, a store, like in the old days—there wasn't even a bathroom. And so we left and caught the red circular tramline. When we were aboard, the driver said to my father, he says, "But are you Jews?" My father, somewhat from . . . from timidity, says to us, "All right, we'll give it all we can." Then to the driver my father says, "Yes." So the man says, "Then don't be afraid, come with me." And he only made one stop from the Garibaldi Bridge to Via Mazzini. Then he said, "Now I can't go on without stopping," he says, "because they'll report me." And we got off there and Papa had an idea. He remembered that one of his representatives, a certain Arturo Borgogna, lived there, someone who during the occupation proved himself to be really like a father, a father . . .

N.C.: Who was he, this man?

O.D.V.: He was a Neapolitan gentleman. He was a representative for our business who supplied us with merchandise. We stayed there for a few hours, then his wife came up and said, "We must send them away because the concierge said that she saw them enter and they must go away immediately." In fact, this man offered us a really good meal and then we left. My father was desperate, especially about mother, who was rather fearful in those days, and we walked for a while. Then he said, "Well, you know what, we're going back, we're going back to the store." And, in fact, we did go back to the store. Two days later my mother remembered that she met a lady, a relative of hers, who, she said, lives on Vicolo del Cinque, number six, I don't know, something that had somehow left an impression on her. Then we went to where these people lived, and they welcomed her, they themselves came to look for us, they welcomed her in their home. I remember that they were very poor people, because he was a strolling musician and she was a washerwoman, they were wretchedly poor. Then these people, to show us that in fact they'd taken us in eagerly, they started to make—in those days the rationing authorities gave I don't know . . . ten, fifteen kilos of potatoes per person and one kilo of sheep cheese—whatever they called pecorino then, that is, who knows what it was? And these people said, "Let's make gnocchi."

Then they made some gnocchi with this cheese—think about that a little—but we ate it also to express, that is, our gratitude. When we'd been there for three or four days, afterward, we really felt well, because nobody said anything and the entire neighborhood was on our side.

N.C.: But did the neighborhood know that you were Jewish? In the Vicolo del Cinque, that is, the entire street knew that you were Jewish?

O.D.V.: Well, I don't know if all of it did, but a good portion, yes, a good portion, yes, they knew it. And someone would bring vegetables, and someone would bring one thing and another would bring something else, so we wouldn't have to leave the house. To such an extent that one day I dared to go to the market to buy some vegetables. One of these women who sell chicory told me, "Yes, take the chicory, but run away, you'll pay me tomorrow or the day after tomorrow or in six months, don't worry, go away." I say, "Excuse me," then I took out a wallet because they advised me when I went out to put a tiny image of the Virgin in it. And after all, I say, the Virgin is always a beautiful thing, then I pulled it out to show conspicuously that I was taking out money. She says, "Let this Virgin be," she says, "because around here not many will look at this." She says, "Take this chicory, we'll even give you more, so you'll have it for two or three days." And I went away.

Four days after we'd been there this woman, let's call her the mistress of the house, got back and had a huge cardiac arrest, and turned all black. Then my father says, "She's in bad shape, we have to call a doctor." Then this other woman who lived here, she lived with them and was a washerwoman from Velletri, she said, "No, no, no, Mr. Enrico, it's not that she's ill," she says. "Just that a woman, I don't know, someone from the neighborhood," she says, "went to call the Fascists and the Germans." Then she says, "Let her calm down and I'll take care of her, I'll put her to bed."

N.C.: And did you go away?

O.D.V.: Yes, we ran away quickly. While running we saw with our own eyes the Fascists the other woman had called. Later, I know, when the Allies came, all the other people in the neighborhood, I don't know what terrible things they wanted to do to her. And okay, it's all past. Then from there we went to Porta Settimiana, to where some clients of ours lived. There they, too, opened the door, gave us some rooms to sleep in and everything, really . . . We were all right, it's not what you'd have to say—but excuse me, first we had been in a convent, at Ponte Rotto. Then when all was said and done in the evening, the sisters sent us all away, because it was said that in the convent there were also some soldiers, and that was true. So they sent everyone away in the evening, really late at night I can say, and from there we went to the house of this lady. Then we went away from there and went to Via Porta Settimiana, to these other clients' of ours, and there we stayed for several months. Then, unfortunately, my father saw some people captured right under our window. He, too, started to be a little frightened, "Not for myself," he says, "but for the children." He says, "When I've arranged something for the two boys who are almost of draft age," he says, "somehow we'll do it." Afterwards, from there we went away and Monsignor Quadraroli placed us . . .

N.C.: Who was Monsignor Quadraroli?

O.D.V.: Monsignor Quadraroli was a secretary at the Vatican. He knew that we were Jewish, so he made some false IDs for both of my brothers and sent the rest of us to the convent on Via Cicerone, where there were sisters. In fact, in Rome they helped us, they opened doors for us. . . . Of course, some had to pay some million lire, some didn't have to pay anything, some were taken inside only out of pity, we've got to say this. But fortunately there were more people who opened their doors selflessly than those who did it with gain in mind. Yes, this has to be told, they really opened not just their doors but their hearts as well; they put on the table the little bit that they had and shared it with everyone.

N.C.: And before September 8?

O.D.V.: From 1938 till 1943 it was almost normal. The kids could no longer go to school, you couldn't go to the movies, you couldn't have a maid, and we were at God's mercy. At a certain hour we were all at home because, what do you want, where could we go? We couldn't go to the movies, we couldn't go to a bar. Now I don't say this for myself, because I was a woman and I was young in those days, and my father wouldn't have allowed me to leave the house anyway, but it was a problem for the boys. Many times at our place my father gathered the boys, four or five lads, youngsters, let's say, in order to have them stay home and not run around.

You could buy chocolate, you could buy fruit, you could buy some homemade ice cream, and he said, "I'm sorry, girls, don't let these youngsters go out, don't let these youngsters go out." There you have it, but this was from 1938 to 1943.

N.C.: And between 1938 and 1943 how were relations with the non-Jews?

O.D.V.: Look, they were good, among the Catholics it wasn't as if they would say, "Go away, you're a Jew," because after all, this friendship had been going on for so many years, they couldn't say it . . . You know . . .

N.C.: And so relations were good . . .

O.D.V.: Yes, at least with the people we knew. . . And to such an extent that they opened so many doors, we didn't know where to go . . . We were embarrassed to choose. Later, though, unfortunately my father was caught. . . .

N.C.: He was caught?

O.D.V.: Yes, he was caught while walking on Via Cicerone with my mother while we were at the convent, because he had no peace if he didn't see all his children. The boys were in another place with them, and so he came to see me, my sister, and my mother, and unfortunately Papa and Mama were arm in arm. Mama always told the story that Papa made a big jump and she says, "What did you do?" He says, "Nothing, walk and don't turn around." He wanted to accompany Mama back to the convent, except that he felt a hand on his back and someone said, "Are you Enrico?" My father says , "No, my name is Nicola Ruda," and he showed him the false ID card. Then this man, who had only one arm because he was wounded in the war of 1915–18, says, "How come you don't recognize me now?" He says, "I'm So and So, how come? On the evening of October 15 you gave me a hundred lire"—in those days a hundred lire were a lot—"You gave me a hundred lire's worth of goods at ten lire a day, which I am to return to you at ten lire a day. Here, this is the paper I still have from your hand." Then my father said, he says, "Look, don't harm me because I have a family." "What harm? What harm? You're a friend," he says. "I'm only taking you for questioning and that's it." Then my mama didn't want to leave him, and my father told her in Hebrew, he says, "Look, let me go alone, look after the children, at least there's one to look after them." Then Mother got in the car, too, and says, "Take me where you're taking my husband," and these men said, "Away, away, get out." Father said, "Sorry, get out, and be good, be good because I'll come back in a very short time." And the other man said, "Lady, it's a question of half an hour," he says. "Wait for him here." Seeing that Mother didn't want to get out, they punched her in the mouth and sent her sideways behind them, with such force in that blow that all of my mother's teeth were broken. And I don't know if I'm using the right term now, her heart was wrenched, and from that time on she always suffered. Then, unfortunately, in 1955 . . .

N.C.: And your father?

O.D.V.: My father did not return again, my sister was taken on October 16 with her children and husband. Then I have some cousins, uncles and aunts, girlfriends, other friends, so many, so many, so many, about sixty people in the immediate and larger family.

It's been a story that, unfortunately, we'll never forget again. We see everything before our eyes.

N.C.: You can't forget.

O.D.V.: Yes. Then I have a cousin, the youngest in the Ardeatine Caves,[25] Michele di Veroli, whom they shot. He was fourteen and was wearing short pants. They shot him together with his father, who was my cousin. And this is a story that, unfortunately, if you had to sit down and write it, you could write and remember everything that happened. In fact, I remember that on October 16 I started to write in my own way, I started to write something. Then my father told me, he says, "What do you want to write? These are days that you will never forget for the rest of your life." In fact, it's been so.

N.C.: And when did you go back? When the Allies arrived?

O.D.V.: I was in the convent and I remember that my sister's husband came, in those days they were engaged, and I say, "Look, are you sure that the Americans have arrived?" He says, "Yes, yes, I'm sure." I went down to Via Cicerone. The first person I saw (I'm not good with faces, but now, after years of distance, I see him vividly) was a soldier. Not an ordinary soldier, he was an officer, a Scot, he had a thin moustache, you know, like the types you often see in the movies. . . .

Then my brother-in-law told me, he says, "Here, you see that the Americans have arrived." I say, "But . . . but is it certain?" Then the officer tells me, "Of course it's certain" (he said *certo,* "of course," in Italian). Then I started to cry, and I say, "Go to find my papa and my sister." And then he said to me, "Good girl, good girl." He took out a handkerchief and dried my eyes and made me blow my nose, and says, "Now wait a moment." He gave me a kiss on the forehead and said to me, "Now, calmly, tell me what you want, because I speak Italian well."

I went to visit those concentration camps, because that's all I have left, because if I had to take a pleasure trip perhaps I wouldn't have the strength, but when I can I make a habit of going to Auschwitz where my family died. The only thing that I might be able to do is place a flower there, and I give you my word of honor that I don't know how to say a prayer. When I arrive there I don't know how to say a prayer. I hope that God, blessed be His name, will give me the strength to return there. Because look, over there a really strange thing happened. Because the first time I went there (I'm speaking about more than twenty years ago) it was raining so hard, and my mother always used to tell me, "I'm convinced that you are the only person who will go to those camps one day, because you have more courage than anyone else." "Remember this," she says. "Bring me a fistful of that soil and kiss the ground for me." And when I went, there are witnesses who saw it. It was raining, and I threw myself down, face forward, spattered with mud, right in the middle where the entrance to the camp was. Then they told me, "Come on, lady, you've fallen." I say, "No, stop." I pulled myself back on my feet. I don't know, look, I was clean the way you are now, look. When I went, unfortunately, my mama was no more, so I brought a fistful of earth from a crematory oven, not that it was from those dead, but it was a fistful of that soil, the soil of Auschwitz. I put it in a little bag and took it to my mother's grave before I returned home. I say, "Mama, I carried out your wish the best way I could."

N.C.: Did you get married later on, did you have children?

O.D.V.: No, I didn't, no, because I was with my sister who had already been engaged for some years, with my brothers who were younger than I—who were students and had interrupted their studies.

They, my brothers and two sisters, were saved; the other sister, no. Then I had my duty, because Mama was ill. Then I worked on the book "The Jews of Rome," where there are some letters written by my father.

N.C.: Then you brought them with you?

O.D.V.: In his last letter, my father was asking me, he says, "Dear Carmela, dear Carmela (because he used to call me Carmela), I know I can count on you." "I know I can count on you," he says, "don't ever abandon your mother, or your brothers, or your sisters. Be brave and strong." And I did what I could, what you must do in the end, I give thanks to God because I feel my soul is calm and at peace. You see, the only thing, the only satisfaction I could give my father is this: enough. I can do nothing else.

N.C.: Good, many thanks . . .

O.D.V.: And your name, please?

N.C.: Caracciolo. . . .

AMBASSADOR ROBERTO DUCCI

NICOLA CARACCIOLO: Well, Ambassador, what do you know about the rescue of the Jews in Croatia?

ROBERTO DUCCI: At that time I was in charge of the Croatian Office of the Foreign Ministry, an office established after the founding of the independent state of Croatia. Our charge was to attend to bilateral relations between Italy and Croatia, over which we were hoping at that time to extend a kind of protectorate or at least hegemony. It was in that capacity, as chief of the Croatian Office, that I found myself confronted with the orders of my chief in that period of time. He was minister plenipotentiary, later ambassador, Luca Pietromarchi, who was responsible for all territories under Italian military occupation. I found myself, I was saying, confronted with the request that was made to us by the embassy of the Reich in Rome, to hand over to the Croatian government the Jews of Croatian nationality and of other nationalities who were in the territories occupied by our troops.

N.C.: And then the Croats would have passed them on to the Germans . . .

Ambassador Roberto Ducci, who died within weeks of the interview

R.D.: As we knew later on, the Croats would have passed them on to the Germans. I've got to stress that in that period, which I am specifying as toward the . . . the spring of 1942, it was not yet very clear what was happening to the Croatian Jews . . .

N.C.: That is, you didn't know about the gas chambers . . .

R.D.: We knew this from a notice that reached us . . . reached us from one of our intelligence services—even at that time there was more than one intelligence service—which was one of the intelligence services that paid particular attention to the Balkans. I believe it was the first, and the chief of the service was an excellent general of the *carabinieri*.

N.C.: Who was he?

R.D.: General Pièche. He came to know, from his agents in Croatia, in the part controlled by the Germans, that the destruction of the Croatian Jews had effectively been decided by the Hitler government. It was made into a memorandum for Mussolini, who, I think, may also have known it from some other service. Certainly he knew it on that occasion.

N.C.: And how did Mussolini react at that time? What happened?

R.D.: Nothing happened. But I'm sure that this had an influence later on Mussolini, who despite having answered the memorandum left through the German Embassy by the Ministerial Councillor Prince Otto von Bismarck[26]—the grandson of the great Bismarck whose first name he also bore—a memorandum in which the handing over of these Jews was precisely requested, Mussolini put "*nulla osta*"[27] on the sheet, and afterwards nothing happened.

N.C.: That is, they were not handed over to the Ustasha and the Germans.

R.D.: The legitimate question is: but then, had Mussolini authorized the thing? My answer to this, not to absolve Mussolini but to explain what happened afterwards, was that *nulla osta* is an Italian expression for saying, "I for my part have nothing against this." Then afterwards, the circumstances . . . It wasn't, "Yes, give the order to the military authorities to do it." In the zone of Croatia we controlled, the civilian authority, along with the military authority, was exercised by our commanders, therefore by the commander of the Second Army,[28] and for him by the commanders . . .

N.C.: Ambassador, what happened then?

R.D.: What happened was that we found, by agreement with the command in Croatia, every possible argument and every possible delay to avoid this ever happening.

N.C.: For example.

R.D.: Now I'll explain to you. In the first place, evidently if the command and the officers had agreed to it the thing would probably have taken place. But they didn't agree, because all the while that was repugnant to their sensibility as men and as Italians, as Christians and, for some of the officers without a doubt, as gentlemen as well. In the second place, because they had already seen the massacres that the Croatian Ustasha, namely those with Pavelić,[29] had done to the Serbs, above all in Bosnia. And we had intervened against these massacres, by removing the powers of civil administration from the Zagreb government in our occupation zone with a move that therefore had been, in effect, not a very friendly one, certainly a most displeasing move to the Pavelić government. This cluster of massacres and other things that happened in the Balkans probably had its psychological influence on our officers who were living in the villages—who were living in contact with the populace and so also with the tiny Jewish minority that existed here and there. At that time General Roatta, who succeeded

O

APPUNTO PER IL DUCE

Bismarck ha dato comunicazione di un telegramma a firma
Ribbentrop con il quale questa Ambasciata di Germania viene
richiesta di provocare istruzioni alle competenti Autorità
Militari italiane in Croazia affinchè anche nelle zone di
nostra occupazione possano essere attuati i provvedimenti
divisati da parte germanica e croata per un trasferimento
in massa degli ebrei di Croazia nei territori orientali.

Bismarck ha affermato che si tratterebbe di varie mi-
gliaia di persone ed ha lasciato comprendere che tali provvedimenti tenderebbero, in pratica, alla loro dispersione
ed eliminazione.

L'Ufficio competente fa presente che segnalazioni della R.Legazione a Zagabria inducono a ritenere che, per desi
derio germanico, che trova consenziente il Governo ustasci:
la questione della liquidazione degli ebrei in Croazia sta-
rebbe ormai entrando in una fase risolutiva.

Si sottopone, Duce, quanto precede per le Vostre deci-
sioni.

Roma, 21 agosto 1942-XX

The note of August 21, 1942, from the Foreign Ministry to the Duce, ordering deportation of Jews from the Italian zone of Croatia, with Mussolini's handwritten *"nulla osta,"* authorizing its execution. This document, discussed by Professor Carpi and Ambassador Ducci, is housed in and photocopied from the Archivo Storico Diplomatico of the Italian Foreign Ministry. (Source: Jonathan Steinberg, *All or Nothing* [London and New York: Routledge, 1990], 2)

General Ambrosio, told us that for reasons of public order and calm in the zone of operations an operation of that sort was clearly ill-advised, that it would have aroused large doubts in the Croatian populace about their future, because they could anticipate their own lot from the lot of the Jews. It was exaggerated, but it made a certain impression. I have to say, moreover, that the Supreme Command even under Cavallero, under Marshal Cavallero, never objected to the position taken by its commander of the army and by his commanding staff. We at the Foreign Ministry, however much I can . . .

N.C.: Yes, what was your role in this turn of events?

R.D.: However much I can try to speak of myself and my office, we found a bunch of reasons that let us keep the thing on the back burner without ever complying with the German request, and at the same time to have plausible enough pretexts or reasons to justify the lack of action before the German authorities. I've got to say that Bismarck, who came every so often to get information on behalf of his ambassador, von Mackensen, on how matters were going, knowing very well that they were going nowhere, was a man of understanding, undoubtedly opposed to this kind of policy on his government's part.

N.C.: Then was he also content that nothing was being done?

R.D.: He helped sufficiently. He stood very well with Ciano, with Ciano's group of friends, without whom we should not have been able to carry out this policy, because if it wasn't at least the foreign minister who backed this policy of continuous postponements, or better covered it up (we're not dealing with backing but with a cover-up), obviously it would have turned out harder for us to carry it out. However, the dissatisfaction of the Berlin government showed itself in various steps that were taken at various levels, and it was necessary to find some reasons to explain why we didn't follow up on their request— indeed, nearly sabotaged it.

N.C.: And what reasons did you give?

R.D.: Well, for example at one point we gave reasons of this sort: we don't really know the nationality of these Jews. You tell us that they are Croatian, but they could also be of another nationality. Some of them could even be Italian nationals. You have to remember that Fascism and Mussolini had obtained from Hitler the concession that the Italian Jews would never be exposed to what was happening to the other Jews, even if the former were residing in Germany. We had some Italian Jews, with Italian passports and Italian citizenship, who continued to reside in Germany during the Holocaust and the persecution. Therefore it was justified to say, "We want to know first if by chance there might not be some Italian citizens." After this we called, I remember, I called on Tommaso Perassi, the great professor of international law, to draw up for me a list of every possible reason for which one more Croat of the Jewish faith, of the Israelite faith, could be granted Italian citizenship. There was a list, there still is, a document that has been published by an Israeli scholar, Daniel Carpi, with five or six cases in which one could recognize Italian citizenship. One of these, the last I think, was "for having performed advantageous actions for the Italian state," advantageous actions—it was enough to have done something of benefit to a platoon of soldiers in a hamlet in Yugoslavia to be able to take advantage of that one.

N.C.: And what else did you do to cause the Germans to lose time?

R.D.: What we did was to start an action that was a lot more complicated and done on the spot. We began to say, temporizing before agreeing to hand over these Jews, that they had been dispersed to every zone occupied by our troops, in Slovenia, in Croatia, in Dalmatia, and we had to bring them together to be able to arrange for the possibility of handing them over, and so they were concentrated in determined areas by the sea.

N.C.: On Arbe, for example . . .

R.D.: Arbe was the last, but first of all at Porto Re,* in temporary camps, camps about which some of these Croatian Jews told me, those I've recently met, who are still full of gratitude to our troops for saving their lives or giving them a chance to save them, camps in which they were authorized to lead rather free lives, as I can tell you. They were allowed their religious functions, the celebration of the Jewish Passover, even a certain education. Italian courses were set up. There are several of these Jews who at that time were children, babies, et cetera, and who learned Italian in these camps. Finally almost all of them were concentrated in the island of Arbe—Arbe is a very beautiful island in the Gulf of Quarnero**—and the reason was to shelter them from a surprise attack. It was easy enough for anyone, let's suppose the Germans, to get to a camp that was on the coast. It was harder to cross over even a strait and go to the island. On the island were gathered quite prob-

---

*Ducci uses the Italian place names rather than the Serbo-Croatian ones. Hence Porto Re = Kraljevice (Dalmatia). For further particulars, see Appendix 1.

**Travel guides would identify it today as Rab, in the Kvarner Gulf.

ably from 3,500 to 4,000 Jews, men, women, old folk, and young-sters, and they stayed there for several months. In the meantime, in March of 1943, Ribbentrop made a trip to Rome, he remained there for three days. . . .

N.C.: And asked that the Jews be handed over.

R.D.: He spoke with Mussolini and asked with a really steadfast insis-tence that the Jews be handed over. And I must say, it was much to the credit there of the ex-governor of Dalmatia, also an ex-Blackshirt, Giuseppe Bastianini,[30]—at that moment the undersecretary of the Foreign Office after Ciano had left the ministry and had been sent to act as ambassador to the Vatican. We owed a lot to Bastianini. He made Mussolini face the deep shame that would result for him, for the coun-try, for the regime, if a deed of that kind should occur. And Mussolini was quite shaken, also because these words came to him from a per-son whom he did not regard as a traitor . . .

N.C.: Who was a friend of his . . .

R.D.: Who was a comrade of his in the youthful struggle, and there-fore was someone who had access to him in a psychological sense. Bastianini had better access than his son-in-law, Galeazzo Ciano, could have, since he already looked at Ciano with great suspicion as a man who did not want the war, as a man who wanted Italy to shift its alli-ance instead to the Anglo-American camp. Therefore Bastianini spoke extremely eloquent words that are reproduced in the diary kept by Ambassador Pietromarchi in those times, recounted to him, because Pietromarchi was not present, by Bastianini himself—for whom that time as well, despite those pressures on the highest level, on the Führ-er's order, and so on, Mussolini hesitated and did nothing. Then came July 25; evidently at that moment the question disappeared. It disap-peared on the diplomatic level, on the level of collaboration between the two armies, and instead it reopened . . .

N.C.: With the eighth of September . . .

I wanted to ask something else, Ambassador. You were acting as you did to save the Jews; you were swimming against the current with respect to the policy of the Axis. Will you explain the reason, then: why did you do this?

R.D.: But this is strange, it's a question that was put to me recently as well in a large meeting that took place in Washington precisely to eval-uate the action of having helped the persecuted Jews in Europe. But why, unlike what went on in other countries, did you Italians take to your hearts not only—here it's the moment to say it—the lot of the Croatian Jews, but also the lot of the Greek Jews, the lot of the Jews who were on the French Riviera? In fact, wherever the Italian occupation was, there we protected the Jews. My answer was, and it seems the normal one, the one that everybody would have to hear, despite Fascism I think that at least the vast majority of the Italian populace had preserved its feelings for humanity, its Christian feelings, for which you don't persecute people without reason. These were a people that had been entrusted to our protection. Many of them had fled from German-controlled territories because they thought that Italy and the Italians would help them, and we didn't want in any way to betray this faith that was put in us. But I meant that, if even this were lacking, there was secondly the sense of all of us, that we have (let's put it this way) a sense of morality and a sense of respect for human dignity, which prevented us from playing a part in a crime of that kind. It was for this reason that I am saying that this group of soldiers, of officers, and of diplomats, with the support . . .

N.C.: And of policemen . . .

R.D.: . . . And of policemen, was able to carry out this operation with the various results that we can see.

N.C.: Another question I wanted to put to you. Ciano supported this policy. Was he convinced of it?

R.D.: Ciano, yes, he was convinced. Ciano had always been, not pro-Jewish but against racial conflict. I recall that in 1938, when the racial laws were passed, he said to his cousin, who was a colleague of mine whom I'd known since he was a boy, "I'm very worried, these are things that bode ill." Maybe he was seeing this from a superstitious perspective, but he was certainly no rabid Jew-hater. After all, his transformation into an anti-German, as a consequence of the famous discussion with Ribbentrop in Salzburg. . . .

N.C.: Yes, in 1939 . . .

R.D.: In August 1939 he saw to it that once something was requested by the Germans, he wanted to do the opposite if there was any way he could. I've got to say of Ciano that he wasn't at the ministry much at that time, in part because he was ill, in part because Mussolini was sending him to the front just to get him out of the way. I can say, however, that Anfuso[31] himself, who even after September 8 remained on Mussolini's side for psychological reasons rather than ideological ones, he, too, did not, *not*, take this thing up. D'Ajeta, who became chief of the cabinet, he, too, was against it, indeed in his discussions with Bismarck he was . . . always between D'Ajeta and Bismarck you saw how you could get Berlin to swallow it, to gulp down another postponement.

N.C.: Bismarck, that is, collaborated quite actively, was part of this— let's call it a conspiracy in defense of the Jews.

R.D.: Yes, de facto. We never asked him to do so, nor did he offer this, but in the end one saw that if he had to explain things in a telegram to Berlin, as he surely was doing after these conversations both with Pietromarchi and with D'Ajeta, he would put things in a convincing way.

N.C.: And your opinion on Mussolini?

R.D.: He was in the usual awful dilemma, in which that man would remain from 1936 on: namely, the alliance on one hand and his "Italianness," if I can put it in a single word, that is, the humanity in which he, too, was not lacking. In his case I wouldn't speak of a Christian spirit or of a spirit of, well, of . . . chivalry, but of the normal humanity in the Italian people, which without doubt he had, even if he didn't show it in some rather sad moments of our history. Therefore I believe he regretted having to affix his signature to the deportation of people who had surely done nothing harmful to Italy, people whom (for reasons we did not understand) we had thus to condemn to a certain death. And on the other hand he maintained that perhaps—in the general framework of a policy toward which we were evolving through the force of circumstances, that is, through the development of the operations of war, which weren't favorable to Italy and weren't yet completely unfavorable to Germany—we couldn't *not* give Hitler every so often some, let's put it this way, some positive answer to his requests. But there was never, to my recollection, a moment when he called anyone from the Foreign Ministry, a Pietromarchi, for example, or others, or called the chief of the General Staff (which would have been more than enough), giving orders to tell the soldiers to hand over the Croatian Jews to the Zagreb government.

N.C.: However one might wish to judge him, he never gave that order . . .

R.D.: That order would have been enough . . .

N.C.: And how did this all end up?

R.D.: Better than what one might think, because in the meantime for a month the camp on Arbe, the island of Arbe, remained free of occupation by the Nazi troops or the troops of the Ustasha.

N.C.: This after September 8 . . .

R.D.: After September 8 some Yugoslavian partisans who arrived there reached some agreements, I think, with the Croatian Jews. Then they went away because they couldn't stay there. And at a certain moment the outflowing of individuals from Arbe first started. A Croatian Jew whom I met in Washington sometime ago told me that he, who was sixteen years old at the time, and other boys came by a dinghy, and going down the Adriatic, a bit with the oars and a bit with the help of the sails, ended up on the island of Lissa.* Lissa by that time had already been liberated, and indeed Tito's headquarters were there. From there they were sent to Bari, after which these boys were in Apulia for two or three years before they could get permission to go to America, and so they all studied in Italian schools and they speak Italian like ourselves. Others, instead, reached the partisans, always a few at a time, and more than a thousand of them, obviously the younger ones, fought against the Germans in the ranks of the partisans.

In the end, unfortunately, the older ones, those who were ill and in bad shape, had to remain on the island. There was no way to transport them, and some of these ended up in the hands of the Germans, and so they met the usual end. But of these 3,500, perhaps 4,000, it's calculated that—without counting the ones who died fighting, with weapons in their hands, which might even be a beautiful and honorable death—about 1,800 to 2,000 were saved. Therefore an ample half were saved, among them the younger ones.

N.C.: You preserved the documentation on what the Foreign Office did to rescue the Jews in Croatia. How?

R.D.: The business with the Jews in Croatia, just like the other business, was characterized by total secrecy. I kept it locked up in my strongbox. It was from there that I removed it on September 9 or 10, when we burned the archives of Palazzo Chigi.[32] I decided not to burn that file and to bring it home, because I felt that it might be well that someone should know later on, in the future, that we had done something good in our lives. And as a matter of fact it stayed there: I went south, to join up with the royal government, the legitimate government, and this file stayed hidden in my father's house, where I retrieved it when I returned to Rome in July of 1944.

*Lissa = Vis, an island in the mid-Adriatic.

NEDO FIANO

NICOLA CARACCIOLO: You, Dr. Fiano, are from Florence, if I'm not mistaken?

NEDO FIANO: Yes . . . Yes. . . .

N.C.: You were deported to Auschwitz . . .

N.F.: Yes. . . .

N.C.: Can you tell me how this happened?
  You were arrested in . . .

N.F.: I was arrested in . . . in downtown Florence. Maybe I was arrested because I couldn't bear to stay hidden. I had thought of moving around a little and then I was brutally accosted on the street by . . .

N.C.: How old were you?

N.F.: Eighteen years old. . . .

N.C.: And your family?

N.F.: My family as well. At different times my entire family was deported and murdered. My mother and my brother, ten people in all.

N.C.: And you are the only survivor?

N.F.: Yes. After a spell in the Florence jail, I was taken to the camp at Fossoli, and from the camp at Fossoli I was taken to Auschwitz. In the camp at Fossoli, I was reunited with Papa and Mama, and so we made the trip from Fossoli to Auschwitz together. There Mama was killed right away, and Papa about two months later.

N.C.: And did you know this, did you see it?

N.F.: Well, not right away, because one couldn't see it. I don't know if you are aware of the structure of the camp? Upon arrival the prisoners went through selection: those who were to be directed to the labor camp and those who were to be eliminated. We didn't know anything about all this. Those who took the opposite direction from ours were immediately eliminated. This we learned that same night in the camp; we arrived in the morning and some prisoners let us know that the fire that came out of the cremation ovens wasn't, they weren't plants, they weren't factories, but it was an annihilation machine, into which my mother, along with so many other mothers, had gone. And . . . do you want to know something about my life in the camp?

N.C.: I would like to ask you, forgive me if I insist, I would like to ask you this: did you know what they had in store for you, did you know what Auschwitz was?

N.F.: You're asking whether we knew it in Italy?

N.C.: Yes.

N.F.: Absolutely not. We were thinking about deportation, we were thinking about living in a concentration camp, something that besides was borne out a little in all European countries during the war, and we were thinking that even let it be through difficulties, through various kinds of privation, we would have . . .

N.C.: That you would have to deal with hard labor camps, perhaps, but not extermination camps.

N.F.: Hard labor up to a point, but in fact . . . just like the camp at Fossoli, moreover, where we stayed for about a month and a half like this, where we were surrounded with difficulties but our lives were not in danger except for some sporadic reprisal episodes, but in fact, in essence, there was no extermination, no genocide. We were not informed about it at all. I have to say that, had we been informed, we wouldn't have gone, we'd have attempted an escape, a revolt, I don't know what, but faced with such a hallucinatory prospect . . .

N.C.: You were telling me that right at the frontier they made you get off the train. . . .

N.F.: Yes, we lived through an unforgettable episode. At the Ora station we got off the train and we were able to freshen up at the local café in the station, where each one of us went in an orderly manner and from where we then returned, all of us got back into our own carriages, and then we left.

N.C.: In other words, you didn't have the slightest idea about what was in store for you.

N.F.: Absolutely. And I must say, everything had been arranged with a lot of skill, with great mastery, with gross orchestration so that nothing would leak out, because they knew that if there had been leaks of any sort, even the most cowardly, even the frailest would not have arrived. And I must say that even at Auschwitz itself the discourse on the killings, the gassing of the people, was carried out with subtle orchestration. Even those who were going to die were guided toward a building all surrounded by majestic-looking trees. In clear letters there was the inscription, "Disinfection Room." Everything was done in such a way that there wouldn't be scenes of terror, and therefore history tells us that at Auschwitz, with the exception of a couple of episodes, the prisoners never participated in any protests because, for the most part, they were to arrive without realizing where they were going to go.

In Italy, until 1943, we all knew that as for the Germans, they had tough, barbarous laws, savagely restrictive to individual freedom, but we didn't know about the destruction, we didn't know about the crematory ovens, we didn't know about the revolt in the Warsaw ghetto, just as we didn't know about the extermination camps. All this was a fact completely unknown both to Jews and non-Jews.

N.C.: I'd like to ask you a last question—what sort of mark did this event leave within you? How do you feel it today, forty years later and more? What effect did it have on your life?

N.F.: But at bottom I would say that I never completely left the camp.

EMILIO FOÀ

NICOLA CARACCIOLO: Well, Dr. Foà, when the first racial measures were taken, where were you and what happened?

EMILIO FOÀ: When the first racial measures were taken in 1938, as is known, I was twelve years old, living with my family at Casale Monferrato. I was going to school regularly like all the children my age, and all of a sudden, because of these laws, I had to leave . . . the school like all the other Jewish children.

N.C.: What did your schoolmates do? How did they act?

E.F.: Let's say that my schoolmates had no idea at first, they couldn't understand what all this was causing, so that the friendships we had in school were kept up later on. Our trauma was that all of a sudden we could no longer attend school as we'd been accustomed to doing by then. But we . . . because we were boys, we didn't understand the gravity and trauma that [all] this could bring about.

N.C.: And the people around you, the friends of the family, generally what was the attitude of the people there?

E.F.: Let's say that friends continued to be friends and maybe better friends than before, and acquaintances, in general, were the same.

Emilio Foà

There was certainly no distancing; rather, in some cases, a drawing closer.

If someone was an enemy, he obviously remained that because, let's say, he was that already. I want to say in this respect that, in my opinion, in the opinion of many others, the attitude of the entire Italian population overall, in the majority of cases, was not helpful to these persecutions.

N.C.: Did you feel some solidarity?

E.F.: We felt a certain solidarity—we were not marginalized: we were marginalized by the state, or rather by the government, to be precise. We were made marginal by the regime, but not by the population.

N.C.: This is valid, let's say, for the period between 1938 and 1943. But how did you live through the eighth of September? What happened?

E.F.: Even without this marginalizing, which didn't really take place, this discrimination left its mark upon us. And as the war progressed, the acts of discrimination got worse and worse.

N.C.: And what, specifically, was happening?

E.F.: Well, every so often there was a new provision—one day the housekeepers couldn't work for a Jewish family. Then so many other regulations came out, regarding school, government employment, and civil servants having to give up their positions even if they had thirty years of seniority. And then the anti-Semitic propaganda.

N.C.: What did your father do?

E.F.: My father was involved in agriculture, on a very small plot of land we had at Monferrato.

N.C.: And therefore they let you hold on to that, because it was small. . . .

E.F.: Yes, and my father was later interned as an anti-Fascist, and if I'm not mistaken, in 1942 at Gioia del Colle above Bari and at Gran Sasso, for having spoken out against Fascism and for being anti-Fascist.

N.C.: And tell me, what happened after September 8?

E.F.: Well, the pace of events sped up after September 8, because some partisan bands began to be formed, some Jews joined the Resistance, and in fact, generally, the Jews did not yet foresee the danger of extermination. In the Social Republic the laws concerning the internment of the Jews were proclaimed in December 1943 and January 1944. At that time we left Piedmont and went to the area near Mantua, where my mother came from.

N.C.: You were then seventeen years old. . . .

E.F.: Seventeen . . . and over there we came into contact with a partisan band from Parma, or rather with a person sent by the group, which was based in the hills of Parma, in order to get my father and me up to where his group was. But we didn't reach an understanding in time, and in a few days we were picked up by the *repubblichini** at Rivarolo Mantovano and taken to a concentration camp in Mantua. It was a shelter for old Jews.

N.C.: Who were these *repubblichini,* what unit was this?

E.F.: I can't tell you exactly. What's certain is that we were entrusted to a marshal of the *carabinieri,* Marshal Sartori, who asked questions of my uncle Aldo Milla, of my father Anselmo Foà, and then said, "The

*These were the uniformed troops of the Fascist Republic of Salò.

boy is very young, yet I've got to take him with me for questioning and then we'll see." At that point—I don't know whether to say it, it's a very personal thing—my father said, "Let's call a spade a spade. Either you ignore who this boy is or if you take this boy along for questioning, it's clear that he'll have the same fate as ours." And this marshal of the *carabinieri* said, "I think it's my duty to take this boy in for questioning as well." After which I went to Mantua, to this concentration camp that was a shelter for the elderly that had been transformed into a camp, and we stayed in this concentration camp till the beginning of April of 1944.

In this camp there was only physical constraint, in the sense that we couldn't leave. But they did not commit any act of violence or harm against us.

N.C.: And was this camp in the hands of the Fascists or the Germans?

E.F.: It was a Fascist camp. But as far as I can tell, the camp commissioner, Martiradonna, gave regular reports to the Mantua police headquarters, but I believe that the Mantua police must have communicated regularly with the German command about the situation in this camp.

The tragedy of this camp is that the majority of inmates were elderly, because it was a Jewish shelter.

N.C.: And what happened then?

E.F.: What happened is that around the first days of April of 1944, an SS came to the camp and then arranged with the Mantua police headquarters for the transfer of these people to Germany, to Poland. In all they were forty-four. Among those were ourselves, about thirty people. I even have the entire list. The majority were between sixty-five and eighty years old, and very few were young, as in my case, precisely because it was a shelter for the elderly. You were talking about my father. Yes, my father and my uncle were deported with me. Like many others we arrived in Auschwitz, rather at Birkenau, on April 10, 1944. And after a trip that by now we all know about, the kind of trip it was, after a five-day journey, we arrived at Birkenau, and there they made a selection. And I think by now it's well known by almost everyone that those able to work went to the left; those unable, to the right—naturally a very generic, swift selection. It could happen that some older person might join the group of the young and vice versa, so the criterion wasn't how many people are able to work, but how many people were needed. For this reason, if on a certain day no one is needed to attain that limit, then there you have it, all the new arrivals can go straight to their deaths because no one is needed to work.

N.C.: And you saw and lived through these things here. . . .

E.F.: Yes, when I arrived at Birkenau, that is to say, three kilometers from Auschwitz, when I arrived at Birkenau, and they still needed a few people for the heavy jobs and also for other work, for which reason let's say that about 150 out of the approximately 1,500 deportees who'd been sent to Auschwitz, after the selection they walked for two kilometers on foot and went to the camp at Auschwitz and to the various jobs. My father and my uncle stayed immediately, straight away, in the group of those put to death.

N.C.: And did they die immediately?

E.F.: Without a doubt.

N.C.: And did you know about this?

E.F.: At the moment I didn't understand anything, at the moment we saw a separation and it seemed as if the older ones were loaded on a truck in order not to have to submit to going that distance on foot.

N.C.: Did it seem an act of kindness?

E.F.: Almost. We didn't understand anything. I think the majority of the deported Italians understood almost nothing at that time. Those who knew the situation in detail were the Jews from Poland, from Czechoslovakia, near the places where this extermination was taking place.

We didn't know these things. At that moment I didn't understand this dividing up, and after a few hours, that is, after the shower, the disinfection and the shaving, the tattooing of the number, afterwards I looked, I tried to find out where my father and the other people I did not see had ended up. Then a fellow who came from Mantua with me but was of German origin and knew everything well from the beginning, told me: "Look, I must tell you how things stand, because in a short while you'll come to know. Think of yourself and of those few you have around you, but don't think about those you don't see— your father and the rest with your uncle and the others stayed at Birkenau, and we don't know if at this moment they are still alive." This was, let's say, the most traumatic moment, if I'm allowed to express a personal feeling—but, as they say, life goes on. At seventeen years of age, one is naturally idealistic and . . .

N.C.: And you have succeeded in some way.

E.F.: I saw the end of the war near and I said: here we have dictatorship, we have what we have, but soon there will be democracy, civilized society, and so this idealism, that's what gave me the incentive to be able to survive, helped also by fortunate circumstances, because later on I went through two other selections.

N.C.: Was it the same thing all over again?

E.F.: The same thing again. Of course, selections among those who were in the camp and who in time grew weaker and became ill and could no longer work. They made a selection. If you were still able to work they kept you, otherwise they put you to death. One of these was made in June and another at the end of August-September 1944.

N.C.: Here, Dr. Foà, is one final question: what thoughts have you drawn out of this? How do you evaluate this awful experience of yours?

E.F.: But my experience is common to so many other experiences, let's say it has nothing specific. Indeed, let's say that I'm among the few survivors. For this reason we can say that for many others the tragedy was much more terrible and more severe. And what has always comforted us, as I believe I said before, was that we weren't marginalized, we didn't live in surroundings, apart from the concentration camp, that were hostile. And this made it much easier to overcome the most difficult times.

N.C.: And how many survived from this group in Mantua?

E.F.: I am the only survivor from the Mantua group.

PRIMO LEVI

PRIMO LEVI: Up until September 8 my experience was practically non-existent. I'd already been graduated. I took my degree in 1941, that is, three years after the racial laws. In other words, I attended university while the racial laws were in place.

NICOLA CARACCIOLO: How was that?

P.L.: It was relatively all right. I mean to say that the university milieu in Turin, my university milieu, had stayed virtually immune to Fascism. Not that the professors didn't wear their black shirts. Yes, they wore them. It was ordered that at exam time both the teachers and the students had to put on their black shirts, and we Jews couldn't and didn't want to wear them. With all this, there were some oppressive rules.

The late author and chemist Primo Levi, whose works have become well known in the United States and Britain.

You had to take the exams last, and it wasn't possible to attend as "internal students," as they called them then, that is, to have access to the labs, which for a chemist (I took my degree in chemistry) was rather serious. I mean that we could attend the obligatory lab, but we weren't allowed to prepare the required thesis, which as a rule is done in a lab, there. But I did it anyway because I had a professor who told me, "What do you care about it, *I* don't care, you come anyway, nobody knows anything about it." I'm convinced that the commendation I received at graduation wasn't due to the worth of my thesis, it was a timid act . . .

N.C.: Of protest . . .

P.L.: Of protest against the racial laws by a very timid professor who didn't dare express himself in a different way and expressed himself that way. I had and still have very good relations with my university colleagues of those days, of whom no one ever expressed a contemptuous remark. I would say quite on the contrary, that among my then fellow students I found a great deal of understanding. Beside everything else there were also the foreign Jews. Paradoxically, until September 8, in Italy there were Hungarian Jews, Polish Jews who had enrolled at the university and were able . . .

N.C.: To study . . .

P.L.: Provided that they were already enrolled at the time of the racial laws, they could go on with their studies.

N.C.: Tell me, in regard to this large question, how did the Italians, let's say the Italian non-Jews, act toward the Italian Jews in that period? Can you offer an opinion . . . ?

P.L.: Generally well—opinions are always approximate—I would say that in large part they acted well. There were several reasons contributing to this. One was that, in those years—I'm talking about 1941–42—it was already perceived that the war had shifted and that the German ally was a losing ally, and therefore Fascism was strongly discredited, especially after the Russian disaster.

N.C.: Let's say before this happened, in 1939–40?

P.L.: The racial laws were looked upon more as a great folly than as a tragedy, as a silly imitation of the German laws. Jews in Italy were and still are very few; they are and were very assimilated, indistinguishable from the rest of the population, either in terms of accent, or dress, or behavior. For the most part there was a "Risorgimento tradition" among the Jewish families, and logically. Many had been active during the Risorgimento; the Risorgimento granted equality, the full acceptance of Jews within the national fabric. Therefore it was, I'd like to say, incumbent upon Jews, in addition to being natural, to take an active part in the Risorgimento.[33]

N.C.: In other words, you didn't have the impression—before that horrendous experience in Auschwitz—you didn't have the impression of having a hostile environment in Italy.

P.L.: I had that most rarely. Only one man who was not a fellow chemistry student, but a former schoolmate from my high school, whom I met on the street and who told me, "Look, I'd rather not see you again." And I accepted it, after which when we met again thirty years later, and he spoke to me again, "I'd like to see you," I answered him, "No, really, really, not *you*."

But that was an isolated case. Beyond which my story from September 8 on coincides substantially with that of the partisans. I went to Val d'Aosta and found assembled in the mountains a number of young men my age. I was twenty-four, for the most part they were disbanded soldiers, I knew some of them because they were from Turin, and in a very artful but very incautious manner we tried to launch a partisan band. But these were beginnings, we had no political contacts, we had very little money and almost no weapons, we were a very disorganized group, and besides all that we were so unwary that we took a spy aboard. . . .

N.C.: For that you were later arrested and sent to the camp at Fossoli. Can you describe it for us?

P.L.: The camp at Fossoli was a former military camp. Earlier there had been English prisoners there. It was relatively well organized, there was food. There was a head of the camp whom I would like to meet again, Dr. Avidabile, who didn't realize that basically the Germans were the bosses. He had excellent relations with us, he was a very pleasant man, he told us, "As long as I'm here, you're fine." He even had some sentimental and more than sentimental relations with some Jewish girls in the camp. You had only to ask to go to Modena or Carpi to see a dentist, but above all to bathe, and he agreed. He would entreat us not to run away.

N.C.: A person who stayed human?

P.L.: A person who was human without a doubt, who was later abruptly deprived of his authority by the Germans when they came a few days before deportation. It seems that it was in fact Eichmann, from what I read, I think I read it in a biography of Eichmann, and the dates seem to correspond. In those days Eichmann was in Italy, therefore it was Eichmann who took away the authority of the Italian police, who took possession of the camp at Fossoli, after which all the Jews, all 650 with no exception, including the dying, the children . . .

N.C.: Later on this will be the subject of your book, *If This Is a Man?*

P.L.: Yes, *If This Is a Man* starts with the departure from Fossoli. Within the course of six or seven days after the Germans arrived, there were SS at the command of the camp. Within the course of a few days this train for Germany was organized.[34]

N.C.: What did Avidabile, the camp commandant, do?

P.L.: Nothing.

N.C.: Nothing?

P.L.: I think I remember that he tried to console us, he tried to say, "You are going to work in Germany," or something like that, some lies that perhaps he believed because the Germans had told them to him.

N.C.: And so the collision with this infernal world of the camps was unexpected?

P.L.: I'd like to emphasize that out of these 650 people some were in their late nineties and were practically in the agony of death. From a certain cynical point of view I understand that the Germans would kill the children, they were among future enemies, but why kill someone already dying? This truly escapes understanding, it's completely irrational. It was really the Jew seen as something monstrous that was being annihilated in the fullest sense of the word.

N.C.: In this whole affair seen again forty years later, there is something incomprehensible, as if UFOs had arrived on earth.

P.L.: Yes, indeed. . . .

N.C.: Then one asks oneself: but how is it possible that people would act that way?

P.L.: But in fact I've noticed that even many celebrated historians throw up their arms when faced with this question. It was truly a flight to the irrational that in my opinion began with Hitler himself, who starting from a certain point in his career launched himself toward the irrational, toward the insane.

N.C.: And the strange thing is that an entire country, or at least a whole state apparatus, followed him.

P.L.: The entire country, the largest part of the country, with few pockets of resistance. But the German people of that time were a people of *Jasagers*, of "Yea-sayers," an obedient people, a people disciplined in good and in evil. They accepted Prussian obedience. I've read some delusive books on the German schooling of that time, how the school contributed in large measure to the building of the Nazi state in a few years. Today Germany is much changed. The borders are less important, the Germans resemble more the French and the Italians. But in those days they were quite different. The cult of discipline, the cult of obedience, the rejection of individuality, seen as a disorder.

N.C.: And then the difference between the German frame of mind and the Italian?

P.L.: It was enormous, but I had very different relations with one group and the other.

The *lager* was so organized that our contacts with the SS were reduced to nothing. The camp was self-managed, the SS appointed functionaries inside the camp.

N.C.: The *kapòs* . . .

P.L.: The *kapòs*, yes, strangely the French pronunciation has prevailed, but instead the word is Italian and the Germans used to say *kàpo,* not *kapò.**[35]

My camp was a special camp. It was an annex of Auschwitz, a *Nebenlager,* that is to say a branch camp, which I later learned belonged even financially to a German trust, to the I. G. Farben industries, something like the setup for the Italian Montedison Company. In essence, I. G. Farben had financed it and paid rent for us to the SS. I believe that they paid four marks a day to the SS for a specialist—I was a specialist—and three marks for a hod carrier. Nine out of ten of the inmates were hod carriers. This money was paid to the SS who spent something like sixty cents a day for our upkeep, clothing, and so on. Therefore it was a good deal for the SS to lend ten thousand workers a day to this industry. And there was in fact a contrast between I. G. Farben and the SS in this sense, that if anyone became ill he had to be taken care of provided the prognosis was under fourteen days. If the prognosis was over fourteen days he had to be killed, and the population in the infirmary couldn't surpass ten percent of the camp. This was a contract.

N.C.: In such a way, in fact, that when someone went to the infirmary (you describe it, besides, in your book), on one hand there was the delight of being able to rest, but on the other, there was a lot of danger.

P.L.: I described a little while ago the irrational blindness of this wave of destruction with respect to the Jews. But the German industrialists weren't so blind and so irrational—not that they were angels, but they simply wanted to have a reasonably efficient work force. Now, a crew, a squad of workers that is renewed constantly isn't efficient. So there existed a certain dyarchy and a certain pressure on the part of I. G. Farben industries not to treat us in too destructive a manner. For instance, corporal punishment was certainly allowed: smacks, blows, and kicks I received in abundance, but not to the point of diminishing my capacity, because it's clear that a worker with a dislocated ankle or a broken nose produces less. Therefore German industry had a moderating influence. They needed labor; they exploited that work force to

* *Capo* (Italian) = "chief."

an extreme; it was accepted that the average life expectancy was three months, but it had to be three months. It was necessary that this human material keep a minimum of efficiency.

N.C.: And how do you explain this characteristic, this mania for order in the camps?

P.L.: It reflected, madly, certain German characteristics. Aside from the known suffering, already described by me and by innumerable others in the *lager,* there was a myriad of further suffering: the fact that you had to have five buttons, the jacket buttons. If anyone lost a button it was a tragedy, you had to find another and you didn't know where to find it, and with what thread or needle to sew it. And your shoes had to be brightly shined, and there was no polish, and so there existed a clandestine traffic in butter, it could be tar or vaseline or axle grease, with which you had to rub your shoes, which were in pieces. They were torture instruments, they were clogs with wooden soles, but every morning they had somehow to be shined. It was the translation or maybe the parody of German military life. And in the morning there was the ceremony of the *Bettenbauen,* of making your bed, this thing that wasn't really a bed, it was a bunk made up of small planks covered with a little mattress of paper chips, with two covers. And two people had to sleep within seventy centimeters, you had to make your bed at ninety-degree angles, and there was even a pair of functionaries to see to it that, after everyone made his bed amid the crowd, in a hurry to arrive on time for the bread handout, that all had made their beds with the pillow exactly measured at a right angle. And so there was a team who looked at the berths horizontally and even carried a thread to see that they were all perfectly aligned, and if one bunk appeared wrong the two tenants were punished, punished by flogging. It was a grave infraction of camp order and world order. The world had to be entirely regulated, entirely prepared minute by minute and centimeter by centimeter.

N.C.: A madness born out of the sense of order.

P.L.: Yes, a madness that doesn't coincide with Nazism. I would say that only in part did it coincide with Nazism, for Nazism partly inherited it, but it existed already in the German tradition. The lore of German proverbs centered, I don't know about today, but it used to center precisely on order and cleanliness. In our washroom in the *lager,* which was foul, was written "Gesund durch Sauberkeit": You'll be healthy if you're clean. And there were the maxims, often rhymed, often in rhyming couplets that exhorted us to order and cleanliness. It's difficult to understand, moreover, the inscription on the main gate to Auschwitz: "Work makes you free." It's difficult to comprehend whether this was derisive. In my opinion it wasn't; in my opinion it was part of the current morality.

N.C.: Yes, but it's a crazed evolution of an overly extended frame of mind, because basically an excessive attention to order, to cleanliness, to discipline characterizes many other northern societies, which nevertheless did not commit the same horrors. I mean that the Dutch, the Swiss, the Scandinavians are very orderly to an Italian mind-set. But they never did anything resembling *that*.

P.L.: Agreed, this sense of order doesn't coincide with Nazism, but it was part of it, and in its Nazi version it constituted further persecution: that of having, above all, the five buttons. Beyond hunger and cold, beyond death and the gas chamber, there was also the torment of the five buttons.

N.C.: Which was no small thing.

P.L.: Which was no small thing, because finding a needle and thread was already a large problem. You had to have bread to buy them, bread that instead of being eaten was spent to find a needle, perhaps for rent—for rent, because you couldn't always find a needle to buy.

N.C.: And you were saved by an Italian at Auschwitz. Can you tell us about it?

P.L.: If I'm alive it's for many reasons, but the main one is this: that I was working, in effect, in a factory for chemical products, and I worked for about a year and ten months as a hod carrier. Now, to my good fortune, on a certain summer day, it was in June 1944, they sent me to be the hod carrier for a crew of bricklayers, to build a wall. Now it wasn't so easy to work as a hod carrier, because you had to lift the lime bucket, which is very heavy, you had to carry it on your back. And I botched it up, that is, I scattered all the lime on my first trip, and the wall was already high and I had to carry it up the ladder. And I realized, with surprise and happiness, that the two men at the top were speaking Italian between themselves, and they spoke a sentence to each other—in fact, one was speaking with a Piedmontese accent, he said to the other, "Ah's capis, cun gent' parei"—"Ah, you understand, what do you want to do with people like these?"[36] And then I said to him, "But you're Italian" . . . and he told me, "S'capis" ("Of course"). "Of course" was from Fossano.

Now, to my further fortune, my family has a branch at Fossano, near Cuneo. We actually had acquaintances in common, and this bricklayer, whose name was Lorenzo Perroni, knew some of my father's aunts.

N.C.: And how did he end up at Auschwitz?

P.L.: In a manner of speaking he ended up there because he volunteered. He was a bricklayer for an Italian firm that did work in France, and when France was occupied, the Germans took over the entire firm en masse. They transferred the operations to Germany, to Auschwitz, in order to build this immense factory about which I spoke to you and where I worked. At that time it was still under construction. There were twenty, thirty construction enterprises there, many of them German, naturally.

N.C.: Were they treated like normal workers?

P.L.: They were treated approximately like soldiers. They had a camp that they could leave, they could go for vacation to Italy. They could send their remittances, their salary in marks, and transfer it to Italy. They could also have correspondence, send letters. They didn't live high, but had a reasonable food ration, approximately what the Germans had. They had their ID card and their own internal mess. Well, this man, who was a very strange man and spoke very little, he seemed virtually a mute, adopted me. He said nothing to me, or almost nothing, but from that day on for as long as I was able he would bring me every day a mess tin with soup, and it was a strange soup in which I found a little bit of everything: once a little sparrow wing with all the feathers in it; another time I found a cooked clipping from *La Stampa*;[37] and still another time some prune pits. Clearly, in fact, as I later learned, he took up a collection among the Italians in his camp and he collected all the leftovers and brought them to me. He realized very well that it was better than nothing, and for me, this complemented the missing calories, because the provisions in the camp, although not nonexistent, were inadequate—there were some fifteen hundred to two thousand calories, which clearly aren't enough. For a man who does heavy labor at least twenty-four hundred to twenty-six hundred are necessary. And he brought me this tin at his risk, because he knew very well that he was taking a risk, that it was forbidden to have contact with us outside of work. A free worker like himself, let's say, a volunteer, was prohibited from speaking with a prisoner except precisely for reasons of "work." But he didn't give a damn. He shrugged his shoulders and said, "What the hell do I care?" I used to tell him, "Look, it's dangerous, I'll bring you trouble." We arranged that instead of giving me the mess tin in hand he would hide it in a certain place, and I would go pick it up. This was a certain precaution on his part. One of the last tins he brought me, he brought in December 1944, when the Russians were at the gates, and there were bombardments. One morning he brought me this tin all misshapen, all dented, and he told me, he only spoke Piedmontese, he said in dialect, "Ah, the soup is a little dirty." In fact there were little pebbles inside some soil, and he said, "Be patient, today it's a little dirty." It even had a twisted handle. Then we saw each other after the liberation. He survived, and we saw each other here at Fossano, after my return, and he told me, as if it were nothing, that during the night there was a bombing in his camp and he had this tin in his hand, he was caught in a bomb crater that smashed one of his eardrums and also smashed the tin. But the eardrum didn't matter to him, what mattered was that the tin should reach [me].

Now this man had a strange homecoming, because there he risked little enough, but he was afraid of the Russians, and when it was learned that the Russians were coming he and a bunch of other Italians ran away and resettled in the midst of a Germany now in full ruin, in January–February 1945, when the Russians were already at the gates, they were already on German territory . . . or just about, in fact . . .

N.C.: Yes, they had arrived in East Prussia.

P.L.: He and someone else walked for three months, from January to April, because they didn't want to go with the Russians, nor with the Germans. They would walk by night and during the day they stopped to sleep. When they had no money, they would work as bricklayers. They would stop in a village, help build a wall and so on, and receive their pay in potatoes or chickens or something else, and then take another step.

N.C.: Did you see him again after the war?

P.L.: After the war I saw him again. He arrived in Italy much earlier than I did. He went to Fossano. Barely returned, I looked for him, found him, tried to help him. I let him have some money, some clothing, I tried to repay my debt, but I found him badly reduced. He was so traumatized by the things he had witnessed there at Auschwitz that he began drinking. He was an extremely sensitive man, even though he hardly spoke, and the things he saw at Auschwitz (at "Suiss," as he used to call it) had struck him, how could you put it, had wounded him profoundly, and he no longer wished to live. He used to say, "In a world like this one, it isn't worth living." And he, who was a bricklayer, a very talented builder, stopped building. He got involved with scrap iron, he bought and sold iron, and all the money he made would be drunk up. And I, who every so often would go to find him at Fossano, would tell him, "But why do you live in this way?" And he would tell me, chillingly . . . : "It isn't worth living, I drink because I'd rather be drunk than sober." So he would sleep, he would get drunk and sleep in the open. He caught pneumonia, and I helped him recuperate at the hospital in Savigliana. But they didn't give him wine, and he ran away, and then they found him dying in a gutter, where he lay in a drunken sleep. In fact he, who wasn't a survivor of Auschwitz, died of the survivors' disease.

GIACOMA LIMENTANI

NICOLA CARACCIOLO: Well, then, can you tell us what was your experience with the persecutions? How old were you then?

GIACOMA LIMENTANI: I was twelve, but the experience starts a little earlier, because I remember perfectly how once I was walking with my cousin to Piazza Mazzini. We were two young girls, she tells me that there was a lot of anti-Semitism. I didn't even know what anti-Semitism was, and the thing left me quite perplexed. Then, a few days later, the magazine *Razza** was going to appear but hadn't yet, and the laws precluding school attendance hadn't come yet, or those precluding having housekeepers, at least that's how I remember it. I remember being on the trolley with my mother and sister, and my mother was very, very beautiful and my sister, too, was rather beautiful. My sister was older than I, and so a young "lady" already; she must have been sixteen. There was a man sitting in the trolley, a creature of an impressive ugliness, holding in his hand the magazine *Razza,* with cover photographs of monstrous-looking Jews. Striking his hand on the journal, he says, "Look here, you can see that they're an inferior race, marked by God, look at this monstrosity." And then my mother, who is the type that always had a short fuse, without thinking that she might have been at risk, said, "Oh, yes? Marked by God, us? I call the entire trolley to be a witness," she says. "Look, I'm Jewish, my daughter is Jewish, we're considered beauties, we *are* beautiful. And look at this monster. This one is really marked by God." The people on the trolley started to laugh.

N.C.: And the matter ended there?

*Razza = "Race."

Giacoma Limentani, another author

G.L.: And fortunately it ended there, because God forbid, God forbid, if it had ended differently given our past, with my father already persecuted as a socialist, the affair would not have been very cheerful.

N.C.: What happened later?

G.L.: What happened later? I have mixed-up, strange memories. You must also figure that all that has happened has marked my life strongly in a certain sense; therefore I have very detailed recollections of some things and confused memories of others. For instance, I have no sense of the passage of time, the facts are all jumbled up in my memory.

N.C.: You, for instance, I believe, didn't want to be Jewish . . .

G.L.: No, no, no, later, this happened much later. . . .

N.C.: When?

G.L.: After the war, afterwards, when everything was over. I had the idea that the Jews will always, somehow, be slaughtered. Among others, it's an idea that I still have today, as when there are, as there have lately been, demonstrations that are called "anti-Israeli." I don't appreciate everything about Israel's politics, I stand apart from it in certain matters, but many people use the excuse of politics really to display anti-Semitism.

N.C.: Tell me, what happened then?

G.L.: Look, as to what happened later than that, I remember something strange. We were on vacation at Pineta di Pescara and the law forbidding Jewish children to go to school appeared.

N.C.: Yes.

G.L.: I remember it like this, vaguely. I still didn't understand exactly what it was. I understood it was a grave thing, but I remember very well that later we returned to Rome, the Jewish school was organized and we went to this Jewish school. The first school was near Celio, a cottage near Celio, and we kids went to school on bicycles. And I remember perfectly a bunch of boys from other schools, who would put sticks through our spokes, so much so that I fell and dislocated a shoulder (and it's still dislocated). That I remember. I must say, the Jewish school was a wonderful experience because we had fantastic teachers, and because they were quite understanding and knew that we were all a little in shock, that in our families . . . Therefore they didn't look too much for discipline, and in turn this "nondiscipline" led us to a splendid scholastic achievement, and so it was really a joy to study at the Jewish school.[38]

N.C.: And tell me, how were your relations with the other people at that time? I'm talking about the period before 1943.

G.L.: Well yes, of course, we are speaking of between 1938 and September 8.

N.C.: Yes.

G.L.: You know, there were people who thought: basically they don't go to school, they don't have a housekeeper, it's not so bad, and who nevertheless were friends and remained friends. Then there were those who would see you, yes, but if they were receiving respectable people you should not have gone to their house. And there were those who simply distanced themselves from you. You know that Jews were not allowed to go to the seashore, don't you? For two very serious reasons: first, they would pollute the water, and second, at the seacoast, while taking a swim, the Jewish children could be spying. Since the Duce was afraid of submarines near the shore, to allow Jewish children there was kind of dangerous. I know people who took this matter lightly and went anyway, and they were denounced, and then they were in a lot of trouble. They were denounced, I don't know, by people taking the little train to Ostia, who saw somebody and said, "That one is Jewish," they called . . . there it is, I know this happened. And then within the Jewish community there was a big upheaval, because at my house for example it was known and accepted that the Fascists were disgusting. Therefore what could Fascists be up to? Only revolting things.

N.C.: That is, your family was anti-Fascist.

G.L.: Namely my father, yes, and for this reason decisively he bore scars of all colors, but there were families who had been Fascist and who believed in nationalism, in this lovely thing. . . . It was a strange Fascism, which came on the trail of a poorly understood Enlightenment. . . .

N.C.: That is?

G.L.: The Enlightenment doesn't accept Jews as Jews, it accepts them because in its exalted theories all men are equal. But to accept them totally meant that the Jews had to assimilate totally, and the idea of equality among people through respect for the differences of peoples, of ethnic groups, through respecting their unique characteristics, that's something reborn later on. The Enlightenment didn't accept this, and therefore these enlightened Jews, or Jews tainted by a misunderstood Enlightenment, thought that Jews ought not to move ahead as Jews, ought not to maintain themselves differently from the rest. There were Jews who were Jewish at home and outside pretended not to be. Understand?

N.C.: In your family, how did you look upon the persecutions? Do you remember your father's words, your mother's words?

G.L.: My father's statements were the statements my father always made. My mother's words: she was terrorized. On one hand, you realized what was happening and on the other, you had the impression of living, you know, in an unreality. That was it, the sensation that there was something unreal, that this wasn't possible, that it was something strange. . . .

N.C.: For instance?

G.L.: I don't know how to explain it to you: the fact that you always used to go to the seashore and at a certain point you couldn't go anymore. And believe me, not that I think it such a calamity not to be able to go to the shore, there are many worse things—I take this as an example, it was something incomprehensible. Why not? Why not?

This invisible yellow star that was pinned on us—and that for some was visible, since they came to put sticks through my spokes when I left school. If they told me, I don't know, I remember a girl in the countryside—we had a house in the country with a tennis court, nothing exceptional, a little court where the children played. There was a girl, I won't tell you her name, the daughter of a famous musician of the RAI who is dead by now, a girl who used to play on my tennis court, and then said, "I'm not playing with you because you're Jewish." . . . There were such absurd things, and you couldn't say anything to her, because if that girl went to denounce you, or if her father did, the trouble would have been greater, there was this subterranean nightmare that I had already lived through before, from the first time they took and beat my father.

N.C.: How did this happen?

G.L.: I don't know exactly how it went, because I *don't* know, I was little, you understand—I know that once . . .

N.C.: But was he beaten up because he was anti-Fascist, because he was Jewish, because of both things?

G.L.: Surely because he was an anti-Fascist—certainly, the fact he was Jewish meant that they held even more against him. I know that once . . .

N.C.: What year was it?

G.L.: It must have been 1936, or maybe 1936–37, I don't remember exactly, I told you. I know I was a little girl . . .

N.C.: No, you know why I ask you this question? Because in 1936 there were no anti-Jewish persecutions . . .

G.L.: It was just beginning . . .

N.C.: The first signs came with the book by Orano in 1937,[39] then very quickly a campaign against the Jews was launched.

G.L.: I can recall one thing for you . . .

N.C.: Tell me . . .

G.L.: That I was wearing short socks, so I was little. I had short socks on and I was walking with my mother in front of Giampaoli on the Corso, and my mother met a friend, an old lady who said, "I learned that they tortured Giovanni," and my mother signaled to her not to talk in front of me. But by then I had heard, and I remember that, in order not to show that I felt ill, since I didn't know what to do, I bent down to roll up my socks. There, this is what I remember. Then, some time later, my father was on a business trip to Milan and my mother was at the hospital with my sister, who . . . [*She pauses, her eyes suffused suddenly with tears at the recollection.*] Excuse me, but I can't talk about this. . . . Excuse me a moment. . . .

Sometime later my father was in Milan, I think he was in Milan, he was on a business trip, and my mother was at the hospital with my sister, who was operated on for appendicitis. I was at home alone with my grandmother . . . who was quite old, and they came. . . . The Fascists were always coming to ask where my father was, to say that he had to show up at the *fascio*,[40] and here and there. And they came and they were four men, I think they must have been around thirty years old. They were from the Fascist party section here at Prati. I know exactly who they are, that is I recognize them, their faces, I see that they walk around, old men by now, and I don't know their names. And they asked me where my father was, and—among other things, aside from the fact that I wouldn't have said it—I didn't know where he was. And they hit me with murderous blows and said that if I didn't tell them they would condemn him by default, a thing that made me retain this horror of condemnation by default—I didn't know what it was, but it frightened me so much. They told me, they made sure to tell me that they beat him, how they beat him, what they had done to him. And they told me that it wasn't true that my father had gone to Florence once when he said that, but rather that they beat him outside of the party headquarters. They hurt him so badly that I later knew it was true, and that my father took refuge with our family doctor, who had taken care of him and called our home to say that he had to go suddenly to Florence.

This is the truth, but it terrified me for another reason. A few years earlier my sister had come of age in a religious sense, and to prepare her for that coming of age my parents found a certain Relles to instruct her, who was a Jew from, I don't know, Germany or Poland, I don't remember. They found him since people were trying to help the refugees that were arriving, who were not well and were hungry. . . . I know that he came to the house, that he was very religious, he even embarrassed my mother because he was so meticulous in following the laws, and my mother was a bit lax in these things. I know that one day this man called my mother. It was known, we knew that he was waiting for a visa to emigrate, to go, I don't know, to Palestine or to America, and the visa wasn't arriving. One evening he called my mother, and he was supposed to come to tutor my sister, and he called her:

"Signora, I cannot come." And she said, "But why, are you ill?" "No, I can't come, because I'm going to throw myself in the river." And we never saw him again.

GUIDO LOPEZ AND
ANNA MARCELLA TEDESCHI

NICOLA CARACCIOLO: There, you're both children of important representatives of the Jewish community in the Thirties, let's say, right?

GUIDO LOPEZ: Well, of the Jewish community, in fact, and let's say we were also among the Italians perfectly integrated within the Italian world.

N.C.: [*to Mrs. Tedeschi*] What did *your* father do?

ANNA MARCELLA TEDESCHI: My father was a law professor at the University of Milan, Professor Mario Falco, and at the same time he belonged to a family that was mindful of its Jewishness—not at all lax in that respect—and therefore my father also had some duties within the Jewish community.

G.L.: My papa was one of the best-known playwrights in Italy, together with Niccodemi and, naturally, Pirandello.[41] Therefore he was a popular fellow.

N.C.: Sabatino Lopez . . .

G.L.: Sabatino Lopez, exactly. He, too, was interested in Jewish matters. In particular, he was president of the Milanese Zionist group and therefore he was perhaps the best-known personality in the Zionist camp.

N.C.: And what happened in 1938, with the racial laws?

A.M.T.: Well, let's say, we had an inkling that things were going badly because from the beginning of 1938, every so often there were some unpleasant things in the press, short features, articles, which let's say put us on alert. . . .

N.C.: For instance Hitler's visit to Rome.

A.M.T.: Hitler's visit to Rome, and in fact, we were somewhat in a pre-alarm state. But our daily life took its normal turn and everything seemed almost normal, except that at a certain point there came the famous statement by Professor Pende that gave birth to the scission between the Aryan race and the Semitic race. This was the big alarm bell. I remember the summer of 1938 as rather disturbing, when we were on holiday at San Vito di Cadore and every morning people went to get the newspaper and we used to say, "Well, let's see what catches our eye next!"

G.L.: Exactly. I, instead, was at Castiglioncello, and we read that we were expelled from the schools, both teachers and students, that very September of 1938. I remember that moment very well. I remember that the next day Silvio D'Amico[42] came immediately to look for my father and show his solidarity with him. At Castiglioncello there was Diaz, the father of Furio Diaz[43]—we hardly knew each other—and he came to invite us to take a boat ride. I would say that the first reaction, at least as far as we were concerned, was one of great solidarity from the outside, and for us, naturally, one of dismay, of fright, no doubt.

A.M.T.: It happened in a very similar way with us, I remember an episode of the same kind: Piero Calamandrei,[44] who was a great friend of my father's, also hastened to show his solidarity, his friendship. For me instead, personally, the big shock was the return to Milan, because on returning to Milan we expected to renew friendships, et cetera. Instead for me personally (this is a very personal fact even though it is not all that isolated, naturally) two girls who were my schoolmates, with whom I used to be very close, extremely good friends—we used to write to one another—seemed not to turn up anymore. Clearly this was a *diktat* by the families, who at that time didn't consider it useful to have anything to do with Jews.

G.L.: These are things that happened. I had better luck as far as my classmates are concerned, and my memories are in fact rather good, indeed quite good in this sense: I remember that there were no break-ups with my friends, I would say with no one in my class. Then soon the Jewish school opened, and it was our great salvation, spiritual, moral, and even material salvation, to continue our schooling. And then naturally the ties with our former classmates became looser, because everyone had to think of his own studies, and his own normal round, and of all the problems caused by this new situation.

N.C.: What happened with the advent of September 8?

A.M.T.: Well, from September 8 on we may immediately have realized what was going on, but then things became frantic. We were in Ferrara. From there, we went to the countryside; unfortunately then, over there, my father succumbed to illness. Certainly the stress and the events did not help him, he was still rather young. After that, things became frantic, and we—that is, my mother, my sister, and I, who remained somewhat cut off from the outside world, accepted an invitation from our friends, the Jemolos—Professor Carlo Arturo Jemolo.[45]

We left for Rome on a trip that was like a bad dream, because we arrived in Rome the day on which the train carrying the Jews from the ghetto was leaving.[46]

N.C.: And did you see it?

A.M.T.: We saw this train on the other track and we heard comments. We arrived with the idea that we were in a grave situation, but not a dramatic one, and so this arrival *was* dramatic. In a corridor of the train, my mother and I destroyed all the documents we had, because we were still carrying all our documents.

N.C.: [*to Mr. Lopez*] And you?

G.L.: We were at Arona, so the notorious issue of the Germans descending there on Meina did involve us. At Meina there was a massacre; there was no massacre at Arona, but they took some Jews away. My father and mother, who'd been alerted, took refuge on a beach on the lakefront and later escaped to the house of some friends of ours, the Calvis; then from the Calvis here to Milan. They were hidden by Catholic friends for a couple of months and then ventured on foot. My father was over seventy at the time and he made it into the mountains with my mother and arrived safely in Switzerland. I had gone there directly.

N.C.: Here's absolutely the last question. During that very period, let's say, in which your lives were in danger, did you feel most strongly the solidarity of the non-Jewish Italians?

A.M.T.: Enormously, very much so. Before, there could have been some small acts of cowardice, some incivilities; but after September 8 we found an awful lot of people who helped us.

MINO MOSCATI

NICOLA CARACCIOLO: And so, how did you escape?

MINO MOSCATI: Right after the curfew, my aunt came to the bar at Monte Savello[47] to get in line for cigarettes and saw . . . this deployment of trucks that were rounding up everyone, men, women, and children and old folks, and then she gave up on the line for cigarettes and left for home, and all of us fled. We were, shall we say, camping out, with our mattresses on the ground, because there were also my father's brothers and sisters, who ran off later, each of us going our own way. We, my family, went to the house of some Catholic neighbors, who gave us refuge right away and treated us well enough. But we had a sister who'd wanted to sleep in the house of our grandmother, who lived here on Via Portico d'Ottavia, and for that reason they mourned her as if she had already been deported. Except that miraculously they were saved, because when they got to the gate with the bundles, someone, a German, passed by and told them, "Wait, I'll go and get the truck." Someone passed by and says, "Why wait, run away," and in fact, they were saved. My father and I spent the first night in the Flaminio district, in the house of a Catholic who'd been evacuated because of the bombardments.

N.C.: A friend? Who was he? . . .

M.M.: A friend, yes. The doorman had the keys and opened the place for us, and let us sleep there, obviously on the floor, and what could you do? Then the second night we spent at the house of the Temple photographer who had his studio in Prati and who let us sleep there, inside the studio.

N.C.: He was Jewish? . . .

M.M.: No, no, no, no, a Catholic, him, too. Emilio, I don't remember the last name, and yet he was the Temple's official photographer. And afterwards, in fact permanently until Liberation Day, we stayed in the home of Catholic friends at San Saba and on Viale Giotto, number 1, and there they gave us shelter until Liberation Day. And all the rest of us in the building were evacuees from the Castelli Romani after the bombardments, and down here instead, later, on the morning of the liberation, we told everyone how things in fact were.

So, then, as far as what I was doing these months is concerned, I did whatever I could. For a month I was a bar boy here, only I had to leave because, as I was telling you, this bar was frequented by the "Black Panther," alias Celeste Di Porto,[48] and by a certain Rosselli, who was a well-known Fascist who lived in Piazza Margana.

N.C.: And how is it that Celeste Di Porto did these things? How do you explain it?

M.M.: For me it's incomprehensible because her family was among the best—"best" in all senses of the word—moral, ethical, hardworking. I saw her brothers, one of whom survived the concentration camps, while the father didn't, and another brother went straight into the

Foreign Legion out of shame. For me she was a woman, I don't know, a little megalomaniacal, who wanted to pose, who wanted, let's say, to get away from the usual treadmill existence.

Then I sold newspapers. I hawked my newspapers right here at Monte Savello. I sold the papers, and the owner of the newsstand, Alfredo, who's dead now, he was an invalid from the war of 1915–18, he says, "Whatever happens," he says, "You're under my protection, don't you worry." . . .

N.C.: And he knew you are Jewish?

M.M.: Yes, he knew my father very well, because papa was his regular customer, every morning he bought *Il Messaggero*.[49]

Oh, then, in the time lapse between the noon edition—because then the newspapers in Rome came out with a noon edition and an afternoon edition, right?—in this time lapse I used to go to Cecchignola and buy bread from the Germans. I used to buy four round loaves; three I'd sell and one was left as earnings, and in fact we'd eat it. I remember that the first one smelled of mildew. Hunger was ugly, though, and so we survived.

N.C.: The story that comes out of these eyewitness accounts we're gathering here in the ghetto is that all those who survived owe that to some Romans who gave them a hand. Do you agree?

M.M.: Without a doubt, all of them, not just some, all of them. Keep in mind that the very morning of October 16 we were living on the Via dei Fienili, behind what is today the city police headquarters. My mother knocked at the door of the convent of nuns facing us. They took in my sisters, just as a baker downstairs took in my brother. . . .

Keep one thing in mind, that my father as a matter of fact was the custodian, the *shammash,* right, and as such he had saved all of what we call the *parochet,* that is, the sacred vessels that he, together with his colleague who was the doorman at that time, had placed under the ritual bath, the *mikvah.* My father's great fear was that the Germans would blow up the Temple with dynamite, with bombs, just as they'd done in other parts of Europe and in Italy itself, and that's why the morning after liberation we came here quickly. I won't tell you how the survivors were hugging each other: "Eh, you were saved, so much the better!" And, let's say, we counted ourselves. At the same time there was a never-ending procession, which lasted three days, of military motor vehicles, which were passing through and heading toward the north of Rome, toward Flaminio. . . .

Those were the Allies. The Germans had headed north on the day before liberation. I milked some cows here because the Germans had stolen a herd of cows, and the animals couldn't move because their udders were full. And we kept the milk. But during the morning we came here, the morning after liberation, and clearly everyone came out, the soldiers as well, English and American and French, all Jewish. But in particular that morning an English captain came, and together with other soldiers and with a pig's foot he opened the door, this lower one, because it had been leveled, because fortunately the Temple had been declared a national monument by the government, precisely so that the Germans, after they got the fifty kilos of gold[50] and after they'd carried off the library,[51] wouldn't blow it up.

Oh, we opened the Temple! The first thing my father did was to rekindle the candle in front of the Sacred Ark, because that's a very important thing, and then, as I repeat, hugs and kisses among the survivors. We gave it a big cleaning, we straightened things up and then in the evening, obviously, we held a ceremony once again. And then slowly, slowly, let's say that life became normal again, but as I repeat we would remember, because every so often then somebody would return from one of the concentration camps. One of these was my brother-in-law, who was in a special unit of the concentration camp where he tells us they used to do the selection of all that the inmates would take with them. And he put away the edibles, in order to give them as presents to the *kapò*,[52] basically in order to get protection, and this was one reason why he was saved. But clearly we all went there with photographs of our loved ones who had been deported, and asked for news. And they saddled him, unfortunately, with the nickname "the informer," because he told everyone, "No, this one was sent to the crematory ovens," which for us was an impossible thing, as if today we were to talk, I don't know, of pirates . . . in the year 2000 to talk about sea pirates: it's a fable, it seems like a fable, and yet unfortunately . . .

N.C.: You didn't believe it. . . .

M.M.: You couldn't believe it. We always thought of how in his time Mussolini had done things, he had captured these people and had put them on the bed of the Tiber to shovel away the sand, but they survived. Hard labor and so on, but . . . whereas these people here did their exterminating in a technical way indeed. . . .

Because they had lists of our names, because we all had to be registered with the regional police headquarters, not because the Germans took the lists here in the Synagogue. We were all listed in every regional police headquarters; in fact, when they arrested me once because I was selling cigarette paper—I was a child, a boy of fifteen—

and the officer said to me, "What are you, Christian or Jewish?" and I told him (I was a little boy), I told him I was Catholic, because later when I gave my real name at the police headquarters at Campitelli, the commissioner (who had me on his list) threw me out. He sequestered the paper but threw me out. In order not to let me suffer other consequences, more serious for him—did you understand?—there it is, that was another kind of help, let's say, don't you think?

AMBASSADOR EGIDIO ORTONA

NICOLA CARACCIOLO: Here then, Ambassador, what do you know about the Jewish question during the war and the attitude of Palazzo Chigi toward this problem?[53]

EGIDIO ORTONA: Well, my charge was such that it allowed me to follow high-level initiatives of Palazzo Chigi close at hand, insofar as I was head of the secretariat of then Undersecretary Bastianini, who had in effect replaced Ciano at the helm of the Foreign Ministry. At a certain point the problem came up of the fate of the Jews evacuated to

Ambassador Egidio Ortona

the French camps under Italian occupation, that is, Menton, Nice, et cetera. I say "the problem came up," because someone pointed out to Undersecretary Bastianini the presence of these Jews and the possibility that, once our troops retreated from the occupation zones, they would be replaced by German troops and the Jews could have been subjected to a different treatment. . . .

N.C.: Handed over to the Germans, that is?

E.O.: Yes, handed over to the Germans. And from then on God only knows what would have happened to them.

N.C.: Did you know at the time about the gas chambers, about these things? Do you think Bastianini knew this or not?

E.O.: I'd say so, I'd say so. Not in great detail, because we were still in a phase rather remote from the discoveries, but some things were known. And certainly, given the influence of the German government on the Fascist government, it was known that the fate of the Jews was indicated, and indicated in an awful way, and therefore one had to do something to avoid disasters for these Jewish refugees. So what we did then, naturally, was send a memorandum to the Duce, as you would do at that time on so many issues. And this matter had great urgency for us, and it also had aspects of human compassion that must certainly be taken into account. And so we worked up a memorandum to the responsible members of the diplomatic corps that we took to the undersecretary, because he was obliged to put his signature to it and go before the Duce, and be received with his proposals by the Duce and be given the instructions that the Duce wanted to send us. We also had many doubts that Mussolini would answer the memo and perhaps also a graver doubt: that he might respond negatively; that he would tell us, "No, let them stay where they are, whatever might or should happen if the German troops were ever to occupy those territories instead of the Italians." I must admit that Mussolini's answer—who generally didn't answer memos with many words, he'd put his initials, he'd put a "yes," he'd put a "no," that was his method—his answer was the one we hoped and wished for, in accord with our proposal. He replied, that is, to act in such a way that the Jewish refugees from those camps would be removed from that zone from which we were retreating, and so protected rather than subjected to what could have been the treatment they would have received from the Germans.

N.C.: A question, Ambassador. I believe there was in March 1943, at the end of February-March 1943, a visit to Rome by Ribbentrop, whose main purpose—at least that's what comes out of the historical studies—was to ask for these very Jews, those Jews of France, of Croatia, and so on. And the hero of this moment, of the refusal given by the Italian government, seems to some extent to have been Bastianini—that is, it was Bastianini who was able to convince Mussolini, after a long and complicated series of events, to say no. Do you know anything about this?

E.O.: I can tell you that even if my recollection is vague, I do remember very well that the visit by Ribbentrop was in part devoted precisely to the racial problem, and on that Ribbentrop found no sympathy, because . . . I knew and still know Bastianini's thinking, in fact I still recall it today. It was that no concession of any kind should be granted to act pitilessly against the Jews because of a solidarity with the Germans with whom we did not see eye to eye on the matter. And it is on that occasion, I believe, that Ribbentrop spoke not only of the Jewish refugees, from the concentration camps and such places, but in fact spoke of a greater severity demanded by the Führer from the Fascist government regarding the Jewish elements in Italy. Yes, yes, I remember this.

N.C.: Can you tell us what the general attitude of the Italian diplomats was?

E.O.: Ah, absolutely identical to the position taken in the memorandum to Mussolini. I must affirm with certainty that none of us had even the slightest inclination to brutalize or compromise in the least the situation of the Jews. . . .

N.C.: And Bastianini felt the same way?

E.O.: Ah, absolutely. . . .

N.C.: Ciano? . . .

E.O.: I can't say, because I didn't work directly with Ciano. I had the opportunity to see him, even to go on a trip or two with him, but I think that basically Ciano, too, was not in favor of treating the Jews in such a way as the Germans demanded. I'm putting it this way as my impression, really, of the atmosphere.

ATTORNEY MASSIMO OTTOLENGHI

NICOLA CARACCIOLO: Your mother, counselor, is Catholic?

MASSIMO OTTOLENGHI: Yes, she was Catholic. . . .

Attorney Massimo Ottolenghi

N.C.: And what did this mean at the start of the racial laws?

M.O.: It meant that there were opportunities to obtain a certificate of "Aryanism" by making someone's paternity unknown.

N.C.: That is, your mother would have had to say that she had had an "Aryan" lover and that you were not your father's son.

M.O.: Clearly my mother never did anything of the sort. But the law would have allowed her to do this.[54] In this way one could get certificates of "Aryanism" that were commonly trafficked with . . .

N.C.: That is, they were sold. . . .

M.O.: There was an organization, the Racial Office of the police department, through which these practices were filtered, just as other bits of information or certain certificates were filtered, very commonly bought and sold.

N.C.: Can you tell me about any episode?

M.O.: I can tell you about an episode that might even have its amusing side, as to how the racial offices did their work. In the Registry Office there was a special department concerned with race. In Turin, for instance, the department chief was a man, let's say, of color, or at least someone from Tripoli,[55] who received the Jews and did the legal assessments, making selections and deciding whether, for instance, marriages would be allowed. I found myself in the situation of hearing myself told that I couldn't marry my wife because I was fifty percent Jewish while my wife was "three-quarters" Jewish, which would have made my children's race inferior.

N.C.: Because if your wife was "three-quarters" she was regarded as Aryan?

M.O.: No, three-quarters *Jewish* . . . Jewish and therefore, counting the fractions, according to Rosenberg's law, my children would have become inferior. . . .

N.C.: And you, at fifty percent, were considered Jewish or Aryan?

M.O.: Ah, I was considered an uncertain case, one that the Ministry of Race held onto for quite sometime.

N.C.: But for instance you could go to school, to the university, you did your military service?

M.O.: In the beginning I was already at the university, but we still had the right to stay there till graduation. It even happened that I received congratulations from Mussolini in 1940 for a degree "of high achievement." Either they forgot, or they didn't understand, or maybe someone wanted to play a trick on the regime. In recompense, they made me take the examinations on the doctrines of Fascism with topics on race, as a separate exam.

N.C.: And did you address these topics on race, or not?

M.O.: I went to answer them because if not, they wouldn't have let me be graduated. And among other things, it's funny that I had a course with a professor from the University of Florence who claimed that Fascism was superior to Nazism because Fascism was pure idealism, in that it wasn't concerned with materialism or the concept of race. I went into the exam with this argument, and evidently the end of the world came about. The professor thought that I was making fun of him and wanted to throw me out.

N.C.: But did he flunk or pass you?

M.O.: He couldn't flunk me because the rector* and another profes-

*Rector, or *rettore magnifico* = president of the university.

sor said, "Look, this one has a thirty average in everything."⁵⁶ And so they found an ingenious way to change the question and they asked me when the Italian Risorgimento started, according to the great Italian historian, De Vecchi of Valcismon.⁵⁷

N.C.: And tell me, what about the military service?

M.O.: I was in service first in Rome, then in the officer training school at Spoleto right at the moment when the first racial laws came out. I stayed in the army and then became an officer. Among other things, I was sent on a mission to Rome when Hitler and Göring came there— I saw them from up close. Our general was Carboni, whose many later adventures in history you know. I remember such episodes from those days: the sergeant who used to send you to clean the latrines, during the Mass hours, you being I and a certain Friedenthal, because we didn't go to Mass; and vice versa, the major from San Marzano whom I met again, later, as commander of a partisan group, who had us called to tell us, "Look, I'm ashamed of what's going on—anything, any abuse they give you, do tell me about it, because I'm with you."

N.C.: Tell me now, what happened after September 8?

M.O.: I'd still like to tell you this first; I think it's important because perhaps it's never been told. Great tragedies occurred among mixed families. Here in Turin we had two Jews who committed suicide in order to remove their own persons from that milieu and make things better for their "mixed-blood" children and their Aryan wives. After September 8 the problem no longer existed, and it's precisely this change of scene that caused even those of "mixed blood," sometimes even the spouses of Jews, to be deported and to end as they ended, which determined and led to far more drastic choices and far more violent positions.

N.C.: What did you do after September 8?

M.O.: I'd already prepared myself. I was moving in anti-Fascist circles and had already prepared myself for the idea of what would happen. And I thought that my position, ambiguous (if you will), could and had to help someone, insofar as it was possible. And then, thanks to all the friendships among anti-Fascists and among so many people who had in the meantime understood the problem on the human level (which they hadn't understood earlier on), and thus almost shared in the discrimination while we were moving toward tragedy, and seeing women and children hurt, and so on. Faced with human cases, they changed attitude, thanks precisely to all these people who showed understanding, particularly among the common people, or among certain circles on a high intellectual level, or among the anti-Fascist military. Stitching together the threads of what was possible from these people, I tried first of all to organize some places of refuge for the prisoners of war who had meanwhile escaped and for the Jews, and this was successful owing to the generosity of many people.

N.C.: Can you name anyone?

M.O.: Oh, yes, gladly: I can name, for example, I don't know, Dr. Mussa, who was chief physician at the hospital of Cirié. He took sick people and others into the hospital knowing they were Jewish, that they were wounded, that they were partisans; pregnant women who went into hiding to give birth. There was also a marshal of the *carabinieri* at the Ceres station, who had been recalled, and who put himself at our disposal and got so well organized that when he received the order to come and arrest us—I had been waiting for this—he put himself at our disposal and organized a system by which he could alert all the people he ought to have arrested. Through my mother and the vicar of Ceres, we would send nuns to warn people at what time they would stop and arrest them. The marshal was going around with two *carabinieri* . . .

N.C.: And he didn't find anyone . . .

M.O.: And exactly, he didn't find anybody. He would get a new address, start out again, and these others would return to their post. Then, little by little, thanks to the availability of a municipal secretary from Coazzolo, whose name was Casasta, we were even able to get authentic (though false) documents, that is, authentic ID files. Unbelievable things happened: neighbors who hid people, peasants and artisans who took people into their mountain huts. Over there in the area of the Valleys of Lanzo I established a liaison with a Salesian father, a certain Monsignor Ulla, and we had a base there, too. Therefore, starting from San Maurizio all the way to Cirié, and then going up to the Nava Valley, the entire Valley of Chialamberto, every subdivision and village had groups of Jews. There were two inns that were full and their patrons were exclusively Jewish and the owners knew it. In Italy, I would say, when faced with the tragedy on a human level, they left no stone unturned. Unfortunately there were exceptions. . . . I had fellow attorneys in Turin who sold out their own high school teacher and his wife and children for two thousand lire each. But the majority of the population had a different response.

CARLA OVAZZA

NICOLA CARACCIOLO: Well, what was your family's experience with the racial persecution?

CARLA OVAZZA: It was a real torment, which indeed touched us, I would say, in every aspect. When the racial laws came to Italy it was dramatic for my father, because they took the bank away from him at once. They could no longer carry on, and it was a bank that went back to my great-grandfather, so everything was closed up between one day and the next. We had trouble meeting with papa's two partners, who were his two brothers, one of whom was just like him, who were so (as he was) let's say of a Fascist tendency, maybe, but never extreme. While we had this brother of my papa's who was really quite a Fascist.

N.C.: Ettore Ovazza. The founder of Nostra Bandiera.[58]

C.O.: Yes, and he created this most difficult situation, because he really split the Jewish community in Turin: on one side, those who want-

Carla Ovazza

ed to be free, wanted to escape, while he insisted that it was necessary to remain.

N.C.: Even after the racial laws came?

C.O.: Yes, to the very end he never wanted to yield to reality and always believed the Fascists would save him. And in the end he was the victim of these same Fascists.

N.C.: What happened?

C.O.: Something awful happened. When we were already in America, we begged him to send us at least his two young children[59] to rescue them, and he wrote us some terrible letters against America, against democracy, saying that we were mad and that his children would always be safe. Until one day, realizing the very grave dangers that they were incurring, he took refuge in a hotel in Gressoney. . . .[60]

N.C.: After the eighth of September?

C.O.: After the eighth of September. The owner of this hotel in Gressoney, I prefer not to tell you his name,[61] knew very well that at that time they were offering two thousand lire for each Jew who was informed against. This man went to Aosta and informed the authorities that the Ovazza family was in his hotel. In the meantime my uncle had sent out his son with a smuggler, giving him money, jewelry, and a scrap of a Hebrew prayer, which this smuggler had promised would be sent back as proof that the boy had crossed the border. Instead the boy was murdered by this smuggler,[62] and this scrap of a prayer was confiscated by the SS.

There was a hotel doctor at Gressoney who was getting ready for the Resistance, and he knew about all of this and knew that they would come that evening to take my uncle and the whole family. Then the SS came to where my uncle was, while he was alone at the table and my aunt was in the room with the little girl. They let him see this scrap of paper and my uncle understood that his son had been killed and that it was over for him. This hotel doctor had the courage to go to the room of my aunt and the little girl and say, "Come with me, I'll save you, come up to the mountains, I can no longer rescue your husband but we'll save the two of you." And she, my aunt, and the little girl didn't accept this.[63] My uncle was skeptical up to the last moment, and the whole family underwent this tragic episode, which everyone knew about later on because it was published everywhere.

They were taken by the SS and brought to Intra, into a school, where they were taken one at a time,[64] cut to pieces one at a time, the little girl, the mama, and he, and the pieces burned in the heating system of this school for days and days, so that all of the people smelled this terrible odor of charring and didn't know where it came from. And so he ended exactly the victim of what had been his grand ideal, of what he believed would save him.

N.C.: How did you live as a girl through the racial persecutions, before going to America?

C.O.: But look, I was really, I've got to say so, a very assimilated Jew, in the sense that I had never thought that there was a difference among my schoolmates. I went to D'Azeglio, which was a well-known high school in Turin where we were mixed; there were Jews, non-Jews, a little of everything, and this question had never come up. I was great friends with the majority of my Catholic schoolmates. So when the racial persecution came, the laws that wouldn't allow us to go to school, for me it was a tragedy. I read the other day in my diary, because I've managed to find it, and I was saying, "It isn't possible that I can no longer be with my classmates, that I can no longer see my teachers." I loved the school a lot, I got on quite well with everybody, and it struck me as something so unjust that it had to end. It struck me as impossible. Yet I had to face the reality, because from one day to the other I could no longer go to school—not only that, but I, who had always been promoted, that year I had a subject in October and had to make it up, because they gave Jews permission even if they were no longer attending school to finish the year they were in. And I remember my humiliation, because my Italian teacher, a woman I had always considered a very intelligent person, was very well known in Turin as an excellent teacher: when I came into the hall in September for the make-up exam, she said to me, "You, Ovazza, who are a Jewess, go to the last desk." And this was the end, for me. You know, for a girl, it seems foolish today, but for me it was something I've carried with me all of my life. I'll never forget it.

CHAIM PAJES, M.D.

CHAIM PAJES, M.D.: I came to Padua because in Poland there was a quota. . . .

NICOLA CARACCIOLO: What do you mean?

C.P.: A quota means that every university could admit a certain number of students; for the Jews the number was almost always zero. . . .

N.C.: Which meant that very few Jews were allowed to study?

C.P.: Four percent.

N.C.: And so you came to Italy.

C.P.: To Italy, yes. I was at Padua, and I could say that for the first time in my life I felt at home.

N.C.: Why?

C.P.: I didn't feel like a stranger.

N.C.: Because there was no anti-Semitism?

C.P.: No.

N.C.: Was it better than in Poland?

C.P.: In Poland, you see, they're a beautiful people, but very religious, and before the war there was a religious anti-Semitism, developed for religious motives and exploited for political ones. At a certain point I had to interrupt my studies for financial reasons; I worked for some years, I saved the money to complete my studies.

N.C.: And you returned to Italy.

C.P.: And then I wanted to return to Italy at the end of 1938, and they answered me that I could no longer study for racial reasons. Then I wrote a letter to Mussolini, and exactly two weeks later I received the answer that I was accepted and that I could stay in Italy until I finished my studies.

N.C.: So then you studied in Italy?

C.P.: Yes, I finished my studies at Padua.

N.C.: How do you explain this?

C.P.: You see, it's hard, it's hard to explain things. For me it was an act of generosity, an act of kindness that saved my life.

N.C.: And how were your relations with the other students at that time?

C.P.: Normal ones. They didn't make me feel anything, let's say, different, and they were relations among friends. Often the head of the GUF* warned me to stay home because they had to have an anti-Jewish demonstration, and he told me to warn my friends, too, because

*The GUF (Gruppi Universitari Fascisti) was the Fascist youth organization for university students.

there were still some foreign Jewish students. We stayed at home, and there, this is all . . .

N.C.: And your professors?

C.P.: The professors I'd say not only treated us well but I'd say showed us favoritism. Instead of asking us questions last, they questioned us among the first and they were demonstrably nice to me. I remember during the exam in clinical surgery they called me and at the same time an officer dressed in a black uniform. Then the professor asked him a question first, and then me, him and me. The other man was tongue-tied, and I was rather well prepared. At the end he said to him, "Excuse me if I give you an eighteen, I'm doing it because of respect for your uniform." And to me he said, "Excuse me, Pajes, I'm only giving you a twenty-seven, because I can't offend the uniform."[65]

N.C.: And your diploma?

C.P.: I got my diploma in a rather dramatic way.

N.C.: When was that?

C.P.: On June 16, 1940. Some days before a police agent came to ask me when I would graduate. I answered him, "The sixteenth of June." Then he told me, "Pajes, try to graduate in time." I understood that he had to arrest me. On the sixteenth of June, exams continued until nine in the evening. At nine o'clock the university porter came out and said enough for today, we should come back the next day in the morning. I was in a bad way. I didn't know what to do, and after about ten minutes I rang the bell and Professor Cagnetto opened, then asked me what I wanted. I told him I didn't know if I could come back the next day. He asked me, "And why?" I replied, "Because tonight they'll probably arrest me."[66] He says, "And for what reason?" I told him, "Because I'm Jewish." Then he told me, "Wait." He and another member of the commission were there, the third member was absent; he called that one and asked him to return. At eleven thirty I had my examination. They embraced me, they wished me well, their words were, verbatim, "Two men and so much hatred,"[67] and then Professor Cagnetto told me, "If you stay in Padua, come back to the clinic, I'll try to help you." I went back to my home, and four hours later they put me in handcuffs at the Padua jail, and everyone was looking at me as if I were mad, because while they were all in tears and despair, I seemed elated.

N.C.: Why so happy?

C.P.: So happy because I had my diploma.

N.C.: Can you tell us, how did the Italians treat you in general? Can you talk about this, or do we run the risk of generalizing too much?

C.P.: You see, I was in nine prisons. The prisons were horrible but the people treated me with kindness and humanity. Then I could also say that in the Italian concentration camps there was no mistreatment. The hunger was enormous, but we had the chance to govern ourselves. We could study, and we had schools for children, adult schools, even courses for medical postgraduates, because we had with us university professors from, you see, Vienna, Berlin; and we had our own newspaper of events. And then, when I escaped from the concentration camp, warned by an agent of public security, Mario Tagliaferri, because after September 8 the Germans were coming, the people outside helped us. They gave us food, hiding places. I can say, you see, it might be an exaggeration, but for me the most beautiful country and the best people in the world I found here, in Italy.

LELLO PERUGIA

LELLO PERUGIA: I feel I'm a citizen of the world. I feel like a Gypsy, a Moor, a Redskin, a Jew.

NICOLA CARACCIOLO: But your origins are Jewish?

L.P.: My origins are Jewish, but I noticed a striking particular in an extermination camp: that among an Italian Jew, a Russian Jew, a Czech Jew, a French Jew there was diversity. And so in practice, this famous ethnic group, as some want to call us, for me doesn't exist.

I fought at Porta San Paolo, and there I met a socialist comrade, Dr. Renzo Golizia. He was a bank officer, and I remember while there was fighting over there at the Cestia Pyramid of Porta San Paolo, where civilians and soldiers were being massacred, and especially the Sardinian grenadiers, Renzo and I went to Villa Borghese because we knew that there were two armored divisions, the Centaur and the Aries. And we introduced ourselves to the officers, explaining that the Germans were engaging in a massacre at Porta San Paolo, and they listened to us and said, "But we don't have orders and cannot move."

N.C.: And afterwards?

L.P.: Sometime later Renzo made me a proposal. He wanted to organize a partisan group made up of English, American, New Zealander, and Russian prisoners, and he asked me whether I wanted to join him, and I accepted. This group was formed in the zone of Carsoli, and I was active in this zone, together with Renzo Golizia, until April 14, 1944. That day I was arrested, together with a group of English, Americans, French, New Zealanders, and Australians. I was taken to a prison of the Gestapo in the hamlet of Collefegato, today called Borgorosi, and there I was interrogated for an exquisite fifteen days. I was tortured, but I got through it. I had the power to withstand these tortures and saved the band.

N.C.: And those guys understood you were Jewish?

L.P.: They knew that I was Jewish even though I had false papers given to me by Monsignor Nobel.

N.C.: How did they know?

L.P.: There was a spy network, because let's say the German espionage service was working perfectly well here in Italy.

N.C.: And then what happened? Were you deported?

L.P.: After fifteen days of interrogation in the village of Collefegato they transferred me to Via Tasso.[68] Oh, let's take a step back: I wasn't arrested alone, my four brothers were also arrested.

N.C.: How did they end up?

L.P.: Three of them were murdered in the Auschwitz camp.

N.C.: An awful thing. . . . And then from Via Tasso?

L.P.: From Via Tasso to the third wing of Regina Coeli—from the third wing of Regina Coeli to Fossoli di Carpi, from Fossoli di Carpi to Auschwitz. The impression that remained for me was this: that there was a collective madness among the Germans, and that held even for the children, because on the lead-covered prison train, children who were all of six or seven years old threw stones at us.

PROFESSOR AUGUSTO SEGRE

NICOLA CARACCIOLO: So, Professor Segre, what did it mean to be Jewish in Italy at the beginning of racial persecution in 1938?

AUGUSTO SEGRE: In 1938 it was the better prepared Jews, a few, the Zionists, who were naturally worried about the situation. Lattes[69] wrote a famous article, "The Hour of Trial," in which he didn't say a word

Professor Augusto Segre

against Fascism. Mussolini, who received the Zionist weekly *Israel,* said that Lattes was walking on the razor's edge because he never said anything bad about anybody, even when he found a way, *some* way, to talk about things that were very grave. In that "Hour of Trial," he said, "It isn't the first time that we Jews have to go through these things, but we must remember also that this moment isn't the time to argue among ourselves, it's the time to organize ourselves, to help each other. We have to set up schools, to give work to our youth, and above all we must remember that the Lord is in history, He is present in history." As if to say: "We'll see something of how this affair is going to end." Oh, this was Lattes, and around Lattes there was a group of young people, myself among them, and we realized that we should be asking ourselves: who knows how it's going to end?

N.C.: Holding on to that thought, did the arrival in Italy of Jews from Germany, from countries where the persecutions were more fierce, give you an idea of how dangerous the situation was and how these Jews were received?

A.S.: Among the Jewish population the idea of persecution has always been quite relative for various reasons. First of all because many times these young people who came to Italy, that is, many who attended the universities, open until 1938 with great latitude, had a life apart from the masses, either because of the language difficulty or because they didn't want to have anything to do with the local Jewish population. And on the other hand, not all but some in the local population naturally didn't want to have anything to do with these foreigners, because yes, their faith was Jewish, but they were still foreigners. And so a good Italian of Mosaic faith, in many cases a Fascist party member, kept his distance.

N.C.: And the people?

A.S.: I'll tell you a story. In 1940 the war had just started when coming toward me one day I see, passing through the main street of the great city of Casale Monferrato, an officer of the Alpine brigade, a former schoolmate of mine. I pretend not to see him because it was the hour of the promenade. We used to be great friends, but in public like this, someone dressed as a lieutenant of the *Alpini* with a bearded Jew—I always wore a beard until my partisan period—and I pass by him like this, pretending not to see him. He comes up behind me and says to me, "Oh," he says, "Friends no longer know each other?" And I tell him, "Excuse me," I say it in a low voice. He says, "Why do you speak *sotto voce*? We were schoolmates, we're friends. Right? Well, we still are at this moment." I say, "But look, watch out, you are putting yourself . . . you can put yourself in danger." He says, "In danger?" He says, "I was on the front, I learned a big lesson. Now you're here with me." I said, "Please," but he grasped my arm and made me rejoin the promenade. Then, under the arcades full of people, he says, "Now we are going get a cup of coffee, an aperitif." I said, "No, please." Nothing. He was talking in a loud voice, saying, "We were schoolmates, we're like brothers and we'll continue to be that." A truly pleasant, truly beautiful thing, which I always recall with gratitude. He became a lawyer later on, then I lost touch for many years now, but this, too, is truly beautiful, I think this is the soul of the Italian soldier (I had the opportunity to write about this)[70]—the fact that he always stood out in an extraordinary way in defense of the Jews, important or not, whoever they were.

N.C.: And what happened after September 8? Is it true, for example, that many Jews—it's a story we often heard—did not realize how dangerous the situation was, and therefore awaited their fate unprepared.

A.S.: When the Germans entered Asti on September 9, with all their weaponry and all their typical, teutonic Nazi organization, I rode my bicycle to all the homes and shops of the Jews, telling them, "Leave everything there"—it was a Friday—"Run away, you still have time, because they're taking up positions in the city. You still have a few hours' time, but not afterward." Well, most reasoned in the following way: we are Italian; we are in Italy; we never did any harm to anyone; we have no quarrel with the law. What can happen to us? And when I explained to them, "Look, unfortunately at this moment you're no longer in Italy, because the Germans are here, and you are only Jews and no longer even Italian Israelites, and if they catch you they'll murder you," I found a wall. That is to say, *I* was becoming their enemy, who put them in danger. Some closed their doors in my face, some started to scream in the street, because I met them in the street. "Don't think about doing who knows what later, because if you behave in this way, not as an Italian . . ."—did you follow all this?—"then you'll pay."

N.C.: After this you joined the Resistance?

A.S.: Yes, I went into the Resistance. But first I want to finish telling you my previous story. I worked for some years for a winegrower in Castagnole Lanze, simply because, though there was a need for teachers of all levels in the Jewish communities, they didn't take me, they didn't give me work. And I would say that it was fortunate that the Germans destroyed my house, because otherwise there would have been letters addressed to my father, who was the rabbi in Casale Monferrato, telling him, "Your son has some very good qualities, but unfortunately he's a friend and collaborator of Lattes's, he's a Zionist, and therefore we don't feel we can run the risk." So I got into being a vintner.

N.C.: What happened after September 8?

A.S.: I was still at the winery, and one day when I was in the cafe in this village, the marshal of the *carabinieri,* whom I knew, comes in. He walks in front of my table and doesn't look at me. I say hello, he doesn't look at me, and he goes straight into the room where the managers of my business were. He comes out after a few minutes, I say hello, he turns to where there were other employees, and he gives them a hello, without looking at me. One of the brothers who owned the vineyards comes out, and I say to him, "But what is going on? Did he lose his wits?" "Segre, stay calm, come here." He closes the door and says, "Marshal Legnano came to me and told me, 'My heart bleeds at the thought of arresting an honest person, but tomorrow morning *at eight o'clock* I've got to arrest Segre.'" Then the owner told me,

"That means that he isn't coming before eight, therefore from now until eight we can arrange something." "I've had an idea," he told me there so as not to tell me that the marshal of *carabinieri* had suggested it: "Look, now I'll get in touch with a peasant at a farm I have in the province of Cuneo. Keep in mind that the *carabinieri* don't go beyond their province, as if it were a border. So when you're in Cuneo stay calm, because no one will bother you."

And the next morning it was snowing. Starting off on country roads for greater safety and in order not to create a mess for those poor devils of the *carabinieri*, we left at seven-thirty and reached this farm. The peasant who accompanied me—it was all a hilly area—made me see in the distance a shed where he put the work implements, and you could see it at some kilometers' distance. And he told me, "Look, every morning you come here. If you see a red signal it means danger; if not, stay calm." I stayed there for two or three days: nothing. On the fourth day he comes and tells me that the marshal had communicated to the province, to Asti, that we weren't there. From Asti, from the prefecture, the order to "go on searching," and after two days he says—I mention this as part and parcel—"I kept on insisting, I made the most careful searches, and I learned that the Segre family went, without a doubt, toward the province of Turin." Case closed.

N.C.: What was the exact date, do you recall?

A.S.: It was December 2, 1943.

N.C.: Then this marshal saved your life.

A.S.: You see, in this life man always understands very little. There are providential forces up above, so that (as I wrote in one of my recent publications) all ends well because everything is well, because over and above man's ideas there is a providence that guides us toward the good and toward happiness. It was a little humiliating for me, with all my diplomas, to go and work in a winery. But in that year and a half or two years I had the opportunity to meet a great number of peasants, and since the winery trusted me with the contracts, I'd been able to help many of the farmers when they were in distress. As a result the peasant, always very discerning when it came to minding his financial affairs, recognized that the employee Segre was trying to handle matters in such a way that the owner of the winery would not throttle the peasants' necks, that he was doing things with the greatest possible fairness. And for that during the two years when I was a partisan and wandered about, many times not knowing where to go, I always found an open house, a bed, a brotherly hug, all the help possible and imaginable from these peasants. That's why, precisely, I told you earlier that man many times doesn't understand at all what he's doing in this life.

N.C.: What is the messianic era?

A.S.: The messianic era—this, too, is a very long speech. Let's say this, insofar as we are looking at David, the Messiah son of David—this one a concept taken over by the New Testament: Jesus son of David, of Abraham and Isaac—was never represented in the Jewish tradition by one person, because we're dealing with an age. Maimonides says it very well in one of his writings: "Don't think that the messianic era ought to shake the world: The world goes on as it was before, only people will be just, they'll be honest. There won't be wars, there won't be violence, life will be normal." Elia Benamozegh[71] used to say, in reference to a talmudic passage, what might seem like a paradox: "The Messiah did not come and won't come, but let's go to meet him." He was referring to a talmudic passage, as I said, which means: all the time of waiting has been exhausted; now everything depends on man. Within Judaism there is, in substance, with respect to the messianic era as well, a great confidence in human potential: man must act, must do. . . . Martin Buber, in one of his better-known writings, says that in the beginning was not the word, nor the faith that characterized Judaism, but there was the act, the doing. And everyone is capable of deeds, everyone can be a precursor of the Messiah. There is a Hebrew tradition that on Passover evening, the famous Passover supper, a glass of wine standing on the table keeps getting filled, and they ask, What is it for? And they are told that the glass is for the prophet Elijah; according to the mystic tradition the prophet Elijah comes on Passover evening and announces the arrival of the Messiah. I remember that my son Dani, when he barely talked, because you start asking questions from a very early age, noting that I was preparing the seder—and I hope, I really wish that you will come here next year to the seder celebration, to this Passover supper, maybe with our friend Renzo De Felice—but I was talking about my son who kept asking me, "But how come, every year, you prepare this glass for this Mr. Elijah, a prophet Elijah who never comes?" And I told him, "Be patient, act in a Jewish way, work for the future like a Jew, and you'll see that one day you'll meet him."

ATTORNEY BRUNO SEGRE

NICOLA CARACCIOLO.: Attorney Segre, you were the son of a Catholic mother. What did this involve for you?

BRUNO SEGRE: Well, it involved the following. After the racist law of November 1938, which defined the characteristics of the Jews, since I didn't profess any religion, I was considered to be of the Hebrew race, because at a certain point, through a ministerial decree, all those without a religion were assimilated to those who practiced the Jewish faith. Instead, my brother, who had been baptized, was declared an Aryan. Thus, even though our parents were the same, the children were of two different races.

N.C.: Then you had some connections with the anti-Fascists, didn't you?

B.S.: Yes, of course, during that period, within the limits of my abilities, I carried on anti-Fascist propaganda and was also arrested, in the winter of 1941, for defeatism.

N.C.: How was it?

B.S.: In prison, you mean? Well, let's see. . . . It was quite a negative experience, because they isolated us as dangerous individuals, and during the aerial bombings that were taking place frequently in Turin, we were not always led to the underground shelters, to such an extent that some of us died right there in the cell. And so we were worried somewhat for ourselves and more also for our families, because we didn't know whether they were destroyed in the bombardments.

N.C.: And with September 8 what happened?

B.S.: On September 8 I didn't think everything was over as it seemed, and I took the road to the mountains.

I, who was evacuated into the Cuneo region, created the so-called committee for Jewish assistance [COMASSEBIT] that received money from Switzerland, from the "Joint," the American organization that helped the Jews,[72] and with the help of my sister and some other friends we moved around like this among the dairy farms, in the most remote places, the farthest away, in order to give some help, some assistance to the Jewish fugitives and refugees.

N.C.: Who were mostly hidden by peasants.

B.S.: Yes, peasants. Those sheltered were doing certain manual labor, and in fact living in very tragic conditions, abandoned, separated from one another, without clothing, it was something really terrible.

N.C.: And who helped you in this, what was the organization like, that is, who kept them in hiding?

B.S.: Yes, then I've got to acknowledge that the clergy had given them a hand. Some were sheltered in a number of convents, toward Carmagnola I believe, toward the province of Turin, and others, instead, lived so to speak on their individual initiative or by some suggestions we gave them. It was a time of great confusion, everyone got along as he could—the peasants behaved magnificently. The population of the Cuneo region, traditionally gentle, hospitable, did some wonderful things on behalf of the Jews. I must also tell you about an impressive thing that perhaps few people saw. During the final moments a group of ten foreign Jews had been captured—that is, Luxembourg, Dutch, and French Jews—while the Nazi and Fascist troops were retreating from Cuneo under pressure from the partisans, and these unfortunate people were led under the viaduct of the Cuneo bridge and were shot. Among them, I well remember, were a father and son from Luxembourg. Later, when a detachment of us partisans was asked to go to the cemetery to honor the remains of these poor victims we heard a loud report, and when we returned to the piazza we saw that a group of twenty *repubblichini** had been shot. I was told they were torturers and informers who had been tracked down by the partisans, and so there was a sinister episode: on one hand, the emotion attending the deaths of these completely innocent victims, gathered that way in the Cuneo cemetery, and on the other, this act of popular vengeance against those most guilty of these massacres, of this situation in Cuneo under the rule of the Nazis and Fascists.

N.C.: Do you remember any other particular episode?

B.S.: Well, among the many tragedies there is always the humorous note. For instance, I recall that when later on the committee for Jewish assistance was no longer clandestine, and therefore everybody went there to get help, a Jewish woman from Yugoslavia came. Her husband had stayed behind in the Balkans as some kind of official, and this woman was left pregnant here as a result of a relation she'd had with some partisan, and she wanted me to track down this partisan at all costs. She only knew his nom de guerre, because we were in hiding and only used such protective names, and it was most difficult to convince her that in reality it was impossible to treat this as a task falling under "assistance"—that is, it was above and beyond our tasks.

N.C.: And so, how did it end?

---

*These were the uniformed army of the RSI, against whom the partisans and Allies waged war between 1943 and 1945.

B.S.: Later on I lost sight of her. I think she had the child at Cuneo and then went back to Yugoslavia.

SION SEGRE AMAR

NICOLA CARACCIOLO: Would you tell us why you were arrested?

SION SEGRE AMAR: I was arrested because I was a member of the so-called Turin group, Giustizia e Libertà.[73]

N.C.: When did it happen?

S.S.A.: In March 1934.

N.C.: How did the Jewish community of Turin react?

S.S.A.: That is the moment when the Jewish community of Turin split into two groups, the group of Jewish Fascists and the group consisting of those we might as well call "the others," because in that period, to be openly anti-Fascist was hardly common.

N.C.: What did the Jews who were Fascists say?

S.S.A.: They said that a good Italian could be Jewish but couldn't be a Zionist, and therefore they set out to distinguish themselves openly from the Jews who called themselves Zionists.

N.C.: And the others?

S.S.A.: The others maintained—apart from the Zionist argument, which wasn't very fashionable yet at that time, let's say—that the Jews had always been good Italians; that there was no reason to discriminate between Jew and Jew, between one Jew who was a better Italian than another. And so they held a position that a posteriori we could call the right one.

N.C.: And the majority of the community was on which side? Can you tell us this?

S.S.A.: The majority? It's very hard to say. Meanwhile you ought to tell me if you mean by this that they sided with their hearts, or with their minds, or with their physical strength.

N.C.: It's not easy. And when the first measures of anti-Semitic persecution came, how did the group that was more openly Fascist react? How did those people feel? What did they say?

S.S.A.: How they felt I can't tell you. What did they say? They didn't all say the same thing. For instance, there was a difference between the most hot-headed person, who was an ex-nationalist (and whose name I prefer not to mention right now), who continued to proclaim himself a Fascist, and instead the more moderate attitude that also existed among those who had always declared themselves Fascists. This attitude was represented by General Liuzzi,[74] who had become the president of the Israelite community of Turin, and who even wrote a very long letter to the king in order to explain his own position and that of the Jews.

N.C.: And returning to the preceding period, were these contrasts between the Fascists and the others harsh?

S.S.A.: They were most harsh and arose precisely in 1934, when many Jews were arrested on the occasion of my arrest. It was a mere coincidence. I had in my pocket a leaflet from a Jewish youth group, so then they raided all the persons who had signed that leaflet, including friends and relatives.

N.C.: And what did the more openly Fascist group—to use this term— say about your positions?

S.S.A.: They said that we were enemies of the country; that we weren't good Italians; that we were anti-Fascists—which was true in some cases and untrue in many others, since many of the people who had been arrested and were later freed relatively quickly were simply Jews who had no interest in politics.

GIULIANA TEDESCHI

NICOLA CARACCIOLO: You were in the camp at Fossoli?

GIULIANA TEDESCHI: Yes, I was deported directly from there to Auschwitz—the trip lasted five days and five nights, and we arrived with this convoy. The train stopped before the actual station, and over there, at the bench, the selection took place of the old Jews who were "loaded" onto trucks together with the children. And the Germans said, "They're going to the family *lagers*." The men like my husband, on the other hand, were separated and entered the men's labor camp, and we women entered the women's labor camp. Certainly the first impression of that camp seen from the outside I won't ever forget, the sight of these shadows without flesh, these limbs all covered with sores and wrapped in paper that might have been our toilet paper because there were no bandages, these eyes filled with crazed terror. I won't

Giuliana Tedeschi

ever forget it, and I was asking myself whether we, too, would become like that.

N.C.: How old were you then?

G.T.: I was thirty years old, in fact I turned thirty right there on the train going to Auschwitz.

N.C.: And then could you describe for us what happened?

G.T.: Well, new arrivals would be quarantined before they were assigned to their various jobs. But there I was at high risk because I was chosen for the experiment detail. The experiment detail worked like this: the Jewish women who had the misfortune to be selected for it were subjected to surgery even wide awake, surgery having mostly to do with female sexuality, and so you can imagine how risky it was for me. Fortunately, since everything occurred in an illogical and irrational way, as I was about to enter that detail the order came to be sent to the labor detail, and thus I avoided the terrible risk and was sent to the labor detail instead.

N.C.: And in the labor detail?

G.T.: This first detail consisted of labor that was possible to do, in the sense that we were working for German factories that paid for the internees' labor. True, they paid the camp and the camp's director, and our work consisted of undoing the rotten shoes, the old shoes from various past convoys, and resewing pieces of the vamps, of leather upper parts, which were then loaded onto trains going to Germany, and I don't really know what they might have done later with these things.

N.C.: Did you know what was happening in the camp—about the crematory ovens, the gas chambers?

G.T.: But of course, because I spent a long part of my imprisonment at Birkenau, right in a block that faced the crematorium. That meant seeing the people entering the crematorium, it meant seeing the path incessantly burning, day and night: that way they could eliminate from eighteen to twenty thousand people. Twenty thousand people a day, and throughout the camp this terrible smell of burnt human flesh was spreading. This exasperated us and devastated us, because we were always thinking that we would end up this way, that there was no way out for us. And yet I must say that I had the strength to resist, especially as I was thinking of my little girls, because I had left two little girls of a very tender age, and I wanted to return for them at all cost. And so I made it my obligation to live. You know, those who let themselves go . . .

N.C.: And did you find your little girls again?

G.T.: Yes, yes, fortunately I found them again. My husband, no; my husband was murdered.

N.C.: And where did your little girls stay?

G.T.: The girls were with us when the SS came at night to arrest us. But since we had false IDs, our housekeeper was able to wipe out all traces of them and to hide them in the home of friends, and this is how they were saved. Later they stayed—I've got to say this because it deserves to be said—they stayed with the Sisters of the Cenacolo here in Turin for several months.

N.C.: They were rescued by the housekeeper and then . . .

G.T.: And by the sisters, yes. . . .

N.C.: What was your housekeeper's name?

G.T.: Annetta Barale. . . .

N.C.: What marks did all of this leave on you?

G.T.: Ah, look, the adjustment was very difficult in the beginning, because I returned and was always hoping that my husband might have survived. Then news began to arrive, people came who had been in his convoy, then the Red Cross itself told me. At first I felt alone like that, after finding the little girls again for whose sake I had lived. I no longer felt them to be my daughters, I was missing my companion. I was missing someone who might have shared my life again, that's it, and so it was very difficult. Then it seemed to me that here, people were getting worried over useless things, things they would talk to me about. And I would say, "But is it possible that people would think about that?" My mother was complaining because she could no longer find the covers to the pots that had been stolen, and I would say, "But then, where are they, in another world?" It struck me that what was lacking was the awareness of what's essential, of exactly what life is in its intimate, deepest form. And then, slowly, I reentered teaching, and I must say that while I was getting started I encountered people who didn't want to know anything, because the Italians, too, had suffered, after all, even those who didn't go to the camps.

They'd suffered a certain hunger—not our hunger, but. . . . Since they didn't want to know, they used to say, "For heaven's sake, it's all over," and so I remained quiet for a long time. And then at the school it was the children who asked me, and they wanted to know. This is how the dialogue unfolded, and I did explain, and they were very affectionate with me.

N.C.: Did your daughters ask you later on? Did you explain to them, did you tell them about what happened? Do they know?

G.T.: Yes, they know. The older one was two and a half years old when I left her and I found her when she was five. She told me, because they brought me back in a car, she says, "When I saw you, you seemed to me to be a beautiful lady, but now you're my mama." And the little one, instead, didn't want me; she was clinging to the skirts of my Annetta.

N.C.: Of Annetta?

G.T.: Of her Nanny "Tata." She said to me, "That one I don't want, that one I don't want." It took a month before I was able to sleep in the same room with her.

RABBI ELIO TOAFF

RABBI ELIO TOAFF: I must say that if the Italians had been anti-Semitic, you would not be talking with me today, because there would no longer be any Jews here. If there had been in Italy the same anti-Semitism that existed in Poland, today there wouldn't be a single Jew here. On the other hand, the Italians have always recognized the Jews as other citizens with whom they were used to living, and whom they regarded as different only because of their customs and religion. But they certainly were perfectly well integrated with the rest of the population. And therefore, since there was no anti-Semitic problem in Italy, anyone who came from the outside would see no difference between Jews and non-Jews.

NICOLA CARACCIOLO: During the Eichmann trial it was said that all the Jews of Italy owe their lives to Italians.

E.T.: There's no doubt, no doubt at all. Look, we've got to pay attention because *somebody* did make up the racial laws, and *somebody* applied them. But it's clear that there are some ways and then other ways

Rabbi Elio Toaff, Chief Rabbi of Rome

to apply them. If you stop to think that there were Italian police officers who were deported for having helped the Jews avoid their fate,
clearly you realize . . .

N.C.: Officials of the Social Republic . . .

E.T.: Of course, of the Ministry of the Interior. There were officials who
were imprisoned and then deported. Naturally there were also those
who for five thousand lire denounced a Jewish family, which ended up
in a concentration camp. But these latter were the exception, while the
former were the rule.

N.C.: Can it be said, Professor, that those who did the denouncing were
more criminals than they were anti-Semites?

E.T.: They were criminals. . . .

N.C.: Then for you, to be a Jew and an Italian at the same time presents no difficulties?

E.T.: No, not at all.

N.C.: Were you already a rabbi when the racial laws came?

E.T.: No. In 1938–39, I was graduated from the University of Pisa and
ordained by the Rabbinical College of Leghorn at the same time. I
became a rabbi in 1939. Therefore I had my dosage of the racial laws
at a crucial moment of my existence, at the very moment when I was
completing my studies.

N.C.: And what happened?

E.T.: And the following happened: that the moment I turned to my
professors at the University of Pisa to obtain a title for a graduation
thesis,* they all acted coy, and no one wished to give me one. Not until
I found a professor with courage—Mossa, professor of criminal law,
who told me, "I know you're looking for someone to supervise your
graduation thesis. Come to me, I'll handle it for you." This pleased
me a lot, because it restored some of my courage. I must say that he
gave me a lot of help in writing my thesis, because, to tell the truth,
I'd got only a smattering of commercial law even if I had done well in
the exam.

Professor Mossa showed courage, and he wasn't alone, for when I
went to argue the graduation thesis I found myself facing Francesco

*Italian undergraduates must submit a *tesi di laurea,* or thesis, as part of their cre-
dentials for a first degree.

Ferrara, who fought, together with Mossa, to allow me to take the exam together with all the rest, and not separately, not with a special oral test, because I was wearing a white shirt rather than a black one. They fought for me, and I argued my thesis in July of 1939 and was the third rather than the last.

After the discussion of the thesis there was an attempt on the life of Professor Mossa, who was shot three times with a revolver. Fortunately the shots were wide. All this is to tell you how . . .

N.C.: A Fascist extremism of some sort . . .

E.T.: Oh yes, there's no doubt, there's no doubt that such things may well have been done not to kill him but rather to intimidate him, because the Fascists were afraid of this opposition, quietly displayed within the university environment.

N.C.: And then you, a young rabbi, went to Ancona. . . .

E.T.: Yes, I was sent to Ancona, where the atmosphere certainly wasn't exactly favorable, since the chief of police of Ancona was Tamburini, who was later shot dead for his misdeeds when Ancona was liberated.[75] But I must tell you, as far as I am concerned, that I would have to bear favorable witness, due to a small incident I was involved in. There was a Jewish man who lay dying in the Ancona community hospital, and they sent for me. I went, and while I was reciting the prayers for this poor unfortunate, two male nurses came to tell me that the director didn't want Jews in his hospital, to which I replied that I was performing my duty and that I wouldn't move till I finished what I had to do. Then they returned and told me that the director was warning me that if I went quietly, fine, but if not he would have me thrown out in way that was anything but gentle. I stayed there, and then they had me thrown out rather ungently. They both picked me up and tossed me down the stairs. Then, at that moment, I decided to go and ask Chief Tamburini whether the law on accepted religious cults . . .

N.C.: Tamburini, the former Fascist *squadrista,* the future chief of police of the Social Republic . . .

E.T.: I went there and asked him whether the law on accepted cults was still in force or had been abrogated, and he asked me why. Naturally he didn't ask me to sit down, this was by now a common thing, and he told me that the law was valid. I answered, relating to him the incident at the hospital, and then he didn't say anything to me. He picked up the telephone and ordered four *carabinieri* and a marshal to come to him. At that moment I thought they might have come for me, there was no need for such an expenditure of force to take me to prison, but on the contrary, he said, "Accompany the rabbi to the hospital and let him perform his duty, and make sure that there are two *carabinieri* in the ward and two others at the gate, so he isn't disturbed in the performance of his functions." This is what Tamburini said. I left and did all I had to with the *carabinieri* protecting me, and this I have to tell for love of truth.

N.C.: This demonstrates the great ambiguity of Fascist policy.—And after September 8? . . .

E.T.: Well, after September 8 many important things occurred, because I, as rabbi of Ancona, realized that the situation was rushing headlong toward disaster. And when I saw the first Germans entering Ancona I decided to have the Jews evacuated from it. The Germans came to the city on the eve of the Yom Kippur fast, and I had the courage to close the Temple on erev Yom Kippur, thus provoking a great rebellion within our very community. I said, "We're going into a private home," and we went to Via della Loggia, to the home of Professor Andreina Coen, who put a large apartment at our disposal. And we didn't go to the Temple. On the Day of Atonement, Yom Kippur, as I had foreseen,[76] the Germans burst upon Via Stannio where the Temple was, blocked the street, went to the Temple, and didn't find a soul. But it didn't end there. They began to comb the city and came to Via della Loggia as well, and even entered the apartment house we were in. They reached as far as the third floor and then went down. Perhaps they were too tired to get to the fourth, and so it seems to me that something touching on the miraculous had occurred. . . .

N.C.: But at first the members of the community were angered by the thought of hiding.

E.T.: A rebellion. This young rabbi, who dared to close the Temple on the eve of the highest holy day of the Jewish year. After this, together with my wife, we tried to rescue the Jews of Ancona, and we got them out also with the help of the president of the community. We had the youngsters board small fishing craft at Ortona on the Adriatic seacoast, and they were later taken to safety at Bari, while we arranged that the older folk and the rest be given refuge in the country with peasants of the Marches, before whom we should all lift our hats, because they took them all in without any objection.

N.C.: These peasants were risking their lives, weren't they?

E.T.: They were risking their lives, and I must say that if I have any reason to be proud, it is that at Ancona not even one Jew was deported,[77] because they [the Germans] could not find them.

N.C.: And were they all hidden?

E.T.: They were all hidden.

GRAZIELLA VITERBI AND
FATHER ALDO BRUNACCI

NICOLA CARACCIOLO: So, Mrs. Viterbi, your story?

GRAZIELLA VITERBI: My story begins in effect on our departure from Porretta, where we were on vacation on September 8, and after a trip full of incidents finally arrived at Assisi, where we found, by chance, a room in a small hotel. And we stayed there without any clue whatsoever as to whom to turn to, because we were totally in the dark. Till one day, walking right toward San Damiano, a monk from that abbey, out for a stroll, asked us whether we were evacuated and if by chance we would want an apartment. We said yes, and this man found for us the house where I still reside when I go to Assisi. Later, also by chance, we met at the Piazza of Assisi other Jews from Padua like ourselves, and they gave us the news about a clandestine movement of assistance to the persecuted, an effective one.

N.C.: And then?

G.V.: And then they introduced us to Don Aldo Brunacci, who was (I would say) one of the three heads of this movement, or rather one of its leaders. And so we entered this circle of clandestine assistance, which meant rescue for us, and rescue for all of the Jews who were in hiding in Assisi.

N.C.: Let's turn to you, then, Don Aldo.* What was this movement?

ALDO BRUNACCI: Well, to understand the existence of this movement and also to understand how in a town as small as Assisi so many Jews could live unnoticed . . .

N.C.: How many?

A.B.: Well, maybe even more than a hundred, even more, more for

---

*Once again the interviewer uses the honorific title "Don," as before with Father Raganella, to address Father Brunacci.

certain. We already had, since 1943, a committee to assist those who were evacuated—think about it, trucks full of evacuees came from the South, and left them in the middle of the piazza—to take an example, the entire village of Guardiagrele in the Abbruzzi: after it was bombed, all the citizens were brought to Assisi. So we had an organization to settle these evacuees in religious buildings and schools—clearly we then realized that it was possible to hide and settle the Jews among these evacuees inadvertently, you see, in a way that went unnoticed in a city of six or seven thousand inhabitants; otherwise, you know, several hundred Jews would have been noticed.

So the center of this organization was the bishopric, but we had, of course, other gathering places, for instance in St. Francis Basilica. There was a priest over there, my friend, a certain Father Todde, who knew every address—clearly I couldn't always receive the people in the same spot, and therefore he knew where I was to receive them and we took care of putting up the new arrivals. The first nucleus was of Jews from Trieste, among whom there were also a few Slavs. They came from Trieste and were placed in a monastery at San Quirico, very near the bishopric. But there were many other religious retreats that took the Jews in—perhaps the first was the convent of the French Poor Clares. There, a curious, curious incident also occurred—a little dangerous at first, then curious. There was a certain Dutch family, Finzi by name, who, having arrived before September 8, were listed in the normal manner on the police files. Therefore the police came looking three times for this family. The third time the sisters called the bishopric, and the bishop told them to "put the family in the cloister." But we have to think what the cloister of this convent was like then: the windows had two grills, with a black cloth in the middle, and the sisters were living barefoot. They set up for us a little apartment inside the cloister, which was also for the children. Even a baby was born there in this convent, and twenty years later the army sent this child a conscription notice, because he was registered in the municipality of Assisi after the liberation, so to speak. . . .

N.C.: And what were the main ups and downs of this rescue work?

A.B.: Well, the main ups and downs had to do with finding hiding places.

N.C.: And the Germans?

A.B.: We were more frightened by the Fascists than we were by the Germans. Assisi was considered a "host city." The commander was a medical officer, a certain Colonel Müller, who was a Catholic, therefore no Nazi. And he had no time to think about these things, nor did the "Jewish problem" ever cross his mind. So he concerned himself with the hospitals.

ELISA DELLA PERGOLA AND
MASSIMO TEGLIO

ELISA DELLA PERGOLA: My father was a civil servant with Ilva.[78] He was dismissed without warning,[79] and therefore Mama found herself with us children and my papa unemployed, and the additional difficulty of finding a position, because in those days you couldn't get back into government employment.[80]

NICOLA CARACCIOLO: Do you remember this?

E.D.P.: Perfectly. I remember, when Papa returned home, his despair and my mama's, both of them sitting on a bench at the entrance. And they were saying, "What are we going to do? How are we going to manage with the little girls?" Then we were sent to school. I was in the first grade, my sister in the third—so these two occurrences are the most upsetting, that is to say, not knowing how to manage and then also the school, which naturally was extremely important.

Massimo Teglio, the "Jewish Pimpernel," and Elisa Della Pergola

N.C.: And then?

E.D.P.: And then indeed my father, with that meager pension he received—because Ilva gave him the minimum, even though my father had worked there for about thirty years—found out just like that, by chance, that there were three shoe repair shops in bad shape. He offered to work for them as kind of a consulting manager; he gave them his pension and in return he had work, he did the bookkeeping for these businesses. There it is, that's the way the "Jewish businessman" originated, the idea of the Jewish businessman: the Jew isn't a businessman, he has to *become* one when the government no longer wants him in its service. There it is—and we were able to manage like this, from 1938 to 1943.

N.C.: What were your feelings about the situation at that time?

E.D.P.: But until that moment—of course, I was a child—I didn't feel particularly Jewish, because in fact I'd lived together with my Catholic girlfriends, and so on. From that moment on I felt Jewish, other people made me feel Jewish, because naturally it was over with the schools. Schools were formed for us Jewish children, so we knew each other, began to care for one another and feel more united. But in practice, life at the time was normal. Then, all this aside, I naturally had my problems: my Catholic friends went to church on Sundays and I was very content to go to Temple on Saturdays. I felt, that is, that I was regaining a certain identity. We now had a Jewish dimension, whereas before I hadn't even felt it as a child; we went to the Temple, we gathered, there was the Jewish circle, et cetera.

N.C.: And what happened in 1943?

E.D.P.: What happened in 1943 was a tragedy, because with the Germans in Italy, from that time on we began thinking seriously about what we had to do to save ourselves. My papa was even warned by the police headquarters that the situation was becoming very dangerous. . . . And then . . .

N.C.: By the police?

E.D.P.: Yes, at police headquarters. Papa had many friends because he was such a good person, so generous to other people, that as a result they all loved him. And so this person said, "Look, be careful, Mr. Della Pergola, because . . . now you've got to get started and leave your house and go away." We started to go around from one house to another with the help of friends.

N.C.: Friends?

E.D.P.: Catholic friends. The Traversos, for example, who put their house at our disposal, telling us, "Come tonight, we'll think about it later." Thus we set out on a maddening kind of pilgrimage.

N.C.: And you felt the solidarity of your friends?

E.D.P.: Yes. The solidarity of our friends, yes, a lot—we felt our friends' solidarity, because if not for that, we wouldn't even have been saved. Where would we have gone that night? It was November 2, 1943, we were standing close to the bar when we heard "Go away, go away . . . go away because the Germans are coming!" And we found friends who saved us.

N.C.: And as young girls you realized what was happening?

E.D.P.: Yes, we realized. Yes, we were frightened, we were all together always, in fact together *physically*. We all slept together because we were scared, and then afterwards things got even worse when they caught Papa. But sure, we were frightened, we all wanted to stay together, we felt this dark threat, even though we didn't know what the concentration camps were, but we were scared. The Germans were something of . . . Those footsteps during the night . . . We were so scared, yes.

N.C.: And then?

E.D.P.: And then came the tragedy when they took my father away. The real tragedy started from September 15, 1944.

N.C.: And how did it happen?

E.D.P.: It happened this way. . . . Because my father, as I told you, had taken over these businesses, his partner gave him a certain amount per month. My father could no longer go to the stores because naturally he was afraid, but at the beginning of each month he went to pick up an amount that allowed us to live. One day he went to this store on the Corso Buenos Aires. The phone rang, and the partner told him, "Look, it's for you." My father came close, and at that moment two SS came up to him and said, "Come with us." That's how they got my father. My father was an extremely good person, extremely generous, an optimist; he didn't think they would be likely to start with him, then search desperately for us—and so I don't know. Anyway, my father was seen while going with the SS, precisely when he was starting toward the Palazzo dello Studente, the student residence; he was seen by the housekeeper of the only lady in Genoa who knew where we were hidden.

The housekeeper ran to the house of her mistress and alerted her. The lady called my mama, who was cooking something—you remember these things—and Mama held up the frying pan, got hold of us, and said, desperately, "Let's run away, let's run." She was crying, "They got Papa, they got Papa, let's run away."

We left—and the emotion of this is still strong—we left by the main door. We took some of the steps, and at that moment we heard the SS jeep arriving that had come for us. Just because my father, especially because my father, in his naïveté, in his infinite goodness, believed the SS who had told him "to give us the address of your family because we want to alert them, in fact we'll take care of your wife and daughters, keep very calm." And my father believed this and gave them the address.

N.C.: And what happened to your father?

E.D.P.: About my father I learned no more. Auschwitz. We received his last letter from Bolzano,[81] and I think it was about October 25, in which he said, "I am rather cold, send me something if you can, the air is cool, and even something to eat, I would like that." I remember that my mama worked at it all night. She packed some socks, some gloves, we sent some food. Then it seems, from eyewitnesses, it seems that he was in Auschwitz and even toward the end when the Russians were about to arrive they had him moved. Then at a certain moment they called, "Out with the Italians!" and they turned machine guns on them.[82] But we learned no more about Papa.

N.C.: And how were *you* saved?

E.D.P.: Let's say that we were saved thanks to Mr. Teglio. . . . Here he is, and I've got to say it with great emotion because he is here beside me, because . . . We were saved because Mr. Teglio came to know about our situation through the archdiocese and took care of us.

N.C.: [*turning to Massimo Teglio*] And your story? Is it true that they used to call you the "Scarlet Pimpernel" of the Jews?

MASSIMO TEGLIO: They called me that a lot later. And yet I ought to tell you the whole story.[83] On the November 2, 1943, when the Jews were arrested, I came back home, near the Jewish Temple, and saw that the Temple was open. I had no idea whatsoever why. Up in my apartment I ate, then I went out, afraid to enter the Temple. But the janitor's two children were playing outside, and so I went down to their lodgings. There was Linda Polacco, the janitor's wife. I said to her, "But what are you doing still here? Go away, they are coming at any moment!" I had a distinct sense of danger. At any rate she told me, "As soon as my husband comes we'll go away." "Do you have relatives?" and so on.[84] Then I went calmly to the office and sent a letter, through two sailors, to my brother-in-law, who was staying with my sister and their children at the Pensione Morini in Montecatini.[85]

N.C.: You were aware that they were getting ready to deport the Jews?

M.T.: Yes. That's why I wrote immediately to my brother-in-law. I told him that they would have to go away without fail. They would have to go to Castiglion Fiorentino, a mere thirty kilometers away.

N.C.: Did he manage to go there?

M.T.: No, they got them all, the children too: the little girl was fifteen months old; the little boy was three years old. And not one of them came back. To think that my brother-in-law didn't leave right away because he was waiting for a car that would take him to Castiglion Fiorentino. But the Germans got there first. . . .[86]

N.C.: And what did you do?

M.T.: I couldn't do anything. However, I went to Don Repetto at the archdiocese of Genoa,[87] and told him what had happened to my sister.

N.C.: And what did he do?

M.T.: And he asks me, "Why do you come to tell me this?" And I told him that attorney Valobra had let me see a letter of his. And he says, "Attorney Valobra? I don't know him."[88] And I tell him, "Listen, Don Repetto, you can ask for information from people who visit the archdiocese, Angelo Costa, the Parodis of Guzzi Motorcycles, and so on."

N.C.: We know from an interview with Bernard Grosser that Don Repetto knew Valobra well and collaborated with DELASEM.

M.T.: But he didn't trust me. At a certain point he left me, went to the hall for a moment, and tells me, "Come back tomorrow. Maybe I'll be able to tell you something." "All right, tomorrow," I told him, "but it would be a miracle." "It will be a miracle if your loved ones return," he told me, because he knew a lot more than we did. The next day Don Repetto let me know that my loved ones had been taken from Montecatini to Florence and from Florence perhaps to Mantua.

N.C.: And how did your work of assisting the Jews commence? You saved many hundreds of people, did you not?

M.T.: I did. By chance I was able to speak with attorney Valobra. He wanted me to go to Switzerland with him, but I told him, "No, I've got my entire family here, my father's family, my brother and sister, and so on. I'm not going away by myself." Then he gave me some information and so my assistance work was started, always in collaboration with Don Repetto. After my sister's deportation I wanted to do something.

N.C.: What?

M.T.: At a certain point it happens that Raffaele Cantoni, the president of the Italian Jews,[89] is caught in Florence and manages to jump from the train at Vicenza, and then comes to Genoa looking for me. He had some trouble finding me, but then met me near the archdiocese. We met in the rain, he without an umbrella and I with one. I quickly brought him to this quiet office and he told me that he was going to Switzerland and therefore I was to head the assistance work all throughout northern Italy. And he proceeded to give me data about people I had to put myself in touch with in other cities: in Milan attorney Sala, president of Catholic Action and of the Society of St. Vincent de Paul;[90] Dottoressa Wittgens of Brera; Cardinal Fossati and his secretary, Monsignor Barale, at Turin;[91] and then the parish priest of San Dalmazzo at Cuneo.

N.C.: In other words you relied mainly on the Catholic organizations?

M.T.: Without question. They had the greatest possibilities for refuge in religious institutions and in convents and monasteries.

N.C.: [*indicating Elisa Della Pergola*] She says that you performed courageous acts, quite extraordinary ones.

M.T.: Well . . . I would rather that others speak about these things. . . . I wasn't able to rescue my sister and her babies. I tried to rescue a few others.

MENOTTI, ERMANNO, AND MARIA DI GIROLAMO

NICOLA CARACCIOLO: What do you remember about Leo Koffler?[92]

MENOTTI DI GIROLAMO: But I was a lad of twelve, though I remember the events of that time well—I remember this young man, this Leo who had come to us by himself, to end up here in this hamlet, and I immediately was caught up in a spirit of great human warmth, of fondness for this boy, who had fit in very well among us. He had really become one of us, you might say, in a very short time.

N.C.: He dressed as a peasant, he came . . .

ERMANNO DI GIROLAMO: Yes, one time my father, just to make him fit even better, let's say, in our environment, had dressed him as a peasant, as a peasant of the Abruzzi with the local high-laced sandals. There came an officer, a German I think, armed with a submachine gun, and the marshal of the *carabinieri* from the village, and they said to Papa, "Go, bring them out because we know . . ."—it wasn't just Leo, we had hidden several of them—"bring them out because we know you hid them someplace, so it won't be the case that you're in fact risking the safety of your family." Also, my family and this marshal knew each other. And Papa said, "Go find them." I remember that I thought at the time, I'm telling myself, "But we're risking our lives with these people here," but fortunately they didn't ask *me* anything. Today I think I might have had some problems.

N.C.: And what did your father say?

E.D.G.: Papa said, "They're not here—this is my house—look for them, if you find them I'm guilty. I don't have them. You were misinformed: I don't have anyone hidden anywhere." Actually, they were in the caves, below, in the valley we saw before.

N.C.: Were you very scared then, Madam?

MARIA DI GIROLAMO: Oh, so scared . . . Very scared. . . .

N.C.: And what did you say?

MARIA D.G.: We were trying to work it out, to get them through the front lines.

N.C.: [*to Menotti*] And you?

MENOTTI D.G.: Well . . . We were boys and saw things from a certain point of view, let's call it a game. And even though, I repeat, we had some intuitive sense of the tragedy that could lie beneath this entire affair.

N.C.: And why did your father do these things?

MARIA D.G.: We found ourselves with these relatives from Fara who brought them here . . .

MENOTTI D.G.: Well . . . And he tried to help them any way he could. . . . And I think above all because of his humanitarian spirit. . . .

SIDI DUIRI SHARON AND SIMI DUIRI

NICOLA CARACCIOLO: What was the attitude of the Italian soldiers?[93]

SIDI SHARON: For us they were the protectors.

N.C.: How were your relations with them?

SIMI DUIRI: Our relations were very friendly. We were seen together with the Italian soldiers; we even went dancing together on holidays. In the camp of Saint-Martin-Vésubie we'd opened a school in which Hebrew was taught.

S.S.: I got married at Saint-Martin-Vésubie. We gave a party for everybody: the French, the Italians, the Jews. The Italians even protected us from the French police. We had a card that stated that we were under Italian protection. When, for instance, we would go to Nice to do some shopping, if the French police stopped us they had to release us instantly. They looked at that card, they were angry, but they couldn't touch us.[94]

N.C.: And later you went to Ondono, near Cuneo?

Sidi Duiri Sharon and her brother, Simi Duiri, interviewed in France

s.s.: On Friday we searched for a place to hide . . .

s.d.: [*interrupting her*] It was Saturday. . . .

s.s.: On Saturday, and we finally found an abandoned shepherds' hut. It was snowing, it was cold, we had some babies with us.

n.c.: How many were you?

s.d.: In the first hut maybe five, in the second nine.

s.s.: All in all we were fifteen or so.
And then on Sunday morning we saw in the mountains a real . . .

s.d.: [*helping her, excited at the memory*] . . . procession . . .

s.s.: A procession of people who came from very far away. We didn't exactly understand, we saw that they were carrying jugs full of milk, buckets, so much stuff. One of them was carrying some straw.

s.d.: [*joining in*] Some straw . . .

s.s.: For sleeping on. We asked them how come and they told us that in church the priest had told them that there were some people on the mountainside and some small children who had nothing to eat, and that it was their duty to help them.

ANNA AND MARIANNA GIORDANA

NICOLA CARACCIOLO: Can you show us where you met those Jews?[95]

ANNA GIORDANA: Up, right on the high mountain . . . behind that bush up there, way, way up, dear.

n.c.: And how did it happen?

MARIA GIORDANA: We were going mushroom gathering . . . and we saw a little girl outside there . . .

a.g.: And up . . . and up . . .

m.g.: And there were the parents and everyone, and ourselves full of curiosity, we started to talk with them. . . .

n.c.: How old were the two of you then?

a.g.: I was eleven. . . .

m.g.: And I, thirteen.

n.c.: What did they tell you?

The two Giordana sisters, Anna and Marianna, in the Alps with Nicola Caracciolo, whose back is to the camera

A.G.: That they were hiding. When they saw us they were nearly hidden and we went behind to see . . .

M.G.: Because we felt sorry to see that little girl who was cold . . .

N.C.: And then?

A.G.: And then we came home. Later on we said, "Grandma and Grandpa, we saw a family, you see that they're hungry," we were sorry for those people, and they gave us right away . . . [*They speak together in dialect.*]

N.C.: What did you bring them?

M.G.: We brought them what we had. My mama gave us a little bread, some things, and we brought that up there fast. . . .

N.C.: Why did you help them like this?

A.G.: Because this is how we were brought up . . .

M.G.: Taught . . .

A.G.: How we were taught. We would see someone suffering and we'd feel sorry about it. . . .

N.C.: And did you become friends with them afterwards?

A.G.: Right away. . . .

M.G.: Right away. . . .

N.C.: And how did things go?

A.G.: Quite well, we used to meet.

N.C.: And they kept in hiding in the hut . . .

M.G.: Because if they were caught it would have been all over.

N.C.: It would have been over . . . And the village knew they were Jewish?

M.G.: Some of them did. . . .

A.G.: Some knew, but anyway there was so much agreement that no one sold out the others. They were all united.

N.C.: And did the little girl come sometimes to sleep at your place?

M.G.: In the winter, when it was really cold, we had her come to our place. . . .

A.G.: We were together in the cowshed, all together over there. . . .

N.C.: All of you . . .

M.G.: As is the custom with a family. The rest of us were happy. . . .

N.C.: And your father knew that he was risking being shot?

A.G.: Oh, yes, he knew it, but it didn't matter to him, even if they'd murdered all of us, if he could rescue seven people.

N.C.: What did he say? Did he explain this to you? . . .

M.G.: Yes, yes, to everyone. Papa always went up there to bring them food. And even if they caught us, patience.

N.C.: And your mother?

M.G.: She, too, even braver. . . .

N.C.: Even braver?

A.G.: Yes, yes. . . .

N.C.: And what happened when they left and he took them to Cuneo?

A.G.: They left, and my father was a bit . . . That morning he didn't feel so brave. Then my mother said, "Go—the Virgin and the Lord will help you."

M.G.: "The Virgin, the Lord, and the souls of the dead will pray for you and for all. Go alone, you go in peace."

ESTHER KICHEL MACHER AND RACHEL KICHEL SCHITZ

ESTHER KICHEL MACHER: And a lady took us[96] to Switzerland across Annemasse.[97] We were in Switzerland for three days. . . .

N.C.: What year was it?

E.K.M.: It was in February of 1943, and since Switzerland only took in children up to ten years of age, and I was . . . I was ten, so that was in 1942, at the end of 1942, I was ten years old and my sister was twelve. . . .

N.C.: Yes. . . .

E.K.M.: But she was very skinny and I was more developed physically.

The two Kichel sisters, Rachel Kichel Schitz (*left*) and Esther Kichel Macher (*center*). She and the man to the right, probably her husband but not identified, each hold a grandchild on their laps. They were interviewed at home (probably Esther's) in France.

There was a lady among us at the time who was saying that it's obvious I'm not ten years old. . . .

N.C.: Yes. . . .

E.K.M.: And on Sunday night, at seven, the Swiss caught us. It was in Geneva. They took us to the border and told us that there's a large camp and on the other side there's a hospital, and the German guards are changing. He said then to run quickly into that hospital. We arrived in this hospital . . .

N.C.: They threw you out of Switzerland . . .

RACHEL KICHEL SCHITZ: They plainly threw us out of Switzerland.

N.C.: Two small girls? . . .

E.K.M.: With Mama, with our mama. And we went into this hospital, we started to cry, they were quite kind and put us in a room for the insane. . . .

R.K.S.: So that if by chance a . . . German passport inspector goes by, they'll say, "They're crazy."

N.C.: What sort of relations did you have at that time with the Italians?

R.K.S.: We were under an Italian "forced residence,"[98] and we stayed there, all of us, a large group of Jews, at Saint-Gervais-Les-Bains.[99]

N.C.: Yes. . . .

E.K.M.: And we stayed there until the armistice, and we were under the Italian administration, and the Germans couldn't take us—in that very hotel there were Germans. But they couldn't do anything. The Italians prevented even the French police from arresting us.

DAN MILLIN

DAN MILLIN: My story begins in the year 1942.[100] We were a Jewish family at Karlovac, near Zagreb, and that was the year when the Germans occupied this Yugoslav region. Then they went away and the Italian Second Army came in. It so happened that an Italian officer, Colonel Luigi Supino, came to take a room in our house. It was a large house and there were ten people in the family. After two months the Ustasha, Yugoslav Nazis, came to take my family away.

The colonel heard that they arrived and said, "No one must enter; no one in this family is going away with you." They left. The com-

Dan Millin, interviewed at home in Israel

mandant of local police in Karlovac came back and said, "I am here and I must take the family." "No," said Colonel Supino, and then he said, "*I* am here and I tell you what to do." And the other said, "No," and after a great deal of quarreling the colonel took out his pistol and said, "If you don't go away I'll shoot you." And the Yugoslav Ustasha saw that this was no longer a joke, and he went away. And that night there were ten of us there, my mama, my grandmother, my aunt, and the children, and the colonel brought two *carabinieri* to guard the house, and told them, "No one gets in here." Next morning we heard that my cousin was able to escape from his house, where they'd taken his whole family, but cannot come to us, he's afraid to come, and we told Supino, the colonel, and he said "I'll do it." And he took an Italian uniform and an Italian car and brought my cousin to our house dressed in the Italian uniform. And after twenty-four hours, using an official car of the Italian army, he brought the entire family into Slovenia, which was under Italian occupation.

We stayed there for three or four months, until we received ID papers for Italy, and they were official papers. Then we went to a place near Vicenza, in a village called Valli del Pasubio. We stayed in Valli del Pasubio for almost two years, until Italy capitulated. But I've got to say something, that we weren't the only group the colonel helped. After us there was another group of ten to fifteen people whom he helped. This is really gentlemanly behavior. I think that day I was born for the second time.

Appendix 1

Historical Personages, Organizations, and Places

GENERAL VITTORIO AMBROSIO (1879–1958) was chief of the Italian General Staff from January 1942 until the armistice of September 1943.

AMERICAN JOINT DISTRIBUTION COMMITTEE, familiarly called "the Joint," provided about $15,000 to DELASEM (see Appendix 2) between its founding in 1939 and the Italian entry into the war and continued clandestinely to funnel money for assistance programs from Switzerland into northern Italy during the war.[1] See the interviews with Bernard Grosser and Bruno Segre.

FILIPPO ANFUSO was cabinet chief in the Foreign Office under Ciano. He remained a Mussolini loyalist to the bitter end.

ARBE was the Italian name of the island off the Dalmatian coast in the Kvarner Gulf that American tourists would know as Rab. Ambassador Roberto Ducci refers to it in his interview.

THE ARDEATINE CAVES, in the series of Christian catacombs along the Appian Way, were the site of a Nazi massacre in March 1944. See the interview with Olga Di Veroli.

MARSHAL PIETRO BADOGLIO (1871–1956) was chief of staff from 1925 to 1940. In July 1943, when the Fascist government fell, he was appointed head of state by the king.

MARSHAL ITALO BALBO (1896–1940) was an early leader of the Fascist movement, who was forced out of the Grand Council in 1933 for counseling moderate policies and who persisted in expressing his opposition to the racial laws passed five years later. In 1939 he was appointed governor-general of the Italian colony of Libya, where the racial laws were not put into effect. After the passage of the racial legislation, he remained friendly with Massimo Teglio, interviewed in this volume.

GIUSEPPE BASTIANINI (1899–1961) was governor of Dalmatia from 1941 to 1943 and then undersecretary in the Foreign Ministry. See the interviews with Ambassador Egidio Ortona, who worked directly under Bastianini, and Ambassador Roberto Ducci.

MINISTERIAL COUNCILLOR PRINCE OTTO VON BISMARCK was the second-in-command to Ambassador Hans-Georg von Mackensen, the German ambassador to Italy. See the interview with Ambassador Roberto Ducci.

CARDINAL PIETRO BOETTO was the archbishop of Genoa, who authorized his secretary, Father Francesco Repetto, to assist Massimo Teglio in rescue efforts.

RAFFAELE CANTONI, a Venetian, was a Jewish leader of importance and courage, who served as a courier for DELASEM and the archdiocese and was arrested for his clandestine activities.[2] In his interview Massimo Teglio inexactly describes him as "president of the Italian Jews," a title more appropriate for Dante Almansi, who was president of the Union of Italian Jewish Communities—a more compromised figure than Cantoni.

VITTORIO CASTELLANI (1902–71) was the Foreign Ministry's liaison officer with the Italian Second Army at its Sussak headquarters in occupied Croatia.

MARSHAL UGO CAVALLERO (1880–1943) was chief of the Italian General Staff until January 1942.

PALAZZO CHIGI in Rome was the office building in which the Italian Foreign Ministry was lodged. See the interviews with Ambassador Roberto Ducci and Ambassador Egidio Ortona.

COUNT GALEAZZO CIANO DI CORTELLAZZO (1903–44), Mussolini's son-in-law, was named foreign minister in mid-1936 and stayed on in that post until early 1943, despite his opposition to Italian entry in the war. Ciano's own role with respect to Jewish issues and to anti-Semitic policy was equivocal. Pro-German in the 1930s but increasingly disaffected with the pact with Hitler, Ciano voted to depose Mussolini in July 1943. He was arrested as a traitor by the RSI, condemned to death, and executed at Verona in January 1944. See the interviews with Professor Daniel Carpi and with Ambassador Roberto Ducci.

MARQUIS BLASCO LANZA D'AJETA (1907–66) was Foreign Minister Ciano's private secretary and chief of cabinet.

MARSHAL EMILIO DE BONO (1866–1944) was an early adherent of Mussolini and a participant in the March on Rome.In his last years he, along with Italo Balbo, Alberto De Stefani, and Luigi Federzoni, was one of the lifelong Fascists who protested against the anti-Semitic policies of the late 1930s. He was executed with Ciano after a military tribunal at Verona.

ALBERTO DE STEFANI was minister of finance in an early Mussolini cabinet. In his later years he opposed the racial laws.

ITALO ANGELO DONATI, who had been director of the Banque France-Italie, served as adviser to Inspector-General Guido Lospinoso. He is mentioned in conjunction with a daring evacuation and rescue plan in the interviews with Professor Daniel Carpi and Father Pierre Marie-Benoît. He died in 1961.

CARDINAL ARCHBISHOP FRANCESCO BORGONCINI DUCA (1884–1954) was the papal nuncio to Italy.

AMBASSADOR ROBERTO DUCCI, who died not long after Nicola Caracciolo interviewed him, was head of the Croatian Department of the Foreign Ministry and one of that ministry's original conspirators who, as J. Steinberg put it, "disobeyed instructions to burn the secret files on the Jews and removed them to his home for safe-keeping."[3] His article published during the German occupation in the foreign policy journal *Politica Estera,* signed with the pseudonym "Verax" (the truthteller), was the first to tell of Italian rescue efforts against the German directives to round up the Yugoslavian Jews.

The FASCIO was the local Fascist party headquarters, where the emblem of the movement, the *Fasci di combattimento*—the ancient Roman bundles of rods enclosing an ax with the blade projecting—was on display in paint or stone relief.

LUIGI FEDERZONI was an early Fascist leader who also protested against the racial laws in Italy.

FERRAMONTI was a concentration camp at Ferramonti Tarsia (Calabria), near Cosenza in southern Italy. It was the largest of the fifteen detention camps and internment centers set up by September 1940. On September 5, M. Michaelis records, "it was learnt that 1,650 out of the 3,000 Jewish refugees in Italy had been taken into custody."[4] See the Ita Lador interview.

FOSSOLI, near the town of Carpi in Emilia-Romagna, formerly the site of a British and Maltese POW camp, became the site of the principal Italian internment camp after the German occupation in September 1943. See Primo Levi's *If This Is a Man* and the interview with Levi here.[5]

PELLEGRINO GHIGI was the Italian minister plenipotentiary in Athens. With General Carlo Geloso, commander of the Italian Eleventh Army in Greece, he protected Jews in the Italian zone and rescued as many as possible from the German-occupied areas, such as Salonica.

ILVA is a large iron- and steelworks complex in Italy, with corporate headquarters located in both Genoa in the North and Taranto in the South. (The name was taken from the Latin name for the Island of Elba, where the iron ore was originally found.) It would be merged in 1961 with Italsider under the IRI, the governmental Institute for the Reconstruction of Industry.

DANTE ABRAMO LATTES (1876–1965) was a longtime leader of the Italian Zionist Federation, whose members, according to M. Michaelis, "courageously stood their ground, flatly refusing to yield to intimidation and pressure."[6] See the interview with Professor Augusto Segre.

PRIMO LEVI (1919–87), interviewed in this volume, was a chemist by profession and a writer by destiny as well as avocation. His books in English include *If This Is a Man, The Reawakening: A Liberated Prisoner's Long March Home through East Europe,* and *The Drowned and the Saved.*[7]

GIACOMA LIMENTANI, interviewed in these pages, is a novelist, the author of *In contumacia.*[8]

LISSA was the Italian name for Vis, an island in the mid-Adriatic, where Tito's headquarters were located after it was liberated.

GUIDO LOPEZ, interviewed here, himself a journalist and novelist, is the younger son of the Italian playwright Sabatino Lopez.

INSPECTOR-GENERAL GUIDO LOSPINOSO was the commissioner of the Italian police. He was sent to Vichy France to "solve" the Jewish problem in the areas under Italian control. Instead, his Commissariat for Jewish Affairs contributed to the policy of obstruction of the "final solution" there. See the interviews with Professor Daniel Carpi and Father Pierre Marie-Benoît.

LVOV, the chief city of eastern Galicia, passed successively from the Austro-Hungarian Empire to Poland to Germany to the Soviet Union. Today it is in the independent Ukraine. At one time, it had a Jewish population of approximately 150,000. See the interview with Marco Hermann.

GENERAL HANS-GEORG VON MACKENSEN was the German ambassador to Italy.

FATHER PIERRE MARIE-BENOÎT (Father Maria Benedetto), interviewed here, was born Pierre Péteul in 1895 and identified later in orders as Marie-Benoît du Bourg d'Iré. This Capuchin priest from France was known to all, according to the chronicler Sam Waagenaar, as "il padre degli ebrei" (the priest of the Jews). For his persistent efforts to save Jewish lives in southern France and later in Italy—efforts that were valiant, tireless, and very dangerous—Father Marie-Benoît would receive a special gold medal from the Hebrew Union of Italy in Milan in 1955 and the Medal of The Righteous from Yad Vashem in Jerusalem in 1967.[9]

SALLY MAYER, whom Bernard Grosser mentions in his interview, was active in Switzerland in assisting Jewish refugees and Italian Jews on behalf of the American Joint Distribution Committee. He evidently settled in Israel after the war. A foundation established in his honor published some of the books on the historical situation discussed in these pages, including one by Rabbi Elio Toaff on the Roman carnival and the Jews and another volume edited by Professor Daniel Carpi and others in memory of Enzo Sereni.[10]

IL MESSAGGERO is a Roman newspaper that carries official notices.

MONFERRATO is a district in the hills of Piedmont, with a notable Jewish presence at one time in the city of Casale. See the interviews with Augusto Segre and Emilio Foà.

The OLIVETTI family of Ivrea was the family of Adriano Olivetti, himself half-Jewish and a notable anti-Fascist, known in Italy as much for utopian communitarian thinking as for the manufacture of office machines. See the Abraham Cohen interview.

PAOLO ORANO was the rector of the University of Perugia and a Fascist deputy. In March of 1937 he published a book entitled *Gli ebrei in Italia* (The Jews in Italy). Though virulently anti-Semitic, Orano's attack on Italian Jews stopped short of Hitler's racial theories. Orano was close to Mussolini and wrote a biography of the Duce called *Mussolini da vicino* (Mussolini Up Close).[11]

ANTE PAVELIĆ (1889–1959), was the chief of the Croatian Fascist party known as Ustasha. He was installed by the Germans as head of a puppet Croatian government at Zagreb after the collapse of the military resistance of the Royal Yugoslavian Army in April 1941. According to J. Steinberg, "He owed his and its [Ustasha's] survival to fascist protection and support during the 1930s when Pavelić and his followers were in exile in Italy."[12]

GIUSEPPE PIÈCHE, general of the *carabinieri* in Croatia, was the first Italian official of standing to file a report to his government on the gassing of Jews deported from Croatia to the "Eastern territories" and to suggest clemency and resistance to further deportation. For General Pièche's actions in the face of German attempts to carry out the "final solution," see the interviews with Izak Itai and Ambassador Roberto Ducci. After the war, J. Steinberg tells us, Pièche received an award from the Italian-Jewish community for his humanity.[13]

COUNT LUCA PIETROMARCHI (1895–1978) was the Foreign Ministry's superintendent of the occupied territories and later the Italian diplomat responsible for the Cabinet of Armistice and Peace. In that capacity he effectively protected the Jews.

IL POPOLO D'ITALIA was the newspaper founded and edited by Mussolini in 1914.

PORTO RE was the Italian name for Kraljevice, the site of an internment camp on the Dalmatian coast to which the majority of the Jews in Italian-occupied Croatia and Slovenia had been sent.[14]

GIOVANNI PREZIOSI, an Italian renegade priest, was, according to M. Michaelis, the "editor of the anti-Semitic review *La Vita Italiana* and [a] future Minister of State . . . [who] was to go down in history as the dean of Italian Jew-baiters and as Hitler's *homme de confiance* in Italy."[15]

REGINA COELI was the name of the prison on the bank of the Tiber, where the Gestapo tortured captured underground resisters during the German occupation. See the interview with Lello Perugia.

FATHER FRANCESCO REPETTO, later Monsignor Repetto, was secretary to Cardinal Pietro Boetto, archbishop of Genoa. He assisted the Jewish relief organization DELASEM. See the interviews with Massimo Teglio and Bernard Grosser.

The RISORGIMENTO, the national uprising in the 1860s that was led by Garibaldi, Mazzini, Cavour, and others, eventually gave Italy political unity under the House of Savoy.

GENERAL MARIO ROATTA (1887–1968) succeeded Vittorio Ambrosio as commander of the Italian Second Army in Yugoslavia.

CARMINE SENISE was the Italian chief of police from 1940 to 1943.

LA STAMPA is the principal newspaper of Turin.

TULLIO TAMBURINI, a *squadrista* in the early days of the Fascist movement, was named chief of police in the period of the Social Republic. Although he was reputed to be a cruel man, his attempts at treating some of the Jewish population humanely ran afoul of German-dictated policy. See the interview with Rabbi Elio Toaff, who mentions that Tamburini was "shot for his misdeeds" after the allies had liberated the Marches.

RABBI ELIO TOAFF, interviewed in this volume, was the spiritual leader of the Jewish congregation in Ancona as a young man during the war. He has for many years been the Chief Rabbi of Rome and the most prominent of Italian rabbis. A recognized scholar in the secular world as well, he has written a book on the Jews of Rome.

USTASHA was the name of the Croatian Fascist party, headed by Ante Pavelić. It was virulently and murderously anti-Semitic. See the interviews with Daniel Carpi, the Noimans, Jossepe Papo, Dan Sternberg, Roberto Ducci, and Dan Millin.

LELIO VITTORIO VALOBRA, a Jewish attorney, administered and organized DELASEM in Genoa with funds received via Switzerland from the American Joint Distribution Committee. See the interviews with Massimo Teglio and Mr. Doron.

VILLA EMMA, where Jewish refugee children were sheltered, was situated in Nonantola, near Modena, in the regional department of Emilia-Romagna. See the interviews with Marcello Hoffman, Izak Itai, and Ariel Leo Koffler.

Appendix 2

Acronyms

ARMIR	Armata Italiana in Russia, the Italian Army on the Eastern Front in World War II.
CDEC	Centro di Documentazione Ebraica Contemporanea (Center for Contemporary Jewish Documentation), the principal archive of documents and most reliable source of statistics on the fate of Italian Jewish communities during World War II. It is located in Milan.
COMASSEBIT	Committee for Assistance to Italian Jews, an organization in Milan whose work with Jewish refugees paralleled the work of DELASEM.
CRI	Croce Rossa Italiana (the Italian Red Cross).
DELASEM	Delegazioni Assistenza Emigrati (Delegation for Assistance to Emigrants), a Jewish relief organization for the victims of the persecutions. Founded in Italy in 1939 with the authorities' permission, it would remain in existence until September 8, 1943.
DL	Decreto Legge, a legal decree or legislative act.
GL	Giustizia e Libertà (Justice and Liberty), a Resistance group of the non-Communist Left, founded by anti-Fascists in exile in France. The *giellisti*, as its adherents were called, were among the first partisan bands to take up armed struggle during the 1943–45 civil war.
GUF	Gruppi Universitari Fascisti, the Fascist youth organization for university students.
ISTAT	Istituto Centrale di Statistica, the Central Institute of Statistics, in which the Italian census bureau is lodged.
OAS	Organisation de l'Armée Secrète, the clandestine organization of military officers in France and Algeria who plotted the attempted right-wing coup against the government of De Gaulle in 1959.

OVRA	Opera Vigilanza Repressione Antifascismo, Work of Vigilance for the Repression of Anti-Fascism, the security police arm of the Fascist state.
RAI	Radio Audizioni Italiane, the government broadcasting network, today expanded into RAI-TV.
RSI	Repubblica Sociale Italiana, the puppet Fascist state established by the Germans in northern Italy in September 1943 in opposition to the Badoglio government in Rome. More frequently referred to as the "Republic of Salò" (after the village in Lombardy where two of its ministries were located), it engaged in the long civil war with the partisans and Resistance forces before the Allies reached the North. Though Mussolini, whom the Germans had rescued from the collapse of his regime in Rome, was reinstated as nominal chief of state of the Social Republic, he would spend his final year and a half more or less confined to the Lake Garda district.

Notes

FOREWORD

1. Marshal Italo Balbo, whose "Germanophobia" and "philo-Semitism" were well known and have been commented on by M. Michaelis, *Mussolini and the Jews: German-Italian Relations and the Jewish Question in Italy, 1922–1945* (Oxford: Clarendon Press, 1978), 205, n. 1, S. Zuccotti, *The Italians and the Holocaust: Persecution, Rescue, Survival* (New York: Basic Books, 1987), 39, and De Felice (here and elsewhere), was a member of the Fascist Grand Council until 1933. Although he ceased to be a member of the government thereafter, he was still close enough to Mussolini to be appointed governor-general of Libya in 1939, a colony with a significant population of Italian Jews even *after* the promulgation of the racial laws, which as discussed later were not enforced there.

2. The acronym RSI stood for the puppet Fascist state established by the Germans in northern Italy in September 1943, after the Badoglio government surrendered to the Allies. More frequently referred to as the Republic of Salò (after the village in Lombardy where two of its ministries were located), it engaged on the German side in a long civil war with the partisans and Resistance forces before the Allies reached the North. Mussolini, rescued by the Germans, was installed and was maintained to the end as the RSI's titular chief of state, more or less confined and carrying out German directives.

3. On this date, by a vote of nineteen to eight, with one abstention, the Fascist Grand Council voted against Mussolini, thus paving the way for his downfall and the forty-five days leading to the armistice, signed by Marshal Badoglio.

4. The two occasions were, first, the Royal Navy's recovery of the ships torpedoed while anchored at Taranto and, second, the transformation of ocean-going submarines into transport submarines for resupplies from the zones occupied by the Japanese.

5. L. Poliakov and J. Sabille, *Jews under the Italian Occupation* (Paris: Centre de Documentation Juive Contemporaine, 1954); D. Carpi, "The Rescue of Jews in the Italian Zone of Occupied Croatia," in *Rescue Attempts during the Holocaust: Proceedings of the Second Yad Vashem International Historical*

Conference, Jerusalem April 8–11, 1974, ed. Y. Gutman and E. Zuroff (Jerusalem: Ahva Cooperative Press, 1977), 465–525; D. Carpi, "Nuovi documenti per la storia dell'olocuasto in Grecia: L'atteggiamento degli Italianai (1941–1943)," *Michael* 7 (1981): 119–200; S. Loi, *Le operazioni delle unità italiane in Jugoslavia (1941–1943): Narrazione, documenti* (Rome: Tipografia regionale, 1978).

6. This statement might have been valid in 1986, when it was first published in the foreword to the Italian text, but it should now be qualified, thanks to the appearance of Zuccotti, *The Italians and the Holocaust,* beginning with chapter 6.

7. R. De Felice, "La Chiesa e il problema ebraico durante gli anni dell'antisemitismo fascista," *Rassegna mensile di Israel* 23 (January 1957): 23–35; R. De Felice, *Storia degli ebrei italiani sotto il fascismo,* 3d ed. (Turin: Einaudi, 1972); G. Mayda, *Ebrei sotto Salò: La persecuzione antisemita, 1943–1945* (Milan: Feltinelli, 1978); M. Michaelis, "On the Jewish Question in Fascist Italy: The Attitude of the Fascist Regime to the Jews in Italy," *Yad Vashem Studies* no. 4 (1960): 7–14; M. Michaelis, "The 'Duce' and the Jews: An assessment of the Literature on Italian Jewry under Fascism (1922–1945)," *Yad Vashem Studies* no. 11 (1976): 7–32; M. Michaelis, *Mussolini and the Jews: German-Italian Relations and the Jewish Question in Italy, 1922–1945* (Oxford: Clarendon Press, 1978).

8. The acronym stands for Centro di Documentazione Ebraica Contemporanea.

9. These are, as indicated, round numbers. The figures gathered by the CDEC (1975) are more precise than De Felice's. See Toscano's Prologue.

10. For Segre, see interview with him. His memoirs, *Memorie di vita ebraica: Casale Monferrato—Roma—Gerusalemme, 1918–1960* (Rome: Bonacci, 1979), like those of G. Sacerdoti, *Ricordi di un ebreo bolognese: Illusionioni e delusioni, 1929–1945* (Rome: Bonacci, 1983), have not been translated.

11. The acronym stands for Delegazione Assistenza Emigrati (Delegation for the Assistance of Emigrants). See the interview with Bernard Grosser.

12. See the interview with Father Marie-Benoît (Padre Benedetto to the Italians).

13. A. Sereni, *I clandestini del mare: L'emigrazione ebraica in terra d'Israele dal 1945 al 1948* (Milan: Mursia, 1973). Ada Ascarelli Sereni, the author of this book about clandestine Jewish emigration to Palestine between the end of the war and the coming into existence of Israel, had herself emigrated in 1927 with her husband, Enzo Sereni, from Italy to British-controlled Palestine. There, as Zuccotti, *The Italians and the Holocaust,* 268–70, recounts the story, they helped found Kibbutz Givat Brenner, near Rehovot. After the outbreak of the war and despite his pacifist ideals, Enzo joined British intelligence in 1940. In 1944 he persuaded the British to train him for a parachute mission behind German lines. His official purpose, Zuccotti tells us, was to attempt to reach Florence and establish contact with partisan units in Tuscany; his additional, private objective was to aid fugitive Italian Jews. Instead he was captured right after the jump that May by the Germans, who interro-

gated him, tortured him, and sent him to Dachau in October, where he was assigned to hard labor and later perished. His widow Ada Sereni's book, published in Italian in 1973 and later in Hebrew and Russian (in Israel) but never in English, deals principally with the postwar emigration, not with the early years of Givat Brenner or with her husband, whose martyrdom is honored and remembered in two countries.

INTRODUCTION

1. L. S. Dawidowicz, *The War against the Jews, 1933–1945* (New York: Free Press, 1986).

2. Nicola Caracciolo, Introduzione, *Gli ebrei e l'Italia durante la guerra, 1940–45* (Rome: Bonacci, 1986), 17.

3. Ibid., 18.

4. F. W. Deakin, *The Bitter Friendship: Hitler, Mussolini, and the Fall of Italian Fascism* (New York: Harper and Row, 1962).

5. That disregard for similar pressures, though not accompanied by similar orders, also held for the Foreign Ministry of the third party to the Axis wartime alliance, the Japanese Empire. Sometimes overtly, sometimes covertly, Japan issued transit visas that allowed Jewish refugees from as far away as Lithuania to resettle in Japanese-occupied Manchuria, China, and Japan itself. M. Tokayer and M. Swartz, *The Fugu Plan: The Untold Story of the Japanese and the Jews during World War II* (New York: Paddington, 1979), 95, quote Yosuke Matsuoka, the foreign minister who signed the Pact of Steel with Joachim von Ribbentrop and Galeazzo Ciano in September 1940, as having told Lew Zikman, a wealthy Jewish businessman from Manchuria who was attempting to intercede for the refugees, *not* to be "overly concerned about this [the Pact]. It is true that I concluded a treaty with Hitler. But I never promised him to be an anti-Semite." The Japanese transit visas and resettlements continued intermittently throughout the war. The story and motivation are complex beyond the scope of this book. Interested readers should also consult D. Kranzler, *Japanese, Nazis, and Jews: The Jewish Community of Shanghai, 1938–1945* (New York: Yeshiva University Press, 1976); S. Lyman, "Nihonism and Judaism—A Dissent," *Midstream* 19 (June–July 1973): 75–80; and B.-A. Shillony, *Politics and Culture in Wartime Japan* (Oxford: Clarendon Press, 1991), along with the memoirs of Setsuzo (later Abraham) Kotsuji, *From Tokyo to Jerusalem* (New York: Random House, 1964), whose role amidst less than friendly Japanese ruling circles somewhat resembled that of Massimo Teglio, interviewed in these pages.

6. Z. Bauman, *Modernity and the Holocaust* (Ithaca, N.Y.: Cornell University Press, 1989), 14–15.

7. See R. G. Weisbord and W. P. Sillanpoa, *The Chief Rabbi, the Pope, and the Holocaust: An Era in Vatican-Jewish Relations* (New Brunswick, N.J.: Transaction, 1991), 35, who comment that Pope Ratti's encyclical "pilloried those who would exalt and worship the nation or race, thereby perverting the divine will."

154 Notes to Pages xxix–xxx

8. We are touching here on a continuing and sometimes acrimonious debate that is not merely historical in its implications. It became an open debate with the production (banned in Italy at that time) and subsequent publication of Rolf Hochhuth's play *The Deputy,* trans. R. Winston and C. Winston (New York: Grove, 1964). The following year the Vatican began to publish an extended though necessarily selective edition of papers, including papal memoranda and correspondence, in *Actes et documents du Saint Siège relatifs à la Seconde Guerre Mondiale,* in eleven volumes, under the editorship of the Jesuit scholars Pierre Blet, Robert A. Graham, Angelo Martini, and Burkhart Schneider. Father Graham's sympathetic portrayal of the actions of Pius XII has recently been published in I. Herzer et al., eds., *The Italian Refuge: Rescue of Jews during the Holocaust* (Washington, D.C.: Catholic University Press, 1989, 231–53; Susan Zuccotti's more critical portrayal appears in the same collection of papers, 254–70. Carlo Falconi attempts to take a balanced view in *The Silence of Pius XII,* trans. B. Wall (Boston: Little, Brown, 1970); Saul Friedländer, *Pius XII and the Third Reich: A Documentation,* trans. C. Fullman (New York: Alfred A. Knopf, 1966), has assembled documents bearing on the papal role; M. Michaelis, "Pius XII and the Third Reich," in *Mussolini and the Jews: German-Italian Relations and the Jewish Question in Italy, 1922–1945* (Oxford: Clarendon Press, 1978), 424–26, disputes Hochhuth's portrait. We are suggesting that, apart from the extraofficial, individual heroism of numerous people in religious orders, the Vatican itself (to paraphrase the Gospel text) had several mansions. While Pius "refused to break his silence even when Dannecker's men rounded up Jews right under his windows," as Michaelis, "Pius XII and the Third Reich," 365, puts it, "the open-door [sanctuary] policy of the Holy See saved the lives of nearly 5,000 Jewish Romans." The Jewish theologian and historian Irving Greenburg, "Cloud of Smoke, Pillar of Fire," in *Holocaust: Religious and Philosophical Implications,* ed. J. K. Roth and M. Berenbaum (New York: Paragon, 1989), 313, pointed out that Angelo Giuseppe Roncalli, the future John XXIII who would succeed Pius, "made representations and protests, issued false baptismal papers, [and] helped Jews escape" when he was a diplomat in the Balkans and the Near East (to 1944) and then nuncio to France (from 1944 on). Clearly Pius, like Franklin D. Roosevelt and Winston Churchill—the latter another instance, for Hochhuth, of moral failure—could have done more; unlike them, confronted with German occupation of his open city and having been warned by Baron Ernst von Weizsäcker, the German ambassador to the Holy See, that "any protest by the pope would only result in the deportations being really carried out in a thoroughgoing fashion" (Michaelis, "Pius XII and the Third Reich," 364), he was also attempting to maintain official neutrality and pursue détente. Obviously, in retrospect, the deportations occurred anyway, but, as Stalin is reported to have asked scornfully, how many legions had the pope?

9. The story of the Di Veroli family has now been told in full detail in A. Stille, *Benevolence and Betrayal: Five Italian Jewish Families under Fascism* (New York: Summit Books, 1991), 167–222.

10. Zuccotti, *The Italians and the Holocaust,* 154ff, recounts the story,

mentioning Father Bernardino by name, as an exception to the pattern of autumn 1943 roundups. Her source is Giuseppe Mayda, *Ebrei sotto Salò: La persecuzione antisemita, 1943–1945* (Milan: Feltrinelli, 1978), 67ff., identified by De Felice as one of the three principal sources on the anti-Semitism of the Fascist era, the others being Michaelis, *Mussolini and the Jews,* and De Felice's own work, *Storia degli ebrei italiani sotto il fascismo,* 3d ed. (Turin: Einaudi, 1972).Unfortunately, neither Mayda's work nor De Felice's is available in English, whereas Michaelis wrote originally in English.

11. Caracciolo, Introduzione, 17.

12. C. Lanzmann, *Shoah: An Oral History of the Holocaust* (New York: Pantheon, 1987); J. Kosinski, *The Painted Bird,* 2d ed. (New York: Random House, 1983).

13. P. P. Hallie, *Lest Innocent Blood Be Shed: The Story of the Village of Le Chambon, and How Goodness Happened There* (New York: Harper and Row, 1979).

14. For more on the Di Veroli family and the Ovazza family, see Stille, *Benevolence and Betrayal,* 167–222 and 17–89, respectively.

15. Stille, *Benevolence and Betrayal,* 79, recounts that Carla's own father, Vittorio Ovazza, did not in fact leave Italy until the summer of 1940, and even then unwillingly, prodded by his immediate family. "We forced him to leave," she tells Stille. "He never did understand." As readers of this book will see, she tells Caracciolo nothing of the kind. Both accounts may be valid: Carla Ovazza emphasizes that which she chooses to emphasize. Or perhaps we have here a further instance of what Lawrence Langer, *Holocaust Testimonies: The Ruins of Memory* (New Haven, Conn.: Yale University Press, 1991), calls "the ruins of memory."

16. Langer, *Holocaust Testimonies,* 5.

PROLOGUE

1. At the end of 1938, the population was 43,610,000. For these data on the population, compare ISTAT, *Sommario di statistiche storiche dell'Italia 1861–1965* (Rome: ISTAT, 1968).

2. E. Ludwig, *Talks with Mussolini,* trans. E. Paul and C. Paul (Boston: Little, Brown), 71.

3. *Popolo d'Italia* was the newspaper founded by Mussolini in 1914, when he had to give up the editorship of the Socialist newspaper *Avanti!* for breaking with its position of neutrality in the war, and was edited by him until the march on Rome in 1922 (except during his brief period of military service and hospitalization in 1917). It remained Mussolini's newspaper, strong in its allegiance to his movement, and he continued to contribute signed and unsigned articles to it. A number of its contributors were Jewish Fascists, as was the editor of its cultural "third page," Margherita Sarfatti, Mussolini's mistress until 1936, the year of the shift Toscano describes. Among other Jewish contributors mentioned by M. Michaelis, *Mussolini and the Jews: German-Italian Relations and the Jewish Question in Italy, 1922–1945* (Oxford: Claren-

don Press, 1978), 52, were the social theorist Gino Arias, the physiologist Carlo Foà, and Giorgio Del Vecchio, rector of the University of Rome.

4. Paulo Orano, *Gli ebrei in l'Italia* (Rome: Pinciana, 1937). See interview with Giacoma Limentani and note 39 in the interviews section.

5. Count Galeazzo Ciano di Cortellazzo (1903–44), Mussolini's son-in-law, was named foreign minister in mid-1936 and stayed on in that post until early in 1943, despite his opposition to the declaration of war against France and Britain in June of 1940. After having to leave the ministry, Ciano served as ambassador to the Holy See, an important diplomatic post in view of the potential role of the Vatican in addressing the treatment of Italian Jews and in directly confronting, had it wished, Hitler's "final solution." Ciano's own role with respect to Jewish issues and to anti-Semitic policy, domestic and foreign, was equivocal in the extreme. See the interviews with Professor Daniel Carpi and Ambassador Roberto Ducci; S. Zuccotti, *The Italians and the Holocaust: Persecution, Rescue, Survival* (New York: Basic Books, 1987), 32–33; and Michaelis, *Mussolini and the Jews,* passim. Pro-German in the 1930s but increasingly disaffected with the "bitter friendship" with Hitler, Ciano voted to depose Mussolini in the Grand Council in July 1943. He was arrested as a traitor by the Social Republic, condemned to death, and shot at Verona in January 1944, despite Countess Edda Ciano's attempt to intervene with her father to save her husband. Ciano was, in short, a most complex and rather tragic figure.

6. A lengthier excerpt from this public announcement, which was published by the Foreign Ministry, is given in Michaelis, *Mussolini and the Jews,* 141–42.

7. Toscano is overstating the case here, if Michaelis's documentation is to be believed. A month later, on May 4 to be exact, Dr. Nahum Goldmann *was* in fact received by Ciano, "who assured him that Italy was not hostile to Zionism and that the anti-Jewish polemics in certain papers in no way reflected the official Fascist attitude." Michaelis, *Mussolini and the Jews,* 136.

8. The actual title was *Manifesto degli scienziati razzisti* (Manifesto of the Racial Scientists), an "infamous" manifesto that, according to Zuccotti, *The Italians and the Holocaust,* 35, "attempted to provide a scientific justification for the coming racial laws." Zuccotti adds, "The manifesto was a fraud in every respect. . . . It was signed by ten 'experts,' of whom at least four were young university assistants just beginning their careers and vulnerable to political pressure. Only one of the ten had national stature." In December Mussolini told a minor official, Bruno Spampanato, that the document was a "piece of pseudo-scientific rubbish concocted by certain scholars and journalists" and was nothing but "a ponderous German treatise translated into bad Italian." Michaelis, *Mussolini and the Jews,* 397.

9. For a tragicomic instance of this office in action, see the interview with Attorney Massimo Ottolenghi.

10. Marshal Emilio De Bono and Luigi Federzoni were, along with Marshal Italo Balbo, Alberto De Stefani, and Giacomo Acerbo (the last two not mentioned by Toscano), the so-called government moderates on the Grand

Council who raised objections to the anti-Jewish measures proposed by the regime. Each of these "moderate" hierarchs had, however, as Michaelis, *Mussolini and the Jews*, 189, notes, been forced out of the government proper, though they retained their advisory roles.

11. See the interview with Feri and Zlata Noiman, Greek Jews interned in the Italian concentration camp at Ferramonti.

12. For DELASEM, see the interview with Mr. Doran and Bernard Grosser.

13. For one such plan, Angelo Donati's, see interviews with Professor Carpi and with Father Pierre Marie-Benoît.

14. See the interviews with Asaf Kansi, Izak Itai, Ariel Leo Koffler, Dan Danko Sternberg, and Yehoshua Halevy, for example. The interview with Ambassador Ducci provides another perspective, that of the Italian diplomatic corps in Yugoslavia.

15. See the interviews with Father Marie-Benoît, Enzo Cavaglion, Sidi Duiri Sharon and Simi Duiri, and Anna and Marianna Giordana.

16. See the interviews with the Noimans and with Emmy Raphael Nachmias.

17. This white paper, the *Carta di Verona*, was the outcome of a Fascist Party Congress convened by the Social Republic on November 14. See Michaelis, *Mussolini and the Jews*, 351.

18. The order for the arrest and internment of all Jews in the RSI and the confiscation of their property was broadcast the following day over the radio. See Michaelis, *Mussolini and the Jews*, 351.

19. See Zuccotti, *The Italians and the Holocaust*, 8–11.

20. See R. Katz, *Black Sabbath: A Journey through a Crime against Humanity* (Toronto: Macmillan, 1969), a book wholly given over to the pillaging, roundup, and deportation of the Jews of Rome. The interviews with Father Raganella and Mr. Dell'Ariccia and with Mino Moscati also convey something of the terror and confusion of that roundup.

21. See Zuccotti, *The Italians and the Holocaust*, 188–89, for the December 31, 1943, onslaught; she also supports Toscano's statement about Italian complicity: "Ninety-three [of the total of 212 Venetian Jews deported] were deported as a result of a single raid conducted entirely by Italians."

22. The entire story of this brutal reprisal by the SS in the catacombs outside of Rome is recounted in R. Katz, *Death in Rome* (New York: Macmillan, 1967), 227, where he gives the figure of 335 victims of the atrocity in the caves, among them the 75 Jews mentioned by Toscano. In 1947 an Italian tribunal convicted SS-Obersturmbannführer Herbert Kappler, who ordered the reprisals (and who had earlier plundered the Roman Jewish community of its gold and irreplaceable books), of war crimes. He was sentenced to life imprisonment for the atrocities.

23. Centro di Documentazione Ebraica Contemporanea, Milan, ed., *Ebrei in Italia: Deportazione, resistenza* (Florence: La Giuntina, 1975), 61. The authority of this research center and the reliability of its Holocaust statistics are acknowledged by all historians in the field, including Zuccotti and, earlier, Michaelis. See the bibliography for other CDEC documentary publications, cited in Italian.

24. See the interview with Bernard Grosser, secretary of DELASEM in Genoa.

25. There are several former partisans among the Jews interviewed in this book: Emilio Foà, Lello Perugia, and Augusto Segre.

INTERVIEWS

1. See the interview with Father Marie-Benoît.

2. See the later interview with Ambassador Ducci.

3. This interview and and all of the interviews through the "Unidentified Voice" were conducted with a group of Jews of Yugoslavian origin in a restaurant in Jerusalem. Not all the witnesses have been identified.

4. In Nonantola, near Modena in Emilia-Romagna, there was a group of about one hundred Jewish children, mainly refugees from Germany but a number also from Yugoslavia. On September 8 they were saved from deportation, some by hiding in a convent, others in dozens of townsfolk's houses.

5. The concentration camp at Ferramonti Tarsia (Calabria), near Cosenza in southern Italy, was the largest of the fifteen detention camps and internment centers set up by September 1940. On September 5, M. Michaelis, *Mussolini and the Jews: German-Italian Relations and the Jewish Question in Italy, 1922–1945* (Oxford: Clarendon Press, 1978), 292, records that "it was learnt that 1,650 out of the 3,000 Jewish refugees in Italy had been taken into custody."

6. See the interview with Ambassador Roberto Ducci.

7. See the interview with Massimo Teglio.

8. For further corroboration of the involvement of Father Francesco Repetto, see the interview with Massimo Teglio, and note 81 to that interview.

9. Compare the interview with Bruno Segre.

10. None of the major extermination camps was located near Lvov. Perhaps Hermann, who speaks of his parents as having been deported, is being unduly precise: he may be referring to the nearest extermination camps, across the Polish border at Belzec. Or perhaps he is referring to the camp the Germans set up in Lvov on the Janowska Road after they captured the city in July 1941. Of the Jewish community of Lvov, which had numbered about 150,000 people before the war, all but a handful perished.

11. See also Josef Ithai, "The Children of Villa Emma," in *The Italian Refuge: Rescue of Jews during the Holocaust,* ed. I. Herzer et al. (Washington, D.C.: Catholic University Press, 1989), 178–202.

12. For General Pièche's actions in the face of German attempts to carry out the "final solution," see also the interview with Ambassador Roberto Ducci, then chief of the Croatian Office of the Foreign Ministry. Pièche was the first Italian official of standing to file a report on the gassing of Jews deported from Croatia to the "Eastern territories" and to suggest clemency and resistance to further deportation. See J. Steinberg, *All or Nothing: The Axis and the Holocaust, 1941–1943* (New York: Routledge, 1990), 75ff.

13. Compare the earlier interview with Marcello Hoffman and the following one with Ariel Leo Koffler.

14. See the interview with the members of the Di Girolamo family.

15. Donati, previously mentioned by Professor Carpi, was the former director of the Banque France-Italie and served as adviser to Inspector-General Guido Lospinoso, the commissioner of police. He died in 1961.

16. The plan anticipated taking the Jews in the summer of 1943 from the Italian zone in France to North Africa, already in Allied hands. An equally bold secret plan devised *within* the Japanese government between 1934 and 1940, the Fugu Plan, aborted after the signing of the Tripartite Pact in September of 1940. See M. Tokayer and M. Swartz, *The Fugu Plan: The Untold Story of the Japanese and the Jews during World War II* (New York: Paddington, 1979).

17. The first step of the transfer, if Father Benedetto's memory is accurate, would have to have been into Spain; however, the historian Susan Zuccotti privately expressed skepticism about this to the translators. She had never heard of this elsewhere and asked whether Donati would have attempted a transfer on this scale through Spain, rather than from southern France to northern Italy and then to North Africa.

18. Less elliptically put, what Caracciolo means is that the collapse of the Mussolini government occurred before it could become acquainted with the plan. The Badoglio government accepted the Donati Plan, but the armistice was proclaimed before it could be launched.

19. This was this same Inspector-General Lospinoso who, in addition to providing a haven for Jewish refugees in Saint-Martin-Vésubie, also served as the government liaison on whose assistance the Donati Plan would have depended for success. See the interviews with Father Pierre Marie-Benoît and Professor Daniel Carpi.

20. See the interview with Sidi Duiri Sharon and Simi Duiri.

21. For the perspective of a student at a Jewish high school set up after the exclusions under the racial laws, see the interview with Giacoma Limentani.

22. Perugia, who fought as a partisan, is interviewed later.

23. Caracciolo calls her *signora* as a sign of respect, though she will confirm that she never married. *Signorina,* "miss," is more commonly used with younger women. Alexander Stille interviewed the late Olga di Veroli for "A Family of the Ghetto: The Di Verolis of Rome," in *Benevolence and Betrayal: Five Italian Jewish Families under Fascism* (New York: Summit Books, 1991), 167–222. There are some variations in what she reported in these interviews, none surprising.

24. This was a typical attitude among Jews at that time: refusing to believe that any kindness could come from Germans.

25. On March 24, 1944, as a Nazi reprisal to a partisan attack on SS troops in Rome, the Gestapo took 70 Jews (and 265 non-Jews) from the prisons of Rome and executed them in the Ardeatine Caves, part of the Christian catacombs along the Appian Way. The story of this massacre is recounted in Susan Zuccotti, *The Italians and the Holocaust: Persecution, Rescue, Survival*

(New York: Basic Books, 1987), and at greater length in two books by R. Katz, *Death in Rome* (New York: Macmillan, 1967) and *Black Sabbath: A Journey through a Crime against Humanity* (Toronto: Macmillan, 1969), with small differences in the number of Jewish martyrs.

26. Bismarck was the second-in-command to General Hans Georg von Mackensen, the German ambassador to Italy.

27. See the interview with Professor Carpi.

28. The commanders of the Italian Second Army in Yugoslavia whose actions Ducci is recalling here were, first, General Mario Roatta and, afterward, when Roatta became chief of staff, General Mario Robotti. On Robotti, L. Steinberg, *All or Nothing: The Axis and the Holocaust, 1941–1943* (New York: Routledge, 1990), 122, recalls the postwar testimony of Colonel Carlà, his first bureau chief of headquarters in Croatia, that when Robotti had learned of Mussolini's promise to Ribbentrop off the record to surrender the Croatian Jews, he "protested so violently that the Duce gave in: '. . . [T]hink of whatever excuse you please, so as not to hand over a single Jew.'" There is a similar account in Michaelis, *Mussolini and the Jews*, 331. The common source is L. Poliakov and J. Sabille, *Jews under the Italian Occupation* (Paris: Centre de Documentation Juive Contemporaine, 1954), 147ff.

29. "During the terrible summer of 1941," writes Zuccotti, *The Italians and the Holocaust*, 76, "Ustasha assassins ran wild in Croatia, destroying entire villages and murdering thousands of Jews and Serbs. Italian policy toward Jews began in response to this rampage." For Ante Pavelić, head of the Fascist movement, see Appendix 1.

30. For Bastianini's role, see the interview with Ambassador Ortona, who served directly under him.

31. Filippo Anfuso was Ciano's cabinet chief in the Foreign Office. He remained loyal to Mussolini to the bitter end.

32. Palazzo Chigi was the site of the Italian Foreign Office. See the interview with Ambassador Ortona for further details.

33. For a parallel view of the role of Italian Jews in the Risorgimento, the national uprising led by Garibaldi, Mazzini, Cavour, and others, which unified the country politically, see De Felice's foreword to this book.

34. Michaelis, *Mussolini and the Jews*, 383, n. 2, notes that "the camp at Fossoli di Carpi (Modena) had originally been set up for British and Maltese prisoners of war; it was taken over by the SS at the end of February or the beginning of March 1944."

35. The Italian word to which Levi is referring was used, of course, for the inmate supervisors, who were also fellow Jews.

36. In Italian, rather than Piedmontese dialect, the bricklayer would have said, "Eh, si capisce, con gente come questa." Levi has to translate for his interviewer to understand the remark.

37. *La Stampa* is a leading Turin newspaper.

38. For a teacher's perspective, see the earlier interview with Lia Corinaldi.

39. In March of that year a book by Paolo Orano, entitled *Gli ebrei in Italia* (The Jews in Italy), was published by Casa Editrice Pinciana in Rome.

Orano was rector of the University of Perugia and a Fascist deputy. Though virulently anti-Semitic, Orano's attack on Italian Jews stopped short of Hitler's racial theories. Orano, it should be mentioned, was close to Mussolini and wrote a biography of the Duce.

40. That is, at the local Fascist party headquarters, where the emblem of the movement, the *Fasci di combattimento*, the ancient Roman bundles of rods enclosing an ax with the blade projecting, were on display in paint or stone relief.

41. Of the three dramatists Guido Lopez mentions in this joint interview, only Luigi Pirandello is known and still produced abroad. Pirandello (1867–1936), a Sicilian playwright and fiction writer, won the Nobel Prize for literature two years before his death. Unlike Croce, he never voiced opposition to Mussolini. Dario Niccodemi (1874–1934) was a playwright and theatrical director. Living abroad in his youth, he wrote some of his earlier work in Spanish and in French. His work, popular in its time, is no longer produced much in Italy. Sabatino Lopez (1867–1951), Guido Lopez's father, was the author of some seventy plays, mostly comedies, that were also widely produced in their time. His younger son, Guido, is a journalist and novelist; his elder son, Robert Sabatino, is a notable medieval historian who writes in English.

42. Silvio D'Amico was a leading theater historian and drama critic of the Twenties and Thirties.

43. We have been unable to determine who Furio Diaz and his father may have been.

44. Piero Calamandrei (1889–1956) was a Florentine lawyer, poet, fabulist, and man of letters. He was briefly involved in national politics in the postwar period. Among his more celebrated books is *Inventario della casa di campagna* (Florence: Le Monnier, 1941; 2d ed., Rome: Tumminelli, 1945), about his childhood in the Tuscan countryside.

45. Arturo Carlo Jemolo was a historian, the author of, among other works, a study of Jansenism in Italy that was published by Croce's publisher, Laterza of Bari, in 1928. Signora Tedeschi has unconsciously reversed the order of Professor Jemolo's names.

46. *If* the Falcos' train from the countryside did pull in as the train transporting the Jews rounded up in the Roman ghetto was departing, they would have arrived at Stazione Tiburtina (*not* the main station) on the morning of October 18, 1943. See Katz, *Black Sabbath;* and Zuccotti, *The Italians and the Holocaust,* 120.

47. Here and throughout Moscati's narrative, the place names refer to well-known streets, squares, and architectural landmarks of the old Roman ghetto and the area around it. The Nazi roundup in the Jewish ghetto that he is describing took place on the "Black Sabbath" of October 16, 1943. In all, the Germans seized and deported 327 men and 800 women and children, mostly ghetto residents, to Auschwitz. Only fifteen of the deportees returned to Rome after the liberation of the camps in 1945. The episode is the subject of Katz, *Black Sabbath.*

48. Celeste Di Porto was at that time an eighteen-year-old Jewish girl,

resident in the old ghetto, who worked as a police informer, handing over about fifty of her fellow Jews to the Fascist police squadrons of the Social Republic for five thousand lire (then worth fifty dollars) per Jew. She is remembered in Italy to this day as the notorious "Black Panther." See Katz, *Black Sabbath,* 179 and 296–97.

49. *Il Messaggero* was and still is a Roman newspaper of no distinction, carrying notices about the civil services.

50. Toward the end of September 1943, SS-Obersturmbannführer Herbert Kappler, the chief Gestapo officer in Rome under the German occupation, had extorted fifty kilograms of gold from the Roman Jewish community in return for promises of safety, which he most likely did not intend to keep. See Katz, *Black Sabbath,* 3–105.

51. In actuality, the Germans looted and carried off *two* libraries in mid-October, just prior to the roundups and deportations, each priceless and irreplaceable collections of rare Jewish books and incunabula, the one belonging to the Jewish community of Rome and the other to the rabbinical college. See Katz, *Black Sabbath,* 105–71.

52. See n. 35 to Levi interview.

53. Palazzo Chigi is, once again, used metonymically for the Italian Foreign Office, which was located there. See the interview with Ambassador Ducci.

54. Attorney Ottolenghi's mother acted on principle. Others, involved in the Fascist party hierarchy, did not. "Apparently some applicants for Aryanization," Zuccotti, *The Italians and the Holocaust,* 292, n. 27, reports, "including Finance Minister Guido Jung and Militia General Maurizio Rava, claimed eligibility on the grounds that their mothers had had sexual relations with Aryans."

55. This official was from the then-Italian colony of Libya and was probably of Arab descent.

56. The top grade in an Italian examination in a university subject is thirty.

57. The question, to an Italian student, would be rather like asking an American college student when the Civil War began. No "great historian" would be required as authority, and the figure Ottolenghi mentioned has been treated with mild irony.

58. Zuccotti, *The Italians and the Holocaust,* 142f., notes that between 1934 and 1938, the years of publication of this newspaper, whose name means "our flag, Ovazza "constantly echoed the government's position that Zionists were disloyal and called upon all Italian Jews to condemn them." For a more complete narrative of the life and death of Ettore Ovazza (1892–1943), member of an assimilated family of bankers, Fascist in his sympathies from the time of the March on Rome, president of the Jewish community of Turin, and vocal opponent of the Zionist newspaper *Israel,* see Stille, *Benevolence and Betrayal,* 17–89. See also the interview with Professor Augusto Segre, a lifelong Piedmontese Zionist and faithful reader of *Israel.*

59. Some forty years later Carla Ovazza recalls her two cousins as "bambini," youngsters, though in reality in September 1943 the brother, Riccar-

do, was already twenty, and his sister, Elena, was fifteen. See Stille, *Benevolence and Betrayal*, 85.

60. In Stille's account of the same events, Ettore Ovazza "did at least leave Turin. He liquidated a good portion of his property, selling two houses and converting at least 6 million lire . . . into precious jewels, gold, cash, and foreign currency. In late September 1943 he took his family to a hotel in Gressoney, a ski resort in the Italian Alps where they had often vacationed, so that they could flee to Switzerland if it became necessary." Ibid., 84.

61. Once again relying on Stille, who has sifted his way through the recollections of eyewitnesses (which, of course, Carla was not) in the archives of the CDEC in Milan, we learn that the hotel was the Lyskamm, whose owner, Arnaldo Cochis, was almost universally disliked for his pro-German views and suspected of having collaborated with the SS. Ibid., 86.

62. Carla's version is, once again, apocryphal in its details. Cochis may have stolen the money and valuables that Ettore Ovazza deposited in the hotel safe, but the Ovazzas remained in the hotel for a full two weeks, during which time Cochis did not betray the family directly. The "smuggler," one Rudy Lercoz—later shot for having collaborated with the SS—may or may not have robbed and betrayed Riccardo Ovazza to the Germans, but he did not murder him. According to other testimony, after Riccardo had successfully crossed the border, he was sent back to Italy by Swiss authorities and arrested by the SS in the train station at Domodossola. In either case, the young man was never seen again, and the SS was able to trace his family's hiding place "from documents in Riccardo's possession and possibly through torture." Ibid., 85–86.

63. The testimony of the medical doctor, a Dr. Raggi, suggests neither the folkloric heroism nor the naïveté on the part of Nella Ovazza, Carla's aunt, or her cousin Elena. "The Ovazzas were locked in their room, the Germans were drunk, and the hotelkeeper had the key." When Raggi and a fellow partisan, Mario Rossi, begged Cochis to give them the key, the hotelkeeper "flew into a rage" and refused to do so, threatening the would-be rescuers. Ibid., 88.

64. Intra is north of Stresa. There, according to the testimony of the custodian of the elementary school, Ida Rusconi, whose account is followed by Mayda, Zuccotti, and Stille, the family was first shot and then the bodies were butchered and burnt as described in Carla's narrative. See G. Mayda, *Ebrei sotto Salò: La persecuzione antisemita, 1943–1945* (Milan: Feltrinelli, 1978), 90–95; Zuccotti, *The Italians and the Holocaust*, 142; and Stille, *Benevolence and Betrayal*, 89.

65. The highest possible grade was thirty.

66. The police in Padua were going to arrest Pajes because he was in Italy on a student visa from Poland, with which Italy had been at war for three-quarters of a year, and because he was a foreign Jew and no longer officially protected. Though subject to arrest and confinement in Italian concentration camps, he was not facing deportation on June 16, 1940, as he would have been after September 8, 1943. The distinction is more than a legal one.

67. One of the men intended by this cryptic remark must have been Hit-

ler; the other, if we assume Cagnetto was an anti-Fascist, would probably have been Mussolini, although Pajes himself would probably not have shared that sentiment at the time.

68. Gestapo headquarters in Rome, where its prisoners were interrogated, was located at 145 Via Tasso.

69. Dante Abramo Lattes (1876–1965) was a longtime leader of the Italian Zionist Federation, whose members in the 1930s "courageously stood their ground, flatly refusing to yield to intimidation and pressure." Michaelis, *Mussolini and the Jews,* 61.

70. Segre put this encounter with the lieutenant of the Alpine Brigade in his *Memorie di vita ebraica: Casale Monferrato—Roma—Gerusalemme, 1918–1960* (Rome: Bonacci, 1979).

71. Elia or Elijah Ben Abraham Benamozegh (1822–1900), an Italian rabbi, philosopher, and student of Kabbalah, was the son of Sephardic parents from Morocco. He was born in Leghorn and spent most of his life in that coastal Tuscan city, preaching in its synagogue and teaching in its rabbinical seminary. He wrote in Italian, French, and Hebrew.

72. Segre is referring to the American Joint Distribution Committee, with an office at St. Gall in Switzerland. See the interview with Bernard Grosser.

73. Giustizia e Libertà (Justice and Liberty) was the name of a political group that endorsed certain liberal ideas and certain other democratic socialist ones. Founded in Paris in 1929 by an Italian Jewish intellectual in political exile, Carlo Rosselli, GL served (to quote Zuccotti) "as a coordinating body for all non-Communist opponents of fascism." See Zuccotti, *The Italians and the Holocaust,* 249–53; and J. D. Wilkinson, *The Intellectual Resistance in Europe* (Cambridge, Mass.: Harvard University Press, 1981), 224ff. The role of GL waned with the German occupation and the armed resistance that began in September 1943.

74. General Guido Liuzzi was commandant of the War School during World War I. See Zuccotti, *The Italians and the Holocaust,* 18, 290, n. 9.

75. Tullio Tamburini, later chief of all the provincial police forces under the Republic of Salò (the RSI), seems to have played an ambivalent role, at one time attempting to "exempt certain categories of Jews from internment, including the aged, the sick, the 'Aryanized,' and those with Aryan spouses." Michaelis, *Mussolini and the Jews,* 351. Afterward he yielded to German pressure to send *all* Jews "even if hitherto exempt or privileged" to concentration camps. Ibid., 380–81.

76. Not, perhaps, through pure clairvoyance: Rabbi Toaff may have been warned in advance of a raid scheduled for October 9, during the High Holy Day service, by a local Catholic priest, Don Bernardino. The story is recounted by Zuccotti, *The Italians and the Holocaust,* 154ff., but the source is second-hand, and she would now defer to Toaff's own account.

77. Strictly speaking, this is an exaggeration. Zuccotti, ibid., 155, reports, citing De Felice's figures, that of the 1,031 members of the Jewish community of Ancona counted in the 1938 census, only 10 Jews were deported and 1 of these returned.

78. Ilva was a large iron- and steelworks complex in Italy, with corporate headquarters located in both Genoa in the North and Taranto in the South. (The name was taken from the Latin name for the Island of Elba, where the iron ore was originally found.) It would be merged in 1961 with Italsider under the IRI, the governmental Institute for the Reconstruction of Industry.

79. Among the twenty-nine articles of the racial laws touched on in several of these interviews, there was a provision that the civil service and defense administrations had to dismiss their Jewish employees. See S. Waagenaar, *The Pope's Jews* (La Salle, Ill.: Open Court, 1974), 341; and Zuccotti, *The Italians and the Holocaust*, 41ff.

80. Although Mr. Della Pergola might have been receiving his salary from private funds, the metal industry would have been considered partially governmental and related to the national defense. In any case, Elisa Della Pergola describes her father as a dismissed Jewish civil servant.

81. The SS had set up a holding camp for prisoners awaiting deportation at Gries, near Bolzano, in the Alto Adige to the far north. Mr. Della Pergola must have been transported directly to Gries, because the concentration camp at Fossoli had been closed in July 1944 and he was arrested in Genoa in September. Since his last letter to the family was dated October 15, he would have been deported to Auschwitz from Gries on October 24, on a train "carrying 300 prisoners, of whom at least 150 were Jewish." Zuccotti, *The Italians and the Holocaust*, 184.

82. Zuccotti, ibid., 184, n. 43, adds to her description of the camp at Gries, "By December 1944, convoys no longer went to Auschwitz. The camp, threatened by the approaching Russians, was in the process of evacuating its prisoners. Auschwitz was liberated on January 27, 1945." Michaelis, *Mussolini and the Jews*, 390ff., carries a related account. Both rely on the published data of the CDEC.

83. The "whole story" is not, assuredly, to be found in Mr. Teglio's summary account in this interview with Caracciolo. But he also spoke with Stille, in the section entitled "The Rabbi, the Priest and the Aviator," in *Benevolence and Betrayal*, 223–78. Teglio—who flew hydroplanes from the Gulf of Genoa and belonged to the Genoa Aviation Club before the war—is "the Aviator." As a dashing, rather lightweight figure, without enemies in the upper social circles of that city, he enjoyed the confidence on which he would draw later to rescue his fellow Jews, such as Mrs. Della Pergola.

84. Unfortunately, the Polaccos were not able to get away in time. Zuccotti, *The Italians and the Jews*, 162, recounts how "two German SS men appeared and seized the two [small Polacco] children, threatening to kill them if their father did not produce the Community lists. He promptly did so. Then the Nazis forced him to telephone everyone on the lists, summoning them to a meeting at the synagogue the next morning. Again he obliged." She cites another interview with Teglio, who had "learned of the seizure of the lists and telephoned warnings" (162). The story of the arrest and detention of the Polaccos, the extortion of the lists by the SS, and the eventual deportation of the family is recounted in Stille, *Benevolence and Betrayal*, 239ff. and 256ff.

85. Montecatini, where Achille and Margherita Teglio Vitale had attempted to take refuge in a small hotel with their two young children, was the site of some celebrated Tuscan spas.

86. As the name suggests, Castiglion Fiorentino is also in Tuscany, well to the south of Liguria. The German army, however, had occupied the entire peninsula, and there were very few safe places left for Jews in November 1943.

87. Father Francesco Repetto was secretary to Cardinal Pietro Boetta, archbishop of Genoa, who allowed the young priest to collaborate with DELASEM and to shelter and rescue Jews. Other instances of Father Repetto's collaboration with DELASEM in rescuing Jews are provided in the interview with Bernard Grosser, who had worked for DELASEM in Genoa. Zuccotti, *The Italians and the Jews,* 211, mentions that Father Repetto "narrowly escaped arrest by the SS" in July 1944 and "was forced to hide for the remainder of the war." Father Repetto is "the Priest" of Stille's section entitled "The Rabbi, the Priest and the Aviator"; after the war, he would be elevated to monsignore. ("The Rabbi," Riccardo Pacifici, and his wife, Wanda, were deported in separate train carriages to Auschwitz, where they died.)

88. Attorney Lelio Vittorio Valobra was president of DELASEM.

89. Raffaele Cantoni, a Venetian, was a Jewish leader of importance and courage who served as a courier for DELASEM and the archdiocese of Florence and was arrested for his clandestine activities. After his close escape from the deportation train, he was able to reach Switzerland. See Waagenaar, *The Pope's Jews,* 393; and Stille, *Benevolence and Betrayal,* 259. It is hard to know what Teglio means in calling him a "president."

90. Attorney Giuseppe Sala, Zuccotti, *The Italians and the Holocaust,* 225, informs us, drawing on CDEC records, "did not die for the help he gave Jews, but he did suffer torture and deprivation for two months at San Vittore Prison in Milan. Both before and after his arrest, he helped hundreds, finding hiding places and delivering food, money, and clothing through a clandestine aid network."

91. Monsignor Vincenzo Barale (who died in 1979), secretary to Cardinal Fossati, archbishop of Turin, was an active figure in the clandestine network of assistance. See Zuccotti, *The Italians and the Jews,* 208, 211, and 213, where Zuccotti advises caution in calling the participants a "network" when they did not know each other for safety's sake.

92. Caracciolo is interviewing Maria Di Girolamo, the wife of Vincenzo Di Girolamo, and Maria and Vicenzo's children, Menotti and Ermanno. Ariel Leo Koffler talks about the family in his interview.

93. The interview with Sidi Duiri Sharon and Simi Duiri, who are sister and brother, was conducted in French, with an interpreter present, and an Italian translation, not entirely faithful to the French text, was then superimposed on the recorded dialogue. This contrasts with the interviews in Israel, which were conducted entirely in Italian.

94. For further particulars on the compulsory residence set up by the Italian army for Jewish refugees at Saint-Martin-Vésubie in the Maritime Alps and the subsequent flight of those refugees to the area near Cuneo in Piedmont, see the interview with Enzo Cavaglion.

95. Caracciolo is interviewing the sisters Anna and Marianna Giordana, peasant women from Ondono, a tiny hamlet of the village of Borgo San Dalmazzo, where Sidi Duiri Sharon and Simi Duiri took refuge.

96. Esther Kichel Macher is referring to her sister, Rachel Kichel Schitz, and their mother.

97. Annemasse was in southeastern France, a zone occupied by the Italian army in November 1942, when the German army was occupying most of southern France.

98. *Forced residence* is the legal term used for an involuntary stay somewhere. See the earlier interview with Enzo Cavaglion.

99. A luxury resort in the Alps.

100. Dan Millin's Italian is weak, so we have had to conjecture in several places what he might have intended to say.

APPENDIX 1: HISTORICAL PERSONAGES, ORGANIZATIONS, AND PLACES

1. S. Zuccotti, *The Italians and the Holocaust: Persecution, Rescue, Survival* (New York: Basic Books, 1987), 65.

2. S. Waagenaar, *The Pope's Jews* (La Salle, Ill.: Open Court, 1974), 393.

3. J. Steinberg, *All or Nothing: The Axis and the Holocaust, 1941–1943* (New York: Routledge, 1990), 9.

4. M. Michaelis, *Mussolini and the Jews: German-Italian Relations and the Jewish Question in Italy, 1922–1945* (Oxford: Clarendon Press, 1978), 292.

5. P. Levi, *If This Is a Man*, trans. S. Woolf (London: Bodley Head, 1960). The second edition of the book was published as *Survival in Auschwitz: The Nazi Assault on Humanity* (New York: Summit Books, 1986).

6. Michaelis, *Mussolini and the Jews*, 61.

7. P. Levi, *If This Is a Man; The Reawakening: A Liberated Prisoner's Long March Home through East Europe*, trans. S. Woolf (Boston: Little, Brown, 1965), 2d ed. (New York: Summit Books, 1986); *The Drowned and the Saved* (New York: Summit Books, 1988).

8. G. Limentani, *In contumacia* (Milan: Adelphi, 1967).

9. Waagenaar, *The Pope's Jews*, 380ff.

10. E. Toaff, *Il carnevale di Roma e gli ebrei* (Milan and Jerusalem: Sally Mayer Foundation, 1956); D. Carpi, A. Milano, and U. Nahon, eds., *Scritti in memoria di Enzo Sereni: Saggi sull' Ebraismo romano* (Milan and Jerusalem: Sally Mayer Foundation, 1970).

11. P. Orano, *Gli ebrei in Italia* (Rome: Pinciana, 1937); P. Orano, *Mussolini da vicino*, 2d ed. (Rome: Pinciana, 1932).

12. Steinberg, *All or Nothing*, 26.

13. Ibid., 75ff., 169.

14. Ibid, 4.

15. Michaelis, *Mussolini and the Jews*, 18.

Selected Bibliography

This bibliography, like the one by Mario Toscano in the Italian edition of this volume that it expands and supplements, is intended to provide the reader with useful suggestions for exploring the themes of this book. No attempt at completeness is pretended. For further references, see the volumes by I. Herzer, M. Michaelis, J. Steinberg, and S. Zuccotti, cited in the Sources in English section.

ITALIAN SOURCES
Books and Other Separately Published Works

Artom, E. *Diari: Gennaio 1940–febbraio 1944.* Edited by P. De Benedetti and E. Ravenna. Milan: CDEC, 1966.

Ascarelli, A. *Le Fosse Ardeatine.* Bologna: Canesi, 1965.

Balsamo, L., and R. Cremante. *A.-F. Formiggini, un editore del novecento.* Bologna: Il Mulino, 1981.

Bedarida, G. *Ebrei d'Italia.* Leghorn: Tirrena, 1950.

Caffaz, U. *L'antisemitismo italiano sotto il fascismo.* Florence: La Nuova Italia, 1975.

Caracciolo, N. *Gli ebrei e l'Italia durante la guerra, 1940–45.* Rome: Bonacci, 1986. [The author's introduction to this work, from which the present translation is derived, is cited but not used here.]

Carpi, D., A. Milano, and U. Nahon, eds. *Scritti in memoria di Enzo Sereni: Saggi sull' Ebraismo romano.* Milan and Jerusalem: Sally Mayer Foundation, 1970.

Cavaglion, A. *Nella notte straniera: Gli ebrei di S. Martin Vésubie.* Cuneo: L'arciere, 1981.

Centro di Documentazione Ebraica Contemporanea, Milan, ed. *Ebrei in Italia: Deportazione, resistenza.* Florence: La Giuntina, 1975.

De Benedetti, G. *16 ottobre 1943: Otto ebrei.* Edited by O. Cecchi. Rome: Editori Riuniti, 1978.

De Felice, R. *Storia degli ebrei italiani sotto il fascismo.* 3d ed. Turin: Einaudi, 1972.

Del Canuto, F. *Il movimento sionistico in Italia dalle origine al 1924.* Milan: Federazione Sionistica Italiana, 1972.

————, ed. *Israel, "Un decennio," 1974–1984: Saggi sull'Ebraismo italiano.* Rome: Carucci, 1984.

Della Pergola, S. *Anatomia dell'ebraismo italiano.* Assisi and Rome: Carucci, 1976.

Eckert, T. *Il movimento sionistico-chalutzistico in Italia fra le due guerre mondiali.* Segre: Kevutzàtlı Yavne, 1970.

Folino, F. *Ferramonti: Un lager di Mussolini; gli internati durante la guerra.* Cosenza: Brenner, 1985.

Folkel, F. *La Risiera di San Sabba.* Milan: Mondadori, 1979.

Formiggini, G. *Stella d'Italia, Stella di David: Gli ebrei dal Risorgimento alla Resistenza.* Milan: Mursia, 1970.

Fortis, U., ed. *Venezia ebraica.* Rome: Carucci, 1982.

Fubini, G. *La condizione giuridica dell'ebraismo italiano.* Florence: La Nuova Italia, 1974.

Gherardi Bon, S. *La persecuzione antiebraica a Trieste (1938–1945).* Udine: Del Bianco, 1972.

Giovannetti, A. *Il Vaticano e la guerra (1939–1940).* Vatican: Libreria Editrice Vaticana, 1960.

————. *Roma città aperta.* Milan: Editrice Ancora, 1962.

ISTAT [National Statistics Office]. *Sommario di statistiche storiche dell'Italia, 1861–1965.* Rome: Istituto Centrale di Statistica, 1968.

Lapide, P. E. *Roma e gli ebrei.* Milan: Mondadori, 1967.

Leone, M. *Le organizzazioni di soccorso ebraiche in età fascista.* Rome: Carucci, 1983.

Loi, S. *Jugoslavia 1941.* Turin: Edizioni de "Il Nastro Azzurro," 1953.

————. *Le operazioni delle unità italiane in Jugoslavia (1941–1943): Narrazione, documenti.* Rome: Tipografia regionale, 1978.

————. *Aggredisci e vincerai: Storia della Divisione motorizzata Trieste.* Milan: Mursia, 1983.

Mayda, G. *Ebrei sotto Salò: La persecuzione antisemita, 1943–1945.* Milan: Feltrinelli, 1978.

Milano, A. *Storia degli ebrei in Italia.* Turin: Einaudi, 1963.

Minerbi, S. *Raffaele Cantoni.* Assisi and Rome: Carucci, 1978.

Momigliano, E. *Storia tragica e grottesca del razzismo fascista.* Milan: Mondadori, 1946.

Morpurgo, L. *Caccia all'uomo.* Rome: Dalmatia, 1946.

Novitch, M. *Il passaggio dei barbari.* Florence: La Giuntina, 1983.

Picciotto Fargion, L., ed. *L'occupazione tedesca e gli ebrei di Roma: Documenti e fatti.* Rome and Milan: Carucci-CDEC, 1979.

Pichetto, M. T. *Alle radici dell'odio: Preziosi e Benigni antisemiti.* Milan: Angeli, 1983.

Preti, L. *Impero fascista, africani ed ebrei.* Milan: Mursia, 1968.

Sacerdoti, G. *Ricordi di un ebreo bolognese: Illusioni e delusioni, 1929–1945.* Rome: Bonacci, 1983.

Segre, A. *Memorie di vita ebraica: Casale Monferrato—Roma—Gerusalemme, 1918–1960.* Rome: Bonacci, 1979.

Sereni, A. *I clandestini del mare: L'emigrazione ebraica in terra d'Israele dal 1945 al 1948.* Milan: Mursia, 1973.

Sorani, S. *L'assistenza ai profughi ebrei in Italia (1933–1947): Contributo alla storia della "Delasem."* Edited by A. Tagliacozzo. Rome: Carucci, 1983.

Staderini, T. *Legislazione per la difesa della razza.* 2d. ed. Rome: 1939.

Toaff, E. *Il carnevale di Roma e gli ebrei.* Milan and Jerusalem: Sally Mayer Foundation, 1956.

Uffreduzzi, M. *Il viale dei Giusti.* Rome: Città Nuova, 1985.

Valabrega, G. *Ebrei, fascismo, sionismo.* Urbino: Argalia, 1974.

Journal Articles and Essays

Boralevi, A. "Angiolo Orvieto, 'Il Marzocco,' la società colta ebraica." In C. Del Vivo, ed., *Il Marzocco, Atti del seminario di studi,* 213–33. Florence: Olschki, 1985.

Canepa, A. M. "Emancipazione, integrazione e antisemitismo in Italia: Il caso Pasqualigo." *Comunità* 174 (June 1975): 166–203.

———. "Cattolici ed ebrei nell'Italia liberale (1870–1915)." *Comunità* 179 (April 1978): 43–109.

———. "L'immagine dell'ebreo nel folclore e nella letteratura del postrisorgimento." *Rassegna mensile di Israel* 44 (May–June 1978): 383–99.

Carpi, D. "Il problema ebraico nella politica italiana fra le due guerre mondiali." *Rivista di Studi Politici Internazionali* 28 (January–March 1961): 35–56.

———. "Nuovi documenti per la storia dell'olocausto in Grecia: L'atteggiamento degli Italiani (1941–1943)." *Michael* 7 (1981): 119–200.

De Felice, R. "La Chiesa e il problema ebraico durante gli anni dell'antisemitismo fascista." *Rassegna mensile di Israel* 13 (January 1957): 23–35.

Di Porto, B. "Ebraismo in Italia tra la 1a guerra mondiale e il fascismo: Esperienze, momenti, personaggi." *Rassegna mensile di Israel* 46 (January–June 1981): 90–119.

———. "Dopo il Risorgimento, al varco del novecento: Gli ebrei e l'ebraismo in Italia." *Rassegna mensile di Israel* 47 (July–December 1981): 19–62.

Di Vita, D. "Gli ebrei di Milano sotto l'occupazione nazista." *Quaderni del Centro Studi sulla deportazione e l'internamento* 6 (1969–71): 16–72.

Ducci, R. [under pseud. "Verax"]. "Italiani ed ebrei in Jugoslavia." *Politica Estera* 1, no. 9 (1944).

Finzi, R. "Gli ebrei nella società italiana dall' Unità al fascismo." *Il Ponte* 34 (November–December 1978): 1372–1411.

Gherardi Bon, S. "Un campo di sterminio in Italia." *Il Ponte* 34 (November–December 1978): 1440–53.

Irico, N., and A. Muncinelli. "Vittime della speranza: Gli ebrei a Saluzzo dal 1938 al 1945." *Notiziario dell'Istituto storico della resistenza in Cuneo e provincia* 28 (2d semester 1985): 59–116.

Kalk, I. "I campi di concentramento italiani per ebrei profughi: Ferramonti Tarsia (Calabria)." *Gli ebrei in Italia durante il fascismo: Quaderni della Federazione giovanile ebraica d'Italia* 1 (1961): 63–71.

Loi, S. "L'esercito italiano di fronte alle persecuzioni razziali." *Revue internationale d'histoire militaire* (1978): 276–87.

Minerbi, S. I. "Gli ultimi due incontri Weizmann-Mussolini (1933–1934)." *Storia contemporanea* 5 (September 1974): 431–77.

Picciotto Fargion, L. "Sul contributo di ebrei alla Resistenza italiana." *Rassegna mensile di Israel* 46 (March–April 1980): 132–46.

Pommerein, R. "Le controversie di politica razziale nei rapporti dell'Asse Roma-Berlino (1938–1943)." *Storia contemporanea* 10 (October 1979): 925–40.

Sarfatti, M. "Dopo l'8 settembre: Gli ebrei e la rete confinaria italo-svizzera." *Rassegna mensile di Israel* 46 (January–June 1981): 150–73.

Sarti, S. "Il mondo protestante e la questione razziale: Note sulla rivista Gioventù Christiana." In G. Valabrega, ed., *Gli ebrei in Italia durante il fascismo: Quaderni del Cdec* 2 (1962): 86–91.

Scalpelli, A. "L'Ente di Gestione e Liquidazione Immobiliare: Note sulle conseguenze economiche della persecuzione razziale." In G. Valabrega, ed., *Gli ebrei in Italia durante il fascismo: Quaderni del Cdec* 2 (1962): 92–104.

Scotti Douglas, R. "Quarantacinque giorni nel campo di concentramento di Borgo S. Dalmazzo Cuneo." *Gli ebrei in Italia durante il fascismo: Quaderni della Federazione giovanile ebraica d'Italia* 1 (1961): 78–89.

Sereni, P. "Gli anni della persecuzione razziale a Venezia: appunti per una storia." In U. Fortis, ed., *Venezia ebraica*, 129–51. Rome: Carucci, 1982.

———. "Della comunità ebraica a Venezia durante il fascismo." In *La Resistenza nel veneziano*, 503–40. Venice: Università di Venezia, Istituto Veneto per la storia della Resistenza, 1985.

Spinosa, A. "Le persecuzioni razziali in Italia." *Il Ponte* 8 (July 1952): 964–78; 8 (August 1952): 1078–96; 8 (November 1952): 1604–22; 9 (July 1953): 950–68.

Tagliacozzo, M. "La Comunità di Roma sotto l'incubo della svastica: La grande razzia del 16 ottobre 1943." In G. Valabrega, ed., *Gli ebrei in Italia durante il fascismo: Quaderni del Cdec* 3 (1963): 8–37.

Tortorelli, G. "L'affare Dreyfus e i socialisti italiani." *Società e storia* 9 (January–March 1986): 105–32.

Toscano, M. "Fermenti culturali ed esperienze organizzative della gioventù ebraica italiana (1911–1925)." *Storia contemporanea* 13 (December 1982): 915–61.

Vaccari, I. "Villa Emma." *Quaderni dell'Istituto Storico della Resistenza in Modena e provincia* 1 (1960).

Valabrega, G., ed. *Gli ebrei in Italia durante il fascismo: Quaderni del Cdec* 2 (1962).

———. *Gli ebrei in Italia durante il fascismo: Quaderni del Cdec* 3 (1963):

Vizio, S. "Gli ebrei croati in Alba, 1942–1945." *Notiziario dell'Istituto storico della resistenza in Cuneo e provincia* 28 (2d semester 1985): 117–27.

SOURCES IN ENGLISH
Books

Archivio Vaticano. *The Holy See and the War in Europe, March 1939–August 1940,* vol. 1 of *Records and Documents of the Holy See relating to the Second World War.* Dublin: Clonmore and Reynolds, 1968.

Arendt, H. *Eichmann in Jerusalem: A Report on the Banality of Evil.* New York: Viking Press, 1964

Bassani, G. *The Garden of the Finzi-Continis.* Translated by I. Quigley. New York: Atheneum, 1965. New ed., translated by W. Weaver. New York: Harcourt Brace Jovanovich, 1977.

Bauman, Z. *Modernity and the Holocaust.* Ithaca, N.Y.: Cornell University Press, 1989.

Bentley, E., ed. *The Storm over the Deputy.* New York: Grove Press, 1964.

Blet, P., R. S. Graham, A. Martini, and B. Schneider, eds. *Records and Documents of the Holy See relating to the Second World War.* Translated and edited by G. Noel. London: Herder, 1968; Washington, D.C., Corpus Books, 1968.

Ciano, G. *The Ciano Diaries, 1939–1943.* Edited by H. Gibson. New York: Doubleday, 1946.

———. *Ciano's Hidden Diary, 1937–1938.* Edited by A. Mayor. New York: E. P. Dutton, 1953.

Dawidowicz, L. S. *The War against the Jews, 1933–1945.* New York: Free Press, 1986.

Deakin, F. W. *The Bitter Friendship: Hitler, Mussolini, and the Fall of Italian Fascism.* New York: Harper and Row, 1962.

Della Seta, F., *The Tiber Afire.* Translated by F. Frenaye. Marlboro, Vt.: Marlboro Press, 1991.

Falconi, C. *The Silence of Pius XII.* Translated by B. Wall. Boston: Little, Brown, 1970.

Friedländer, S. *Pius XII and the Third Reich: A Documentation.* Translated by C. Fullman. New York: Alfred A. Knopf, 1966.

Ginzburg, N. *Family Sayings.* Rev. ed. Translated by D. M. Low. Manchester, England: Carcanet, 1984.

Hallie, P. P. *Lest Innocent Blood Be Shed: The Story of the Village of Le Chambon, and How Goodness Happened There.* New York: Harper and Row, 1979.

Herzer, I., K. Voigt, and J. Burgwyn, eds. *The Italian Refuge: Rescue of Jews during the Holocaust.* Washington, D.C.: Catholic University Press, 1989. [Contains an excellent bibliography by M. Sarfatti in addition to references in notes to individual contributors' articles.]

Hilberg, R. *The Destruction of the European Jews.* Rev. ed., 3 vols. New York: Holmes and Meier, 1985.

Hochhuth, R. *The Deputy.* Translated by R. Winston and C. Winston. New York: Grove Press, 1964. [See particularly Hochhuth's essay, "Sidelights on History," published as an author's epilogue with the translation of the text.]

Hughes, H. S. *Prisoners of Hope: The Silver Age of the Italian Jews, 1924–1974.* Cambridge, Mass.: Harvard University Press, 1983.

Katz, R. *Death in Rome.* New York: Macmillan, 1967.

———. *Black Sabbath: A Journey through a Crime against Humanity.* Toronto: Macmillan, 1969.

Kosinski, J. *The Painted Bird.* 2d ed. New York: Random House, 1983.

Kotsuji, A. *From Tokyo to Jerusalem.* New York: Random House, 1964.

Kranzler, D. *Japanese, Nazis, and Jews: The Jewish Community of Shanghai, 1938–1945.* New York: Yeshiva University Press, 1976.

Langer, L. *Holocaust Testimonies: The Ruins of Memory.* New Haven, Conn.: Yale University Press, 1991.

Lanzmann, C. *Shoah: An Oral History of the Holocaust.* New York: Pantheon, 1987.

Levi, P. *If This Is a Man.* Translated by S. Woolf. London: Bodley Head, 1960. 2d ed., *Survival in Auschwitz: The Nazi Assault on Humanity.* New York: Summit Books, 1986.

———. *The Reawakening: A Liberated Prisoner's Long March Home through East Europe.* Translated by S. Woolf. Boston: Little, Brown, 1965. 2d ed. New York: Summit Books, 1986.

———. *The Drowned and the Saved.* New York: Summit Books, 1988.

Lewy, G. *The Catholic Church and Nazi Germany.* New York: McGraw-Hill, 1964.

Ludwig, E. *Talks with Mussolini.* Translated by E. Paul and C. Paul. Boston: Little, Brown, 1932.

Marrus, M. R., and R. O. Paxton. *Vichy France and the Jews.* New York: Basic Books, 1981.

Michaelis, M. *Mussolini and the Jews: German-Italian Relations and the Jewish Question in Italy, 1922–1945.* Oxford: Clarendon Press, 1978. [Contains the most complete bibliography available for readers in English, with references for original documents. Needs supplementing for 1979 to the present.]

Nolte, E. *The Three Faces of Fascism.* New York: New American Library, 1969.

Ophuls, M. *The Sorrow and the Pity: A Film.* Translated by M. Johnston. New York: Outerbridge and Lazard, 1972.

Poliakov, L. *Harvest of Hate: The Nazi Program for the Destruction of the Jews of Europe.* 1954. Reprint. Westport, Conn.: Greenwood Press, 1971.

Poliakov, L., and J. Sabille. *Jews under the Italian Occupation.* Paris: Centre de Documentation Juive Contemporaine, 1954.

Reitlinger, G. *The Final Solution: The Attempt to Exterminate the Jews of Europe, 1939–1945.* Rev. ed. South Brunswick, N.J.: Thomas Yoseloff, 1968.

Roth, C. *History of the Jews of Italy.* Philadelphia: Jewish Publication Society, 1946.

Roth, J. K., and M. Berenbaum, eds. *Holocaust: Religious and Philosophical Implications.* New York: Paragon House, 1989.

Rothchild, S., ed. *Voices from the Holocaust.* New York: New American Library, 1982.

Segre, D. V. *Memoirs of a Fortunate Jew.* Washington, D.C.: Adler and Adler, 1987; New York: Dell Books, 1988.

Shillony, B.-A., *Politics and Culture in Wartime Japan.* Oxford: Clarendon Press, 1991. /

Steinberg, J. *All or Nothing: The Axis and the Holocaust, 1941–1943.* New York: Routledge, 1990. [Contains extensive bibliography of oral and published sources, primarily for the Balkans.]

Steinberg, L. *Not as a Lamb: The Jews against Hitler.* Translated by M. Hunter. Farnborough, England: Saxon House, 1974.

Stille, A. *Benevolence and Betrayal: Five Italian Jewish Families under Fascism.* New York: Summit Books, 1991.

Tokayer, M., and M. Swartz. *The Fugu Plan: The Untold Story of the Japanese and the Jews during World War II.* New York: Paddington, 1979.

Trunk, I., ed. *Jewish Responses to Nazi Persecution: Collective and Individual Behavior in Extremis.* New York: Stein and Day, 1979.

Urquhart, C., and P. L. Brent. *Enzo Sereni: A Hero of Our Times.* London: Robert Hale, 1967.

Waagenaar, S. *The Pope's Jews.* La Salle, Ill.: Open Court, 1974.

Weisbord, R. G., and W. P. Sillanpoa, *The Chief Rabbi, the Pope, and the Holocaust: An Era in Vatican-Jewish Relations.* New Brunswick, N.J.: Transaction, 1991.

Wilkinson, J. D. *The Intellectual Resistance in Europe.* Cambridge, Mass.: Harvard University Press, 1981.

Zuccotti, S. *The Italians and the Holocaust: Persecution, Rescue, Survival.* New York: Basic Books, 1987. [Contains valuable references in notes and updates Michaelis thoroughly but lacks a bibliography.]

Journal Articles and Essays

Carpi, D. "The Rescue of Jews in the Italian Zone of Occupied Croatia." In Y. Gutman and E. Zuroff, eds., *Rescue Attempts during the Holocaust: Proceedings of the Second Yad Vashem International Historical Conference, Jerusalem, April 8–11, 1974,* 465–525. Jerusalem: Ahva Cooperative Press, 1977.

Deák, I. "The Incomprehensible Holocaust." *New York Review of Books* 36 (September 28, 1989): 63–72. [This review of recent accounts by survivors and scholars of a later epoch, and the other reviews published by Deák some three years later (listed below), represent more than the sum of their parts and should be read carefully by anyone attempting historical work on the Holocaust in the future. Several of the books under consideration deal specifically with Italy.]

———. "Strategies of Hell." *New York Review of Books* 39 (October 8, 1992): 8–13.

———. "Witnesses to Evil." *New York Review of Books* 39 (October 22, 1992): 40–42.

———. "Holocaust Heroes." *New York Review of Books* 39 (November 5, 1992): 22–26.

Graham, R. A. "Relations of Pius XII and the Catholic Community with Jewish Organizations." In I. Herzer, K. Voigt, and J. Burgwyn, eds., *The Italian Refuge: Rescue of Jews during the Holocaust,* 231–53. Washington, D.C.: Catholic University Press, 1989.

Ithai, J. "The Children of Villa Emma." In I. Herzer, K. Voigt, and J. Burgwyn, eds., *The Italian Refuge: Rescue of Jews during the Holocaust,* 178–202. Washington, D.C.: Catholic University Press, 1989. [This author appears as an interviewee in the present volume as Izak Itai.]

Ledeen, M. A. "The Evolution of Italian Fascist Antisemitism." *Jewish Social Studies* 37 (January 1975): 3–17.

Lyman, S., "Nihonism and Judaism—A Dissent." *Midstream* 19 (June–July 1973): 75–80. [A review essay on Isaiah Ben-Dasan, pseud., *The Japanese and the Jews.*]

Michaelis, M. "On the Jewish Question in Fascist Italy: The Attitude of the Fascist Regime to the Jews in Italy." *Yad Vashem Studies* 4 (1960): 7–41.

———. "The 'Duce' and the Jews: An Assessment of the Literature on Italian Jewry under Fascism (1922–1945)," *Yad Vashem Studies* 11 (1976): 7–32.

Shelah, M. "The Italian Rescue of Yugoslav Jews." In I. Herzer, K. Voigt, and J. Burgwyn, eds., *The Italian Refuge: Rescue of Jews during the Holocaust,* 205–17. Washington, D.C.: Catholic University Press, 1989.

Zuccotti, S. "Pope Pius XII and the Holocaust: The Case in Italy." In I. Herzer, K. Voigt, and J. Burgwyn, eds. *The Italian Refuge: Rescue of Jews during the Holocaust,* 254–70. Washington, D.C.: Catholic University Press, 1989.

SOURCES IN OTHER LANGUAGES

Blet, P., R. A. Graham, A. Martini, and B. Schneider, eds. *Actes et documents du Saint Siège relatifs à la Seconde Guerre Mondiale.* 11 vols. Vatican City: Editrice Libreria Vaticana, 1965–81. [This edition of the documents in the Archives of the Secretariat of State of the Catholic Church for the years 1939–45 consists of official correspondence, memoranda, diplomatic records, and other state papers. The documents are in Latin, Italian, French, German, and English; the introduction and annotation are in French.]

Shelach, M. *Blood Account: The Rescue of Croatian Jews by Italians, 1941–1943.* Tel Aviv: Sifriat Poalim, 1986 [in Hebrew with summary in English].

NICOLA CARACCIOLO is a journalist engaged in historical programming for the Second Network of RAI-TV, the government-owned radio and television service. He drew heavily on his two-part RAI documentary *Il coraggio e la pietà* for the interviews that are the focal point of this book. Earlier, working as a foreign correspondent for the weekly *L'Espresso* and the daily newspaper *Il Giorno,* he covered the war in Algeria; later, he was the Washington correspondent for *La Stampa,* one of the leading dailies in Italy. He is the author of two earlier books, *Il piccolo Re* (The Little King) and *Tutti gli uomini del Duce* (All the Duce's Men).

FLORETTE RECHNITZ KOFFLER is an associate professor of Romance languages and literatures at St. Thomas Aquinas College. She has taught at Wesleyan University and before that at the University of Pennsylvania, from which she holds two graduate degrees. She also served as program director for the Soros Open Society Fund and as a translator for the Office of Special Investigations of the U.S. Department of Justice, which looks into illegal entry by war criminals. Her longer-range projects have dealt with comparative oral balladry, particularly the traditions of Spain and Romania.

RICHARD KOFFLER, who has a Ph.D. in comparative literature from Rutgers, is executive editor for the social and behavioral sciences at Aldine de Gruyter and an adjunct lecturer in Italian and English at St. Thomas Aquinas College. He has taught at Rutgers, Syracuse, Temple, and MIT. Apart from translating books for scholarly and trade publishing houses, he has edited a volume of essays, *The Rarer Action,* with Alan Cheuse. He has also published in journals ranging from scholarly quarterlies to the *Nation* and the *Spectator.*

RENZO DE FELICE, a historian, has published a multivolume biography of Mussolini and many other significant books on the era, including a history of the Jews in Italy under Fascism, critical interpretations of the historiography of the Fascist period, and a history of Jews in the colony of Libya.

MARIO TOSCANO, a diplomatic historian, is the author of books on the diplomatic origins of the Pact of Steel and on the question of the Alto-Adige region, long contested between Italy and Austria.